Level **D** Mathematics

Measuring Up®

to the

New York State Learning Standards

and Success Strategies for the State Test

This book is customized for New York, and the lessons match the
New York State Learning Standards for Mathematics.
The Measuring Up® program includes instructional worktexts plus
ePath Assess™ online assessments and print Diagnostic Practice
Tests, which are available separately.

800-822-1080
www.PeoplesEducation.com

Peoples Education
Your partner in student success®

REVISED to match the latest NYS test format

Executive Vice President, Chief Creative Officer: Diane Miller

Editorial Development: Fox Run Press

Managing Editor: Kerri Gero

Copy Editor: Katy Leclercq

Editorial Assistant: Amy Priddy Wierzbicki

Vice President of Marketing: Victoria Ameer Kiely

Senior Marketing Manager: Christine Grasso

Marketing Manager: Victoria Leo

Production Director: Jason Grasso

Production Manager: Jennifer Bridges Brewer

Assistant Production Managers: Steven Genzano, Jennifer Tully

Director of Permissions: Kristine Liebman

Cover Design: Joe Guerrero, Todd Kochakji

New York Advisors:

Maria Fusco, retired teacher
Mechanicsville MIddle School,
Mechanicsville, NY

Karleen Adam-Comrie
Assistant Principal
Jean Nuzzi IS 109, Queens, New York

Your partner in student success®

Copyright © 2011
Peoples Education, Inc.
299 Market Street
Saddle Brook, New Jersey 07663

ISBN 978-1-61602-057-6

Manufactured in Ann Arbor, MI in August 2011 by Edwards Brothers, Inc.

Printed in the United States of America.

10   9   8   7   6   5   4   3

Measuring Up® Contents

This section provides information about the Grade 4 **New York State Test** for Mathematics and reviews the Grade 4 New York State Learning Standards for Mathematics. It also provides test-taking tips and stategies for answering multiple-choice, short-response, and extended-response questions.

May/June Review

Grade 3
May/June Review

Part 1 Number Sense and Place Value, Addition and Subtraction, Multiplication, Division, and Algebra

Chapter 1 Number Sense and Place Value

Chapter 2   Addition and Subtraction

Chapter 3   Multiplication

Chapter 4   Division

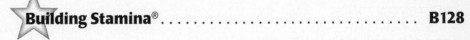

Chapter 5   Algebra

PART 2   Fractions, Decimals, Geometry, Measurement, and Data Analysis
Chapter 6   Fractions

Chapter 7   Decimals

Chapter 8   Geometry

Chapter 9   Measurement

Chapter 10   Data Analysis

*This Performance Indicator was designated as Post March prior to the 2009-10 school year and will now be taught during the **September-April** instructional periods.

This Performance Indicator was designated as Post March prior to the 2009-10 school year and will now be taught during the **May-June instructional periods.

Student Resources

DPTs (Diagonstic Practice Tests) . . . . Measuring Up® Supplement

> Your teacher may choose to give Diagnostic Practice Tests that assess your standards knowledge and identify areas where you may need extra support. These tests will help you prepare for the New York State Test for Mathematics.

ePath Assess™ . . . . Measuring Up® Supplement

> Your teacher may choose to assess your standards knowledge with Measuring Up ePath Assess™—an online diagnostic and formative assessment system customized to the New York State Learning Standards.

Lesson Correlation to the New York State Learning Standards for Grade 4 Mathematics

This worktext is 100% customized to the New York State Learning Standards and will help you prepare for the *New York State Test*!

New York State Learning Standards for Mathematics	Measuring Up® Lessons
Problem Solving Strand	
Students will build new mathematical knowledge through problem solving.	
4.PS.1 Explore, examine, and make observations about a social problem or mathematical situation	25, 38
4.PS.2 Understand that some ways of representing a problem are more helpful than others	21
4.PS.3 Interpret information correctly, identify the problem, and generate possible solutions	21, 33, 39, 58, 61, 62
Students will solve problems that arise in mathematics and in other contexts.	
4.PS.4 Act out or model with manipulatives activities involving mathematical content from literature	36
4.PS.5 Formulate problems and solutions from everyday situations	9, 37–39, 53, 54
4.PS.6 Translate from a picture/diagram to a numeric expression	13, 22–23, 38, 43–44
4.PS.7 Represent problem situations in oral, written, concrete, pictorial, and graphical forms	13, 15, 30–31, 45, 50, 61
4.PS.8 Select an appropriate representation of a problem	16, 21, 32, 43–44
Students will apply and adapt a variety of appropriate strategies to solve problems.	
4.PS.9 Use trial and error to solve problems	10
4.PS.10 Use process of elimination to solve problems	49
4.PS.11 Make pictures/diagrams of problems	35, 45, 47, 50
4.PS.12 Use physical objects to model problems	34, 47, 49
4.PS.13 Work in collaboration with others to solve problems	52
4.PS.14 Make organized lists to solve numerical problems	8
4.PS.15 Make charts to solve numerical problems	1, 8, 33, 40, 42, 61
4.PS.16 Analyze problems by identifying relationships	29, 33, 48
4.PS.17 Analyze problems by identifying relevant versus irrelevant information	27
4.PS.18 Analyze problems by observing patterns	19, 26, 28–29, 33
4.PS.19 State a problem in their own words	12
Students will monitor and reflect on the process of mathematical problem solving.	
4.PS.20 Determine what information is needed to solve a problem	27, 39
4.PS.21 Discuss with peers to understand a problem situation	48
4.PS.22 Discuss the efficiency of different representations of a problem	58
4.PS.23 Verify results of a problem	10, 12, 15, 27, 62
4.PS.24 Recognize invalid approaches	20
4.PS.25 Determine whether a solution is reasonable in the context of the original problem	11, 12, 57, 62
Reasoning and Proof Strand	
Students will recognize reasoning and proof as fundamental aspects of mathematics.	
4.RP.1 Use representations to support mathematical ideas	39, 45
4.RP.2 Determine whether a mathematical statement is true or false and explain why	3

New York State Learning Standards for Mathematics	Measuring Up® Lessons
Students will make and investigate mathematical conjectures.	
4.RP.3 Investigate the use of knowledgeable guessing by generalizing mathematical ideas	11
4.RP.4 Make conjectures from a variety of representations	59
Students will develop and evaluate mathematical arguments and proofs.	
4.RP.5 Justify general claims or conjectures, using manipulatives, models, and expressions	36
4.RP.6 Develop and explain an argument using oral, written, concrete, pictorial, and/or graphical forms	50, 52
4.RP.7 Discuss, listen, and make comments that support or reject claims made by other students	15, 52
Students will select and use various types of reasoning and methods of proof.	
4.RP.8 Support an argument by trying many cases	14
4.RP.9 Disprove an argument by finding counterexamples	20
Communication Strand	
Students will organize and consolidate their mathematical thinking through communication.	
4.CM.1 Understand and explain how to organize their thought process	8
4.CM.2 Verbally explain their rationale for strategy selection	21, 27, 39, 45, 57
4.CM.3 Provide reasoning both in written and verbal form	8, 52
Students will communicate their mathematical thinking coherently and clearly to peers, teachers, and others.	
4.CM.4 Organize and accurately label work	59
4.CM.5 Share organized mathematical ideas through the manipulation of objects, drawing, pictures, charts, graphs, tables, diagrams, models, symbols, and expressions in written and verbal form	8, 29, 32, 45, 50, 59
4.CM.6 Answer clarifying questions from others	47, 54
Students will analyze and evaluate the mathematical thinking and strategies of others.	
4.CM.7 Restate mathematical solutions shared by other students	36
4.CM.8 Consider strategies used and solutions found in relation to their own work	16
Students will use the language of mathematics to express mathematical ideas precisely.	
4.CM.9 Increase their use of mathematical vocabulary and language when communicating with others	46
4.CM.10 Describe objects, relationships, solutions and rationale using appropriate vocabulary	46, 49
4.CM.11 Decode and comprehend mathematical visuals and symbols to construct meaning	1, 3, 15, 34–36, 48, 55–56
Connections Strand	
Students will recognize and use connections among mathematical ideas.	
4.CN.1 Recognize, understand, and make connections in their everyday experiences to mathematical ideas	6, 49, 54
4.CN.2 Compare and contrast mathematical ideas	25
4.CN.3 Connect and apply mathematical information to solve problems	16
Students will understand how mathematical ideas interconnect and build on one another to produce a coherent whole.	
4.CN.4 Understand multiple representations and how they are related	2
4.CN.5 Model situations with objects and representations and be able to make observations	2, 34, 35, 45, 50
Students will recognize and apply mathematics in contexts outside of mathematics.	
4.CN.6 Recognize the presence of mathematics in their daily lives	6, 10, 51, 54, 56
4.CN.7 Apply mathematics to solve problems that develop outside of mathematics	24

continued

New York State Learning Standards for Mathematics		Measuring Up® Lessons
4.CN.8	Recognize and apply mathematics to other disciplines	62
Representation Strand		
Students will create and use representations to organize, record, and communicate mathematical ideas.		
4.R.1	Use verbal and written language, physical models, drawing charts, graphs, tables, symbols, and equations as representations	1, 4, 29–30, 33–35, 40-45, 50, 56, 61
4.R.2	Share mental images of mathematical ideas and understandings	48–49
4.R.3	Recognize and use external mathematical representations	5, 43–44
4.R.4	Use standard and nonstandard representations with accuracy and detail	53
Students will select, apply, and translate among mathematical representations to solve problems.		
4.R.5	Understand similarities and differences in representations	2
4.R.6	Connect mathematical representations with problem solving	32
4.R.7	Construct effective representations to solve problems	13, 16, 21, 32, 33, 35, 39, 61
Students will use representations to model and interpret physical, social, and mathematical phenomena.		
4.R.8	Use mathematics to show and understand physical phenomena (e.g., estimate and represent the number of apples in a tree)	7
4.R.9	Use mathematics to show and understand social phenomena (e.g., determine the number of buses required for a field trip)	25
4.R.10	Use mathematics to show and understand mathematical phenomena (e.g., use a multiplication grid to solve odd and even number problems)	14
Number Sense and Operations Strand		
Students will understand numbers, multiple ways of representing numbers, relationships among numbers, and number systems.		
4.N.1	Skip count by 1,000's	1
4.N.2	Read and write whole numbers to 10,000	1
4.N.3	Compare and order numbers to 10,000	3, 4, 8
4.N.4	Understand the place value structure of the base ten number system: 10 ones = 1 ten 10 tens = 1 hundred 10 hundreds = 1 thousand 10 thousands = 1 ten thousand	2
4.N.5	Recognize equivalent representations for numbers up to four digits and generate them by decomposing and composing numbers	2
4.N.6	Understand, use, and explain the associative property of multiplication	15
*4.N.7	Develop an understanding of fractions as locations on number lines and as divisions of whole numbers	34
*4.N.8	Recognize and generate equivalent fractions (halves, fourths, thirds, fifths, sixths, and tenths) using manipulatives, visual models, and illustrations	35
*4.N.9	Use concrete materials and visual models to compare and order unit fractions or fractions with the same denominator (with and without the use of a number line)	36
*4.N.10	Develop an understanding of decimals as part of a whole	40, 41
*4.N.11	Read and write decimals to hundredths, using money as a context	40
*4.N.12	Use concrete materials and visual models to compare and order decimals (less than 1) to the hundredths place in the context of money	42
4.N.13	Develop an understanding of the properties of odd/even numbers as a result of multiplication	14

continued

New York State Learning Standards for Mathematics	Measuring Up® Lessons
Students will understand meanings of operations and procedures, and how they relate to one another.	
4.N.14 Use a variety of strategies to add and subtract numbers up to 10,000	9, 10, 12
4.N.15 Select appropriate computational and operational methods to solve problems	11
4.N.16 Understand various meanings of multiplication and division	13–18, 21–25
4.N.17 Use multiplication and division as inverse operations to solve problems	23
4.N.18 Use a variety of strategies to multiply two-digit numbers by one-digit numbers (with and without regrouping)	17, 19, 20
*4.N.19 Use a variety of strategies to multiply two-digit numbers by two-digit numbers (with and without regrouping)	18, 21
4.N.20 Develop fluency in multiplying and dividing multiples of 10 and 100 up to 1,000	19, 20, 26
4.N.21 Use a variety of strategies to divide two-digit dividends by one-digit divisors (with and without remainders)	22, 24, 25, 27
4.N.22 Interpret the meaning of remainders	25
*4.N.23 Add and subtract proper fractions with common denominators	37–39
*4.N.24 Express decimals as an equivalent form of fractions to tenths and hundredths	41
*4.N.25 Add and subtract decimals to tenths and hundredths using a hundreds chart	43–45
Students will compute accurately and make reasonable estimates.	
4.N.26 Round numbers less than 1,000 to the nearest tens and hundreds	5, 8, 11, 20
4.N.27 Check reasonableness of an answer by using estimation	7, 11, 12, 17
Algebra Strand	
Students will represent and analyze algebraically a wide variety of problem solving situations.	
4.A.1 Evaluate and express relationships using open sentences with one operation.	30–32
Students will perform algebraic procedures accurately.	
*4.A.2 Use the symbols $<$, $>$, $=$, and $\neq$ (with and without the use of a number line) to compare whole numbers and unit fractions and decimals (up to hundredths)	3, 4, 31, 36
4.A.3 Find the value or values that will make an open sentence true, if it contains $<$ or $>$	31
Students will recognize, use, and represent algebraically patterns, relations, and functions.	
4.A.4 Describe, extend, and make generalizations about numeric ($+$, $-$, $\times$, $\div$) and geometric patterns	28
4.A.5 Analyze a pattern or a whole-number function and state the rule, given a table or an input/output box	29, 33
Geometry Strand	
Students will use visualization and spatial reasoning to analyze characteristics and properties of geometric shapes.	
4.G.1 Identify and name polygons, recognizing that their names are related to the number of sides and angles (triangle, quadrilateral, pentagon, hexagon, and octagon)	48, 50
4.G.2 Identify points and line segments when drawing a plane figure	46, 48
4.G.3 Find perimeter of polygons by adding sides	55
4.G.4 Find the area of a rectangle by counting the number of squares needed to cover the rectangle	56, 57
4.G.5 Define and identify vertices, faces, and edges of three-dimensional shapes	49, 50

continued

New York State Learning Standards for Mathematics	Measuring Up® Lessons
Students will identify and justify geometric relationships, formally and informally.	
**4.G.6 Draw and identify intersecting, perpendicular, and parallel lines	46
**4.G.7 Identify points and rays when drawing angles	47
**4.G.8 Classify angles as acute, obtuse, right, and straight	47
Measurement Strand	
Students will determine what can be measured and how, using appropriate methods and formulas.	
4.M.1 Select tools and units (customary and metric) appropriate for the length measured	51, 57
4.M.2 Use a ruler to measure to the nearest standard unit (whole, ½ and ¼ inches, whole feet, whole yards, whole centimeters, and whole meters)	51
4.M.3 Know and understand equivalent standard units of length: 12 inches = 1 foot 3 feet = 1 yard	51, 57
4.M.4 Select tools and units appropriate to the mass of the object being measured (grams and kilograms)	52
4.M.5 Measure mass, using grams	52, 57
4.M.6 Select tools and units appropriate to the capacity being measured (milliliters and liters)	53
4.M.7 Measure capacity, using milliliters and liters	53, 57
Students will use units to give meaning to measurements.	
4.M.8 Make change, using combined coins and dollar amounts	6
4.M.9 Calculate elapsed time in hours and half hours, not crossing A.M./P.M.	54
4.M.10 Calculate elapsed time in days and weeks, using a calendar	54
Statistics and Probability Strand	
Students will collect, organize, display, and analyze data.	
**4.S.1 Design investigations to address a question from given data	58, 59
**4.S.2 Collect data using observations, surveys, and experiments and record appropriately	58, 59, 61
4.S.3 Represent data using tables, bar graphs, and pictographs	58, 59, 61
*4.S.4 Read and interpret line graphs	60, 62
Students will make predictions that are based upon data analysis.	
4.S.5 Develop and make predictions that are based on data	59–61
4.S.6 Formulate conclusions and make predictions from graphs	59, 60, 62

*This Performance Indicator was designated as Post March prior to the 2009-10 school year and will now be taught during the **September-April** instructional periods.

** This Performance Indicator was designated as Post March prior to the 2009-10 school year and will now be taught during the **May-June** instructional periods.

Dear Student,

How do you get better at the things you do? You practice! Just as with sports and other activities, the key to success in school is practice, practice, practice.

This book will help you review and practice skills in mathematics. These are the skills you need to know to measure up to the New York State Learning Standards and Performance Indicators for your grade. Practicing these skills now will help you do better in your work all year.

There are two parts in this book. Part 1 focuses on number sense and place value, addition and subtraction, multiplication, division, and algebra. Part 2 focuses on fractions, decimals, geometry, measurement, and data analysis.

Each lesson consists of four main sections:

- **Focus on the NYS Learning Standards** introduces the skills covered in the lesson.

- **Guided Instruction** shows you the steps and skills you need to solve problems.

- **Apply the NYS Learning Standards** helps you practice the important concepts and skills you learned in each lesson.

- **NYS Test Practice** gives you experience in answering test-type questions.

There are many chances for you to practice your mathematical skills. At the end of each chapter are **Building Stamina**® sections. Each **Building Stamina**® includes multiple-choice questions and extended-response questions. The Part 1, Part 2, and End-of-Book **Building Stamina**® also have short-response questions. Many of these questions are more difficult and will help you prepare for taking mathematics tests.

Grade 3 May/June Review covers skills from the prior grade level that may appear on the Grade 4 **New York State Test** for Mathematics.

Here are symbols you will see to help you solve some problems in the book.

This picture means that you will need to use a ruler.

This picture means that you will need to use a protractor.

This school year you will take the New York State Test. It will be an important step forward. The test will show how well you measure up to the New York State Learning Standards for Mathematics. It is just one of the many important tests you will take.

Have a great year!

Peoples Education®
Your partner in student success®

to the
New York State Learning Standards
and Success Strategies for the State Test

Dear Families,

All students need mathematics skills to succeed in school and in life. New York educators have created grade-appropriate standards called the New York State Learning Standards and Performance Indicators for these skills. These standards describe what New York students should know at different grade levels. Students need to meet these standards as measured by the **New York State Test** for Mathematics, which your child will take this school year.

The **New York State Test** for Mathematics is directly related to the New York State Learning Standards. The Mathematics standards comprise 5 Content Strands and 5 Process Strands. Each Strand has some specific Performance Indicators that are used to show how well the student has mastered mathematics concepts and skills. The standards emphasize higher-order thinking skills. Students must learn to use mathematical reasoning, analysis, and interpretation instead of just recalling facts.

Measuring Up® will help your child review the New York State Learning Standards and prepare for all mathematics exams. It contains:

- **Lessons** that focus on the New York State Learning Standards and Core Curriculum;

- **Guided Instruction,** in which students are shown the steps and skills necessary to solve a variety of mathematical problems;

- **Apply the NYS Learning Standards,** in which students apply the skills they have learned;

- **NYS Test Practice,** in which students practice answering test-type questions;

- **Building Stamina®,** which provides practice with multiple-choice, short-response, and extended-response questions that require higher-order thinking.

- **Grade 3 May/June Review,** which covers skills from the prior grade level that may appear on the Grade 4 **New York State Test** for Mathematics.

You play a crucial role in your child's success in school as well as in the rest of the world. Below are a few suggestions for helping your child meet the educational challenges with interest and enthusiasm!

- Keep mathematics alive in your home. Involve your child in activities that use mathematics such as mixing recipes, counting coins, telling time, and identifying geometric shapes and patterns.

- Look for ways in which mathematics is used when you are out with your family. Encourage your child to count your change after making a purchase, read the items and prices on a restaurant menu, identify shapes such as spheres and cubes in real objects, and add or subtract to find how many there are or how many are left in real-life situations.

- Ask your child to talk and write about what he or she has learned in mathematics. Always encourage your child to use mathematical language.

- Encourage your child to take time to review and check his or her homework. Finding a solution is just one part of solving a problem. Ask your child to tell why his or her answers are reasonable and make sense.

Work with us this year to ensure your child's success. Mathematics skills are essential skills for success throughout your child's life.

Your partner in student success®

What's Ahead in Measuring Up

This book was created for New York students just like you. Each lesson and question is aimed at helping you master the New York State Learning Standards for Mathematics and do well on the **New York State Test** in Mathematics for grade 4. It will also help you do well on other mathematics exams you take during the school year.

About the Test

New York educators have set up standards for mathematics. They are called the New York State Learning Standards and Core Curriculum. These standards spell out what students at each grade level should know. New York educators have also created a statewide test for mathematics, which you will take in May. It is called the Grade 4 **New York State Test** for Mathematics. The test will assess your conceptual understanding, procedural fluency, and problem-solving abilities. Test questions are based on Performance Indicators from the following Content Strands within the New York State Learning Standards for Mathematics:

The Five Content Strands:

Number Sense and Operations Strand
Algebra Strand
Geometry Strand
Measurement Strand
Probability and Statistics Strand

The New York State Learning Standards and Core Curriculum also include the following Process Strands, which are meant to be integrated throughout all mathematics concepts taught during the school year.

The Five Process Strands:

Problem Solving Strand
Reasoning and Proof Strand
Communication Strand
Connections Strand
Representation Strand

Format of the Test

The Grade 4 **New York State Test** for Mathematics is given in May and is broken up into two sections. You will see many question types on the **New York State Test,** such as multiple-choice, short-response, and extended-response questions.

Section 1 of the **New York State Test** for Mathematics includes 45 multiple-choice questions, which you will have 70 minutes to complete. Section 2 has 8 short-response questions and 4 extended-response questions that you will have 70 minutes to answer.

Many questions include a picture, a graph, a number line, or another type of graphic that is used to solve the problem. This book gives you practice in reading and using these types of graphics.

Measuring Up on Multiple-Choice Questions

A multiple-choice question has two parts. The first part is the stem, or question.

It has a number in front of it. The second part is made up of the answer choices. Each answer choice has a letter in front of it. You will be asked to read each question and then circle the letter of the best answer.

Some of the multiple-choice questions have a graph or table. You will need to read information from the graph or table to solve the problem.

For example, in the question below, you will need to read the information in the table, select the answer choice that seems most reasonable, then circle the letter next to that answer.

1 The table below shows the cost of flowers in a flower shop.

Number of Flowers	Cost
4	$1.00
5	$1.25
6	$1.50
7	$1.75

How much does one flower cost?

A 10 cents   **C** 25 cents

B 20 cents   **D** 50 cents

By studying the pattern in the table, you can see that each flower costs 25 cents. So C is the correct answer. Notice how to mark your answer.

Here are some strategies for answering multiple-choice questions:

- Try to work the problem without looking at the answer choices. Once you have solved the problem, compare your answer with the answer choices.

- Eliminate answer choices you know are wrong. Then choose from the answers that are left.

- Some questions will be more difficult than others. The problem may require an extra step, or you may need to look for those answers that do not apply.

- Even if you don't know the answer, you can make a good guess based on what you know and get the right answer.

- Check and double-check your answers before you turn in the test. Be sure of your answers.

Measuring Up on Short-and Extended-Response Questions

For short- and extended-response questions, you may be required to write an answer to an open-ended question and to show your work. In some cases, you may be required to explain, in words, how you arrived at your answer.

Here are some tips for answering short- and extended-response questions:

- Carefully work the problem. You do not have answer choices as a way to check your work. Use your time wisely and follow all the steps carefully.

- When you have an answer, carefully write it down.

- Use information from the problem and your answer to help you write an explanation of your work and reasoning. Show all of your thinking.

- Read over your explanation. Does it say what you wanted to explain?

Higher-Order Thinking Skills

Higher-order thinking skills are important on the **New York State Test.** When you use higher-order thinking skills, you do more than just recall information. On the **New York State Test,** some questions ask you to find and continue a pattern, understand and use information in a table or graph, or use a number line. Instead of adding or subtracting to solve a problem, you may need to solve a two-step problem and use both operations. In Measuring Up, the higher-order thinking skills questions are starred.

Measuring Up with Building Stamina

A special feature of Measuring Up is **Building Stamina.** It was created to give you practice and build your confidence for taking hard tests. The more you practice answering hard questions, the more prepared you will be to succeed. At the end of each part and the end of the book is a longer **Building Stamina.** These review the New York State Learning Standards covered in the lessons.

Measuring Up with May/June Review

Measuring Up includes a section in the front of the book called Grade 3 May-June Review. This section will help you review mathematics skills that you learned in Grade 3 but that may appear on the Grade 4 **New York State Test** that you will have to take this year.

Tips for Measuring Up

Here are some more test-taking tips for you to keep in mind. These tips will help you do better on the tests you will take this year.

- Start getting ready now. Spend a few minutes a day answering practice test questions.

- Get a good night's sleep the night before the test.

- Eat a good breakfast.

- Keep telling yourself that you will do well. Then you probably will. That's what it means to "think positively."

You will learn a lot in Measuring Up. You will review and practice the skills included in the New York State Learning Standards. You will practice for the Grade 4 **New York State Test** for Mathematics. Finally, you will build stamina to answer tough questions. You will more than measure up. You will be a smashing success!

What's Inside: A Lesson Guide

The lessons in this worktext first introduce individual content standards and then explain, apply, and assess the concepts and skills that are needed to meet those standards.

Focus on the NYS Learning Standards

Introduces the standards and important terms and concepts covered in the lesson. These terms are defined in a glossary at the end of the book.

Guided Instruction

Allows you to work with your teacher to learn the steps needed to solve different types of mathematical problems.

Focus on the NYS Learning Standards

Chapter 6
Lesson 34 Understand Fractions

NYS Performance Indicators: 4.N.7, 4.PS.12, 4.CN.5, 4.CM.11, 4.R.1

A **fraction** is a number that names part of a whole or part of a group.

The first model shows a whole with 6 equal parts. The second model shows a group with 6 equal parts. The fraction $\frac{2}{6}$ names the shaded part of each model.

$\frac{2}{6}$ ← numerator
$\frac{2}{6}$ ← denominator

The **numerator** tells the number of equal parts shaded. The **denominator** tells the total number of equal parts.

The arrow points to the location of the fraction $\frac{2}{6}$ on the number line.

$$\frac{0}{6} \quad \frac{1}{6} \quad \frac{2}{6} \quad \frac{3}{6} \quad \frac{4}{6} \quad \frac{5}{6} \quad \frac{6}{6}$$

Guided Instruction

Problem | What fraction of the marbles are striped?

Step 1 Write the number of striped marbles as the numerator. Then write the total number of marbles as the denominator.

← numerator
← denominator

Step 2 Read the fraction. $\frac{3}{8}$ is read "three eighths."

Solution What fraction of the marbles are striped? _____

Another Example

You can use models to find $\frac{1}{2}$ of 10.

The denominator, 2, tells you to separate the 10 counters into 2 equal groups.

2 groups

The numerator, 1, tells you to count the number in 1 group.

$\frac{1}{2}$ of 10 is 5.

142 Mathematics • Level D   Copying is illegal.   Measuring Up® to the New York State Learning Standards

---

Apply the NYS Learning Standards

Provides practice for the important concepts and skills learned in the Guided Instruction section of the lesson.

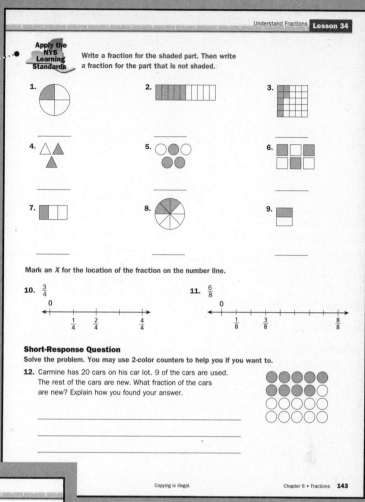

NYS Test Practice

Gives multiple-choice questions that will test understanding of the concepts and skills taught in the lesson.

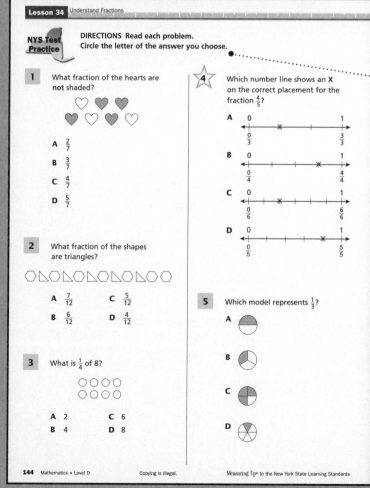

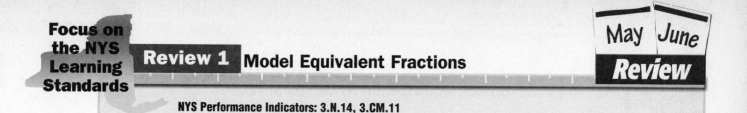
You can use models to help you understand equivalent fractions.
Equivalent fractions are fractions that name the same amount.

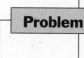
Guided Instruction

Problem Rob folded his paper in 2 equal parts. He shaded 1 of the parts. Kathy folded her equally sized paper in 4 equal parts. Then she shaded 2 of the parts. Who shaded more of the paper?

You can make models to compare the parts.

• Model of Rob's paper

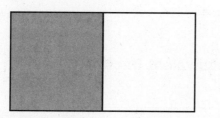

How many equal parts in all? _____

How many parts are shaded? _____

What fraction of the paper

did Rob shade? _____

• Model of Kathy's paper

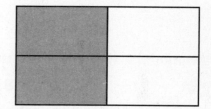

How many equal parts in all? _____

How many parts are shaded? _____

What fraction of the paper did

Kathy shade? _____

Compare the parts that are shaded.

They are the same size.

$\frac{1}{2}$ and $\frac{2}{4}$ name the same amount.

They are equivalent fractions.

$\frac{1}{2} = $ _____

Solution Who shaded more of their paper?

_____

Apply the NYS Learning Standards

Are the fractions equivalent? Write *yes* or *no*.

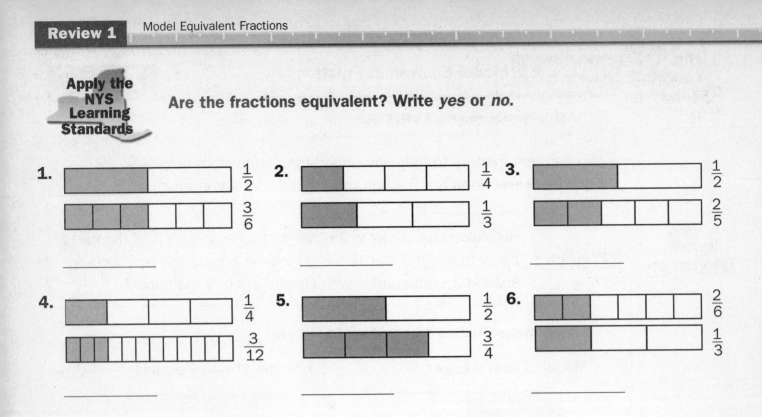

1. $\frac{1}{2}$
   $\frac{3}{6}$

   _____

2. $\frac{1}{4}$
   $\frac{1}{3}$

   _____

3. $\frac{1}{2}$
   $\frac{2}{5}$

   _____

4. $\frac{1}{4}$
   $\frac{3}{12}$

   _____

5. $\frac{1}{2}$
   $\frac{3}{4}$

   _____

6. $\frac{2}{6}$
   $\frac{1}{3}$

   _____

Use the models at the right to name an equivalent fraction.

7. $\frac{2}{8}$ = _____

8. $\frac{1}{2}$ = _____

9. $\frac{8}{8}$ = _____

10. $\frac{3}{4}$ = _____

$\frac{1}{2}$				$\frac{1}{2}$			
$\frac{1}{4}$		$\frac{1}{4}$		$\frac{1}{4}$		$\frac{1}{4}$	
$\frac{1}{6}$	$\frac{1}{6}$	$\frac{1}{6}$	$\frac{1}{6}$	$\frac{1}{6}$	$\frac{1}{6}$
$\frac{1}{8}$	$\frac{1}{8}$	$\frac{1}{8}$	$\frac{1}{8}$	$\frac{1}{8}$	$\frac{1}{8}$	$\frac{1}{8}$	$\frac{1}{8}$
$\frac{1}{10}$	$\frac{1}{10}$	$\frac{1}{10}$	$\frac{1}{10}$	$\frac{1}{10}$	$\frac{1}{10}$	$\frac{1}{10}$	$\frac{1}{10}$	$\frac{1}{10}$	$\frac{1}{10}$

Short-Response Questions

Solve each problem. Shade the models to help you.

11. Carl ate $\frac{1}{4}$ of the pie. Sam ate $\frac{2}{8}$ of the pie.
    Did they eat the same amount of the pie?

    _____

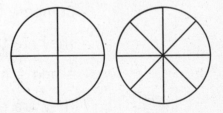

12. Jared planted $\frac{3}{6}$ of the garden with tomatoes.
    He planted $\frac{1}{3}$ of the garden with flowers.
    Did he plant the same amount of tomatoes
    and flowers?

    _____

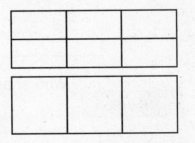

Measuring Up® to the New York State Learning Standards

NYS Test Practice

DIRECTIONS Read each problem.
Circle the letter of the answer you choose.

1 The picture below best shows which statement?

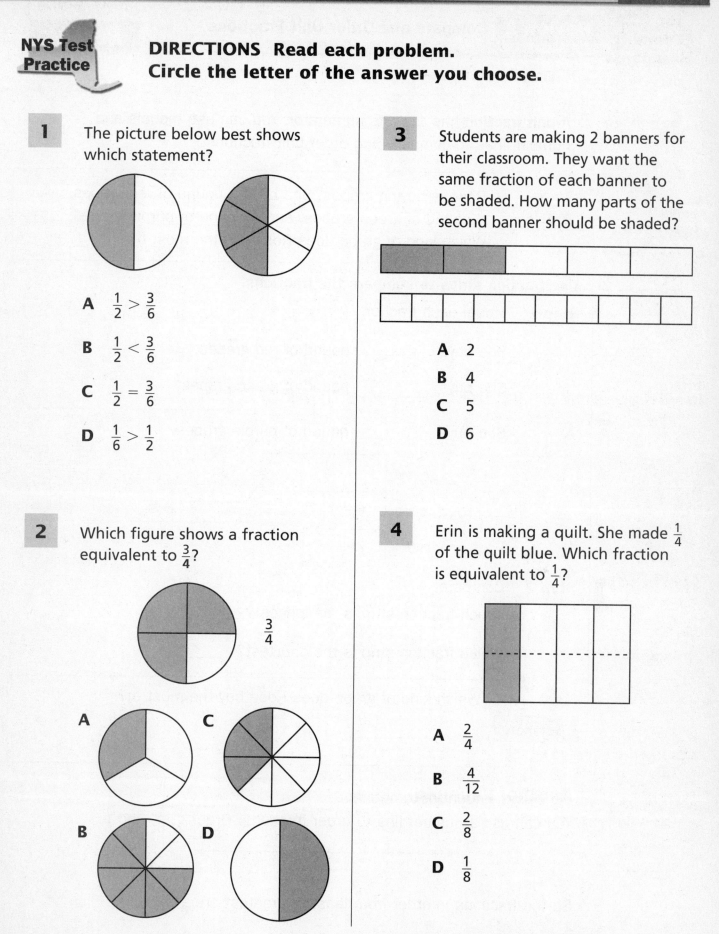

A $\frac{1}{2} > \frac{3}{6}$

B $\frac{1}{2} < \frac{3}{6}$

C $\frac{1}{2} = \frac{3}{6}$

D $\frac{1}{6} > \frac{1}{2}$

2 Which figure shows a fraction equivalent to $\frac{3}{4}$?

$\frac{3}{4}$

A

B

C

D

3 Students are making 2 banners for their classroom. They want the same fraction of each banner to be shaded. How many parts of the second banner should be shaded?

A 2

B 4

C 5

D 6

4 Erin is making a quilt. She made $\frac{1}{4}$ of the quilt blue. Which fraction is equivalent to $\frac{1}{4}$?

A $\frac{2}{4}$

B $\frac{4}{12}$

C $\frac{2}{8}$

D $\frac{1}{8}$

A **unit fraction** has 1 as its numerator. You can use models and number lines to compare and order unit fractions.

Guided Instruction

Problem Rosa is buying grapes. She buys $\frac{1}{2}$ pound of red grapes, $\frac{1}{4}$ pound of green grapes, and $\frac{1}{3}$ pound of purple grapes. Which kind of grape does Rosa buy the most of?

Use fraction strips to compare the fractions.

Step 1 Model each fraction.

She buys _____ pound of red grapes.

She buys _____ pound of green grapes.

She buys _____ pound of purple grapes.

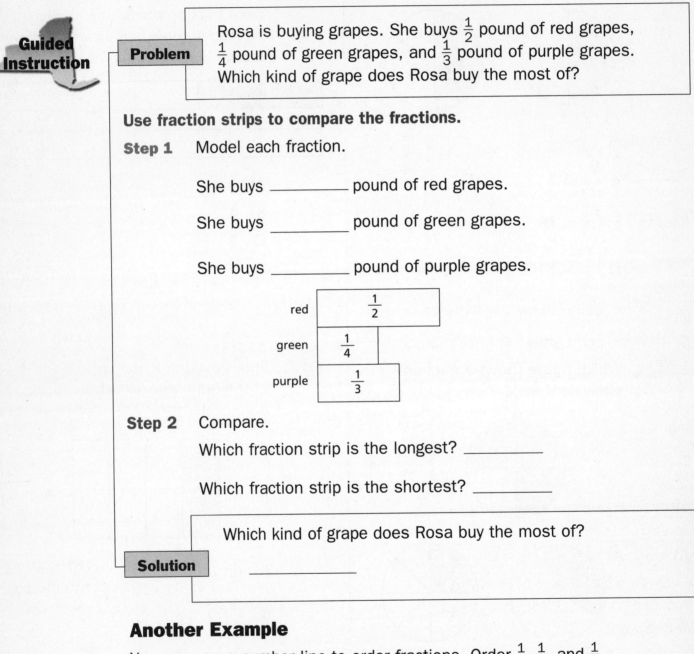

Step 2 Compare.

Which fraction strip is the longest? _____

Which fraction strip is the shortest? _____

Which kind of grape does Rosa buy the most of?

Solution _____

Another Example

You can use a number line to order fractions. Order $\frac{1}{2}$, $\frac{1}{6}$, and $\frac{1}{5}$.

So the fractions in order from least to greatest are $\frac{1}{6}$, $\frac{1}{5}$, $\frac{1}{2}$.

$\frac{1}{6} < \frac{1}{5} < \frac{1}{2}$

Measuring Up® to the New York State Learning Standards

Apply the NYS Learning Standards

Use the models to compare the fractions.

1. Which is greater, $\frac{1}{4}$ or $\frac{1}{5}$?

_____

2. Which is greater, $\frac{1}{6}$ or $\frac{1}{10}$?

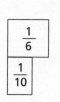

_____

3. Which is greater, $\frac{1}{3}$ or $\frac{1}{2}$?

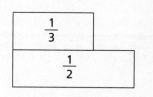

_____

Locate each fraction on the number line.

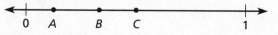

4. Which point shows the location of $\frac{1}{3}$? _____

5. Which point shows the location of $\frac{1}{2}$? _____

6. Which point shows the location of $\frac{1}{8}$? _____

Use the number line above. Write <, =, or > to compare.

7. $\frac{1}{3}$ ◯ $\frac{1}{2}$ **8.** $\frac{1}{2}$ ◯ $\frac{1}{8}$ **9.** $\frac{1}{8}$ ◯ $\frac{1}{3}$

Short-Response Question
Solve the problem.

10. Max's family had pizza night. They ate $\frac{1}{8}$ of a pepperoni pizza, $\frac{1}{6}$ of a white pizza, $\frac{1}{2}$ of a veggie pizza, and $\frac{1}{4}$ of a supreme pizza. The pizzas were all the same size. List the pizzas in order from the least amount eaten to the greatest amount eaten. Explain how you found your answer.

_____

_____

_____

NYS Test Practice

DIRECTIONS Read each problem.
Circle the letter of the answer you choose.

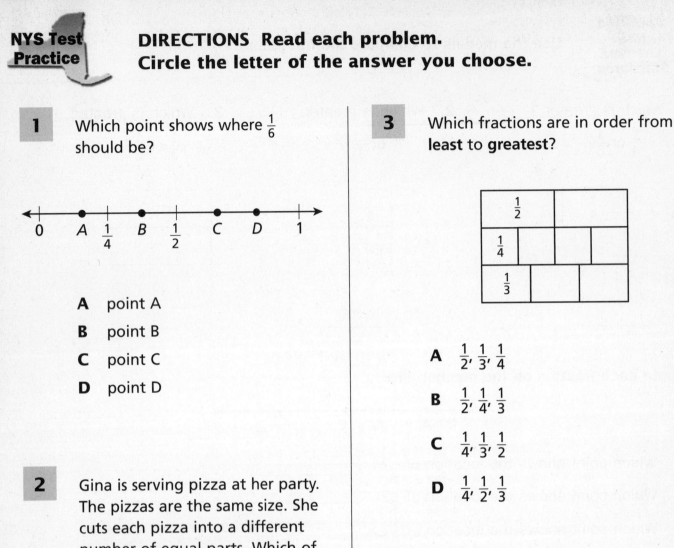

1 Which point shows where $\frac{1}{6}$ should be?

A   point A

B   point B

C   point C

D   point D

2 Gina is serving pizza at her party. The pizzas are the same size. She cuts each pizza into a different number of equal parts. Which of the following shows the pizza with the largest slices?

A   a pizza cut into 4 parts

B   a pizza cut into 5 parts

C   a pizza cut into 6 parts

D   a pizza cut into 10 parts

3 Which fractions are in order from **least** to **greatest**?

A $\frac{1}{2}, \frac{1}{3}, \frac{1}{4}$

B $\frac{1}{2}, \frac{1}{4}, \frac{1}{3}$

C $\frac{1}{4}, \frac{1}{3}, \frac{1}{2}$

D $\frac{1}{4}, \frac{1}{2}, \frac{1}{3}$

4 Which number sentence is correct?

A $\frac{1}{10} > \frac{1}{2}$

B $\frac{1}{3} < \frac{1}{4}$

C $\frac{1}{3} > \frac{1}{10}$

D $\frac{1}{2} = \frac{1}{1}$

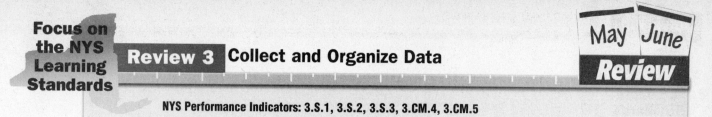
NYS Performance Indicators: 3.S.1, 3.S.2, 3.S.3, 3.CM.4, 3.CM.5

Data is information. A **survey** is one way to collect data. When you conduct a survey, you ask a question and record the answer. You can display the results from a survey in a tally chart or in a table. Remember

I = 1   II = 2   III = 3   IIII = 4   ℋ = 5

Guided Instruction

Problem

Gina took a survey to find the favorite fruit of her classmates. The tally chart shows the results for berries, grapes, and bananas. Apples were chosen by 8 students. Complete the tally chart. Which fruit did the greatest number of students choose?

FAVORITE FRUIT

Fruit	Tally	Number
Grapes	ℋ II	
Berries	ℋ ℋ	
Bananas	IIII	
Apples		

Interpret the data in the table.

Step 1   How many students chose apples? _____

Fill in the tally marks for apples.

Step 2   Write the numbers that the tallies represent to complete the chart.

Step 3   Compare the numbers. Which is the greatest number? _____

Solution

Which fruit did the greatest number of students choose?

_____

Apply the NYS Learning Standards

Use the information below to complete the tally chart.

Juan asked his classmates which ice cream flavor was their favorite. These are their answers.

vanilla	strawberry	chocolate	vanilla
cotton candy	chocolate	vanilla	vanilla
vanilla	chocolate	cotton candy	chocolate
chocolate	cotton candy	strawberry	chocolate

Complete the tally chart to show how many children picked each flavor. You may cross off each vote as you tally.

FAVORITE ICE CREAM FLAVOR

	Flavor	Tally	Number
1.	Vanilla		
2.	Chocolate		
3.	Strawberry		
4.	Cotton candy		

Short-Response Questions

Fill in the chart below by completing problems 5–8.

5. Write a survey question about pets to ask 11 of your classmates.

   _____

6. Fill in the title for your chart.

7. Fill in the labels across the top row of your chart.

8. Survey your classmates and record their answers in the chart below.

_____

NYS Test Practice

DIRECTIONS Read each problem. *teac theater*
Circle the letter of the answer you choose.

1 The tally chart shows the number of votes students received for Student Council Representative.

STUDENT COUNCIL CANDIDATES

Name	Tally	Number
Sheila	IIII	5
Heidi	IIII III	8
Taylor	IIII I	6
Marco	IIII IIII	? =9

What number should be next to the tally marks by the student with the greatest number of votes?

A 5

B 6

C 8

D 9

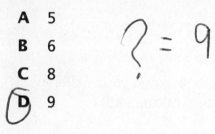

? = 9

2 What number would you record for the tally marks shown below?

A 5

B 6

C 8

D 9

3 Brian has his friends each draw their favorite shape. The results are below.

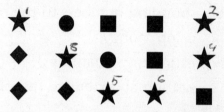

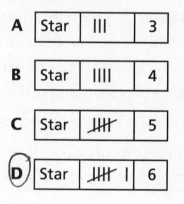

Brian wants to make a tally chart of this information.

Which shows what the row for *star* should look like?

A	Star	III	3

B	Star	IIII	4

C	Star	IIII	5

D	Star	IIII I	6

4 Which do you think would be the **best** survey question?

A How would you explain why it rains?

B What are your favorite memories of being 5 years old?

C How many rooms are in your house?

D Why do you go to bed at night?

Chapter 1 Number Sense and Place Value

In Chapter 1, you will study and practice:

- understanding place value to ten thousand;
- finding equivalent forms of numbers;
- comparing whole numbers to ten thousand;
- ordering whole numbers to ten thousand;
- rounding numbers to the nearest ten, hundred;
- using money;
- estimating quantities;
- writing an extended response to solve problems.

★ **Building Stamina**® This section gives you a chance to sharpen your skills in number sense and place value while strengthening your test-taking skills.

Chapter 2 Addition and Subtraction

In Chapter 2, you will study and practice:

- adding whole numbers;
- subtracting whole numbers;
- estimating sums and differences;
- determining a reasonable solution to solve problems.

★ **Building Stamina**® This section gives you a chance to sharpen your skills in addition and subtraction while strengthening your test-taking skills.

Chapter 3 Multiplication

In Chapter 3, you will study and practice:

- understanding multiplication;
- finding patterns in multiplication;
- using multiplication properties;
- using the distributive property;
- multiplying by one- and two-digit factors;
- multiplying by multiples of 10 and 100 using patterns;
- estimating products;
- solving a simpler problem to solve problems.

★ **Building Stamina**® This section gives you a chance to sharpen your skills in multiplication while strengthening your test-taking skills.

Chapter 4 Division

In Chapter 4, you will study and practice:

- understanding division;
- relating multiplication and division;
- using divisors to 10;
- interpreting and applying remainders;
- dividing multiples of 10 and 100;
- identifying relevant and irrelevant information to solve problems.

★ **Building Stamina**® This section gives you a chance to sharpen your skills in division while strengthening your test-taking skills.

Chapter 5 Algebra

In Chapter 5, you will study and practice:

- describing, extending, and creating patterns;
- analyzing patterns and functions;
- using variables;
- using simple equations or inequalities;
- writing expressions or equations;
- making a table to solve problems.

★ **Building Stamina**® This section gives you a chance to sharpen your skills in algebra while strengthening your test-taking skills.

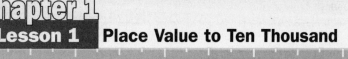
Place value can help you read and write numbers.

A place-value chart shows the value of each digit in a number. In larger numbers, commas are used to separate groups of three digits.

Guided Instruction

Problem

Mount Marcy, the highest mountain in New York state, is 5,344 feet high. How would you read the number 5,344?

You can use a place-value chart to help you read the number.

Step 1 Write the number in the place-value chart.

Thousands		Ones		
ten thousands	thousands	hundreds	tens	ones
		,		

What value does the digit 3 have? _____

Step 2 Read the number in the place-value chart from left to right. Say "thousand" instead of the first comma.
How many thousands are there? _____

Solution

How would you read the number 5,344?

_____

Write each population in words.

NEW YORK TOWN POPULATIONS

Town	Population
Amboy	1,312
Hornell	9,019
Knox	2,647

1. Amboy _____

2. Hornell _____

3. Knox _____

Write the value of the underlined digit.

4. 6,349 _____

5. 4,009 _____

6. 9,899 _____

7. 6,570 _____

8. 1,342 _____

9. 364 _____

Use the number line.

10. Mark the number that is 1,000 greater than 2,500.

←—————————————————————————————————————→

2,000 2,100 2,200 2,300 2,400 2,500 2,600 2,700 2,800 2,900 3,000 3,100 3,200 3,300 3,400 3,500 3,600 3,700 3,800 3,900 4,000

Short-Response Questions

Solve the problems.

11. By how much would the value of 7,409 change if the digit 4 were replaced with the digit 2? _____

12. In the number 6,547, how much will I have to add to change the digit 6 to an 8? _____

13. Which digit in the number 1,983 has the greatest value? Explain.

_____

_____

_____

NYS Test Practice

**DIRECTIONS Read each problem.
Circle the letter of the answer you choose.**

1 What is another way to write three thousand four hundred seven?

A 3,047

B 3,407

C 3,470

D 3,704

2 What is the value of the underlined digit of 9,845?

A 9

B 90

C 900

D 9,000

3 By how much would the value of 7,324 change if the digits 7 and 3 were both replaced with the digit 5?

A 18

B 55

C 1,800

D 5,500

4 How do you write the number 9,506 in words?

A nine thousand fifty six

B nine thousand five hundred six

C nine thousand five hundred sixty

D nine thousand six hundred fifty

5 The table below shows the number of pages read by students in each grade during a reading contest.

Grade	Pages Read
First	7,042
Second	8,420
Third	5,240
Fourth	5,042
Fifth	5,204

Which grade read five thousand two hundred forty pages?

A first grade

B second grade

C third grade

D fourth grade

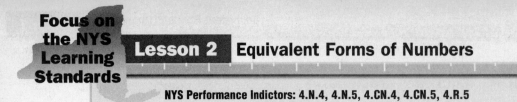
You can show a number in different ways. Numbers are **equivalent** when they describe the same amount.

Guided Instruction

| Problem | What are three different ways to show the number 482? |

You can show a number by using a model, using place value, and using computation.

Step 1 Use a model to show 482.

What number is shown? _____

Step 2 Use place value to show 482.

_____ hundreds _____ tens _____ ones

Step 3 Use computation to show 482. Write a mathematical expression using addition, subtraction, multiplication, or division.

500 − _____ = 482

| Solution | Three different ways to show 482 are _____ _____. |

Another Example

Do 3 hundreds 1 ten 8 ones and 300 + 300 equal the same number?

3 hundreds 1 ten 8 ones = 318

300 + 300 = 600

Apply the
NYS
Learning
Standards

Complete the table. Write an equivalent form for each number.

	Number	Model	Place Value	Computation
1.	187		1 hundred 8 tens 7 ones	
2.	302			310 − 8
3.	38		3 tens 8 ones	19 + 19

Write *true* or *false*.

4. 7 hundreds 3 tens 8 ones is equivalent to 600 + 138. _____

5. is equivalent to 4 hundreds 7 tens 1 one. _____

Two number forms are equivalent and one is not.
Cross out the one that is not equivalent.

6.

5 tens 9 ones		100 − 50

7.

182 + 208		3 hundreds 9 tens 0 ones

Short-Response Question

Solve the problem.

8. John said that 3 hundreds 6 tens 5 ones is equivalent to
565 − 100. Is this true? Explain your thinking.

_____

NYS Test Practice

DIRECTIONS Read each problem.
Circle the letter of the answer you choose.

1 Which is an equivalent form of
8 hundreds 3 tens 3 ones?

A $800 + 30$

B $700 + 133$

C $830 - 3$

D $933 - 10$

2 Which model is another way
to show $371 + 15$?

A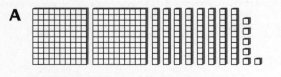

B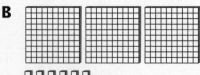

C

D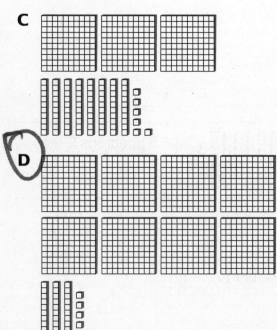

3 Which two number forms
are not equivalent?

A $70 + 5$ and 7 tens 5 ones

B $128 - 28$ and 1 hundred 0 tens
0 ones

C $253 + 105$ and 3 hundreds
5 tens 8 ones

D $446 - 200$ and 2 hundreds
2 tens 6 ones

4 Which is the same as 6 thousands?

A   60 tens

B   600 ones

C   6 hundreds

D   60 hundreds

Lesson 3 **Compare Whole Numbers to Ten Thousand**

NYS Performance Indicators: 4.N.3, 4.A.2, 4.RP.2, 4.CM.11

You can use place value to compare whole numbers.

Compare, or examine, whole numbers to see if one is *greater than* (>), *less than* (<), or *equal to* (=) another. (Hint: The greater than and less than symbols point to the lesser number.)

Guided Instruction

Problem Two music stores are in the same shopping mall. The first music store had 9,641 customers in one month. The second music store had 9,956 customers during the same month. Which music store had more customers in that month?

You can use a place-value chart to help you compare. Compare the digits in each number from left to right until you find an unequal pair.

Step 1 Write both numbers in the place-value chart.

thousands	hundreds	tens	ones
9	6	4	1
9	9	5	6

Step 2 What is the greatest place value where the digits are different?

_____

Step 3 Compare the digits in the hundreds place.

Which number has more hundreds: 9,641 or 9,956?

_____

Step 4 Use >, <, or = to compare the numbers.

9,956 ◯ 9,641

Solution Which music store had more customers in that month?

_____

Apply the NYS Learning Standards

Compare. Write >, <, or = for each.

1. 9,462 ◯ 9,624

2. 4,567 ◯ 3,456

3. 3,576 ◯ 5,675

4. 5,000 ◯ 6,000

5. 7,845 ◯ 7,845

6. 1,500 ◯ 1,005

7. 4,125 ◯ 4,125

8. 10,000 ◯ 9,999

Write _true_ or _false_.

9. 5,898 is less than 8,598. _____

10. 2,539 > 2,359 _____

11. 2,098 = 4,098 _____

12. 2,089 < 9,980 _____

Compare. Use the table for questions 13–15.

13. Which dog is more popular, the poodle or the beagle? _____

14. Which dog is most popular? _____

15. Which dog is least popular? _____

POPULAR BREEDS OF DOGS

Breed	Votes
Poodle	5,852
Rottweiler	1,776
Beagle	9,080
Dachshund	9,712

Short-Response Questions
Solve each problem.

16. A movie theater had 9,753 customers this year. Last year, the movie theater had 9,537 customers. In which year did the movie theater have more customers?

_____

17. An amusement park had 3,665 visitors in June. In July, 6,098 people visited the amusement park. In which month were there more visitors? Explain your answer.

_____

_____

     Measuring Up® to the New York State Learning Standards

NYS Test Practice

DIRECTIONS Read each problem.
Circle the letter of the answer you choose.

1 The table shows the average monthly income for various businesses.

AVERAGE MONTHLY INCOME

Business	Income
Video store	$7,822
Ice cream shop	$7,228
Clothing store	$8,225
Coffee shop	$8,125
Computer store	$2,522

Which business had the greatest average monthly income?

A video store

B ice cream shop

C clothing store

D computer store

2 Which number has the **greatest** value in the hundreds place?

A 7,185

B 5,409

C 3,286

D 2,623

3 The movie theater sold 1,020 tickets on Thursday, 1,220 tickets on Friday, 1,340 on Saturday, 1,267 on Sunday, and 1,165 on Monday. On how many days were more tickets sold than were sold on Sunday?

A one

B two

C three

D four

4 Which statement is true?

A $1,437 = 1,438$

B $1,758 > 1,672$

C $1,758 < 1,672$

D $2,543 < 2,542$

You can use a number line to **order** whole numbers. Sometimes you order numbers by listing them from least to greatest. Sometimes you order numbers by listing them from greatest to least.

Guided Instruction

Problem

Sam's town recycles aluminum cans. What are the numbers of recycled cans in order from greatest to least?

CANS RECYCLED BY YEAR

Year	Number of Cans
1999	1,046
2000	1,404
2001	1,334
2002	1,227

You can order the numbers by locating them on a number line.

Step 1 Write each number from the table on the number line.

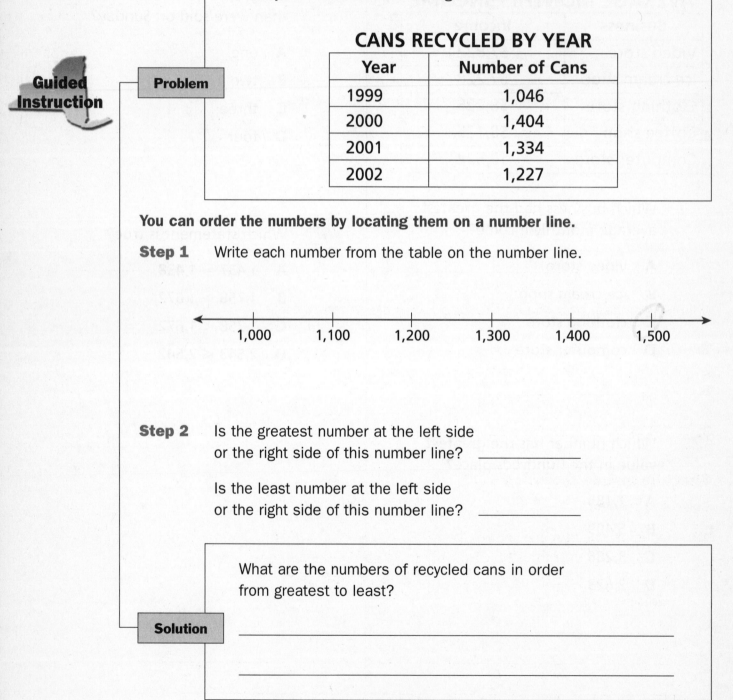

1,000   1,100   1,200   1,300   1,400   1,500

Step 2 Is the greatest number at the left side or the right side of this number line? _____

Is the least number at the left side or the right side of this number line? _____

What are the numbers of recycled cans in order from greatest to least?

Solution _____

_____

Measuring Up® to the New York State Learning Standards

Apply the NYS Learning Standards

Order the numbers from *least* to *greatest*.
Use each number line to help you.

1. 8,901; 8,739; 8,886

←———|——|——|——|——|——|———→
   8,500 8,600 8,700 8,800 8,900 9,000

_____

2. 2,336; 2,199; 1,990

←———|——|——|——|——|——|———→
   1,900 2,000 2,100 2,200 2,300 2,400

_____

Write each group of numbers in order from *greatest* to *least*.

3. 5,571; 5,759; 5,330

_____

4. 2,900; 2,980; 2,908

_____

5. 6,883; 3,555; 4,839

_____

6. 3,992; 2,841; 3,997

_____

Choose a number from the box to make each statement true.

7. 3,112 > 1,997 > _____

8. _____ > 7,216 > 7,119

9. 2,808 > _____ > 2,008

7,113	
	1,401
9,922	
	2,088

Short-Response Question

Solve the problem.

10. Tanesha bought a DVD player for $289, a television set for $785, and a VCR for $219. How would you order the items Tanesha bought from most expensive to least expensive? Explain your thinking.

_____

_____

_____

_____

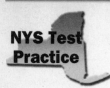

NYS Test Practice

DIRECTIONS Read each problem.
Circle the letter of the answer you choose.

1 The table below shows the number of visitors to a zoo during four months.

ZOO VISITORS

Month	Number of Visitors
June	7,113
July	6,923
August	7,012
September	6,994

Which list shows the number of visitors from **least** to **greatest**?

A   6,994; 6,923; 7,113; 7,012

B   6,923; 6,994; 7,113; 7,012

C   6,994; 6,923; 7,012; 7,113

D   6,923; 6,994; 7,012; 7,113

2 The Video Store had sales of $9,167 in January, $8,990 in February, and $9,583 in March. Which list shows the months in order from **greatest** sales to **least** sales?

A   March, February, January

B   March, January, February

C   February, March, January

D   January, February, March

3 Which dot on the number line shows 897?

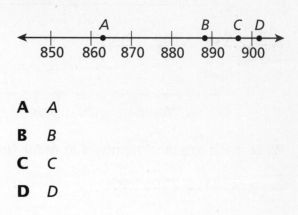

A   A

B   B

C   C

D   D

4 Which of the following statements is not true?

A   8,944 > 8,551 > 7,873

B   5,021 = 5,021

C   9,826 > 9,895 > 9,899

D   5,669 < 5,696 < 5,966

Measuring Up® to the New York State Learning Standards

You can use place value to round whole numbers to the nearest ten or hundred.

Guided Instruction

Problem

Mary Sanchez is writing a report about her company's monthly sales. The company sold 728 electric parts in May. What whole number would Mary report if she rounds 728 to the nearest ten? What whole number would Mary report if she rounds to the nearest hundred?

You can round whole numbers to any place value.

Step 1   Underline the digit in the place value you want to round to.

Which digit would you underline if you want to round 728 to the nearest ten? _____

Which digit would you underline if you want to round 728 to the nearest hundred? _____

Step 2   Circle the digit to the right of the underlined place.

If the digit is 5 or more, round up.

7<u>2</u>8 rounded to the nearest ten is _____.

If the digit is less than 5, round down.

<u>7</u>28 rounded to the nearest hundred is _____.

Solution

What whole number would Mary report if she rounds 728 to the nearest ten? _____

What whole number would Mary report if she rounds to the nearest hundred? _____

Another Example

You can also use a number line to help you round numbers.

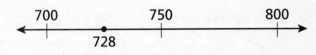

728 is closer to 700 than to 800.

Apply the NYS Learning Standards

Round each number to the nearest ten.

1. 876 _____

2. 273 _____

3. 889 _____

4. 114 _____

5. 348 _____

6. 927 _____

Mark each number on the number line below. Then round the number to the nearest hundred.

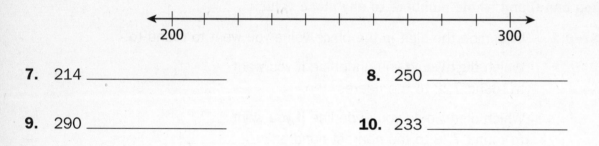

7. 214 _____

8. 250 _____

9. 290 _____

10. 233 _____

Use the numbers in the box below to answer questions 11–14.

| 348 | 338 | 375 | 341 | 418 | 345 |

11. Which numbers round to 340?

_____

12. Which numbers round to 300?

_____

13. Which numbers round to 350?

_____

14. Which numbers round to 400?

_____

Short-Response Question
Solve the problem.

15. Sam estimated that 800 people attended the game. If he rounded to the nearest hundred to get his estimate, what is the greatest number of people who could have attended? Explain how you found the answer.

_____

_____

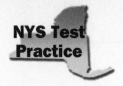

DIRECTIONS Read each problem.
Circle the letter of the answer you choose.

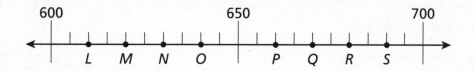

Use the number line above to answer problem 1.

1 Which point represents the **greatest** number that rounds to 600?

   A *M*

   B *O*

   C *R*

   D *S*

2 Washington Elementary School has 554 students. What is 554 rounded to the nearest 10?

   A 580

   B 570

   C 560

   D 550

3 A restaurant sold 326 ice cream cones in one year. To the nearest hundred, about how many ice cream cones were sold?

   A 300

   B 320

   C 330

   D 400

 About 720 people live in a town in New York state. If this estimate was made by rounding the actual number of people to the nearest ten, what is the **fewest** number of people that could be living there?

   A 700

   B 710

   C 715

   D 800

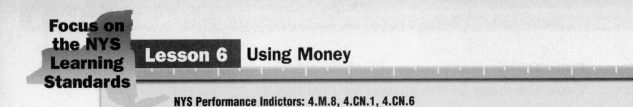
To find the value of a group of coins or to make change, you need to know the value of each coin.

Guided Instruction

Problem Jake paid for some fishing lures with a ten-dollar bill. The total cost of the lures was $7.54. How much change did Jake receive?

Count on to find the coins and bills.

Step 1 Begin at the cost, $7.54. Use coins to count up until you get to the next dollar.

Then count by dollars until you get to the dollar amount paid.

Receipt						
$7.54	$7.55	$7.65	_____	_____	_____	

_____

Step 2 To see how much change was given, go back and count the bills and coins in order from the greatest value to the least value.

What is the total value? _____

Solution How much change did Jake receive? _____

Measuring Up® to the New York State Learning Standards

Apply the NYS Learning Standards

Write the value of each group of coins and bills.

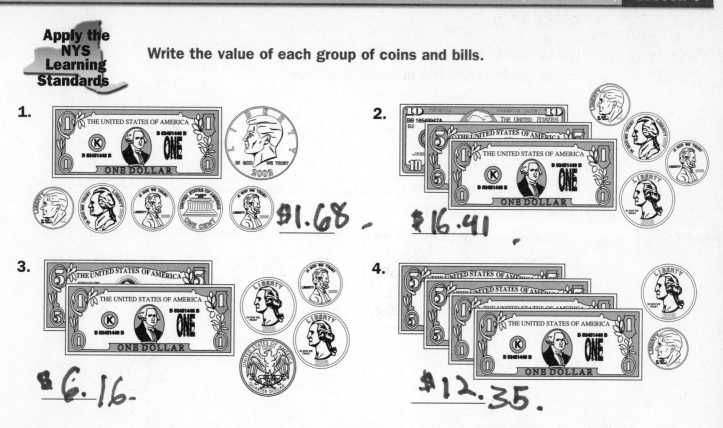

1. $1.68

2. $16.41

3. $6.16

4. $12.35

A $20 bill was used to pay for each item named below. List the coins and bills you would use to make change.

5. One shirt for $14.81 _____

6. One ball for $5.55 _____

7. One cap for $9.98 _____

Short-Response Questions

Solve each problem.

8. Josh kept a record of money he spent from Friday to Sunday on his birthday weekend. Fill in the missing amounts in the table.

RECORD OF BIRTHDAY SPENDING FOR THE WEEKEND

Day	Total Cost of Items	Bill Given to Cashier	Change
Friday	$8.45	$20	
Saturday	$10	$10	
Sunday	$7.54	$10	

9. What is the fewest number of bills and coins that Josh can receive as change on Sunday? Explain how you found your answer.

_____

_____

NYS Test Practice

DIRECTIONS Read each problem. Circle the letter of the answer you choose.

(handwritten: 40 + 35 = 75)

1 Maggie is buying a game. It costs $13.64. She gave the clerk a twenty-dollar bill. How much change should Maggie receive?

(handwritten: $20.00 − 13.64 = $6.36)

A

B

C

D

2 Sam received a $35 gift certificate and a $40 gift certificate for a sports store. He bought a glove for $49.99. Which amount will he have left to spend on his certificates?

A $29.01

B $25.01

C $20.01

D $15.01

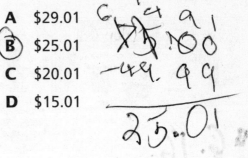

(handwritten: $75.00 − 49.99 = 25.01)

3 Joshua buys $32.60 worth of CDs. He gives the clerk 2 twenty-dollar bills. What bills and coins could he receive as change?

A 1 ten-dollar bill, 2 one-dollar bills, 4 dimes

B 1 five-dollar bill, 2 one-dollar bills, 1 quarter, 1 dime, 1 nickel

C 1 five-dollar bill, 2 one-dollar bills, 3 quarters

D 2 five-dollar bills, 3 quarters

 Measuring Up® to the New York State Learning Standards

Lesson 7 Estimate Quantities

Benchmark numbers can help you estimate quantities.

A **benchmark** is a measurement that you know, which you can use to estimate other measurements.

Guided Instruction

Problem Ramon has a jar filled with marbles. What is a reasonable estimate of the number of marbles in his jar?

You can use a benchmark to help you estimate.

Jar A: Benchmark   Ramon's jar:
100 marbles   ? marbles

Step 1 Compare the amount of marbles in Ramon's jar to the amount of marbles in Jar A.

• Ramon's jar holds about _____ times the number of marbles in Jar A.

Step 2 Use the benchmark to estimate the number of marbles in Ramon's jar.

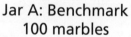

4 × _____ = _____

About how many marbles are in Ramon's jar? _____

Solution What is a reasonable estimate of the number of marbles in Ramon's jar? _____

Apply the NYS Learning Standards

Use each benchmark to find a reasonable estimate.

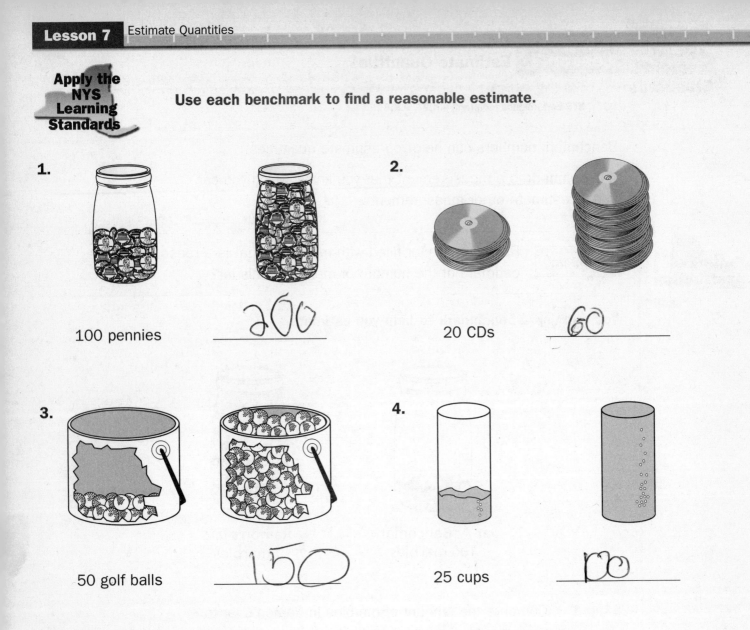

1.

100 pennies   200

2.

20 CDs   60

3.

50 golf balls   150

4.

25 cups   100

Short-Response Questions

Solve each problem.

5. Maria has a jar full of jellybeans. After she takes out 10 jellybeans, the jar is about half full. About how many jellybeans were in the full jar? Explain your thinking.

_____

_____

6. There are about 10 crackers in one layer of a container. If 5 layers of crackers fit in the container, about how many crackers does the container hold? Explain your thinking.

_____

_____

NYS Test Practice

DIRECTIONS Read each problem.
Circle the letter of the answer you choose.

1 There are 100 paper clips in the jar shown below.

100 paper clips

About how many more paper clips are needed to fill the jar?

A 100
B 120
C 200
D 500

2 Which is the **most** reasonable number of dollar bills in the stack below on the right?

10 $1 bills   ? $1 bills

A 100
B 90
C 75
D 30

3 Mark has circled 50 dots.

Which is the **most** reasonable number of dots on the whole piece of paper?

A 54
B 200
C 500
D 1,000

4 Paul has a jar full of coins. After he takes out 25 coins, the jar is about half full. About how many coins were in the full jar?

A 10
B 25
C 50
D 100

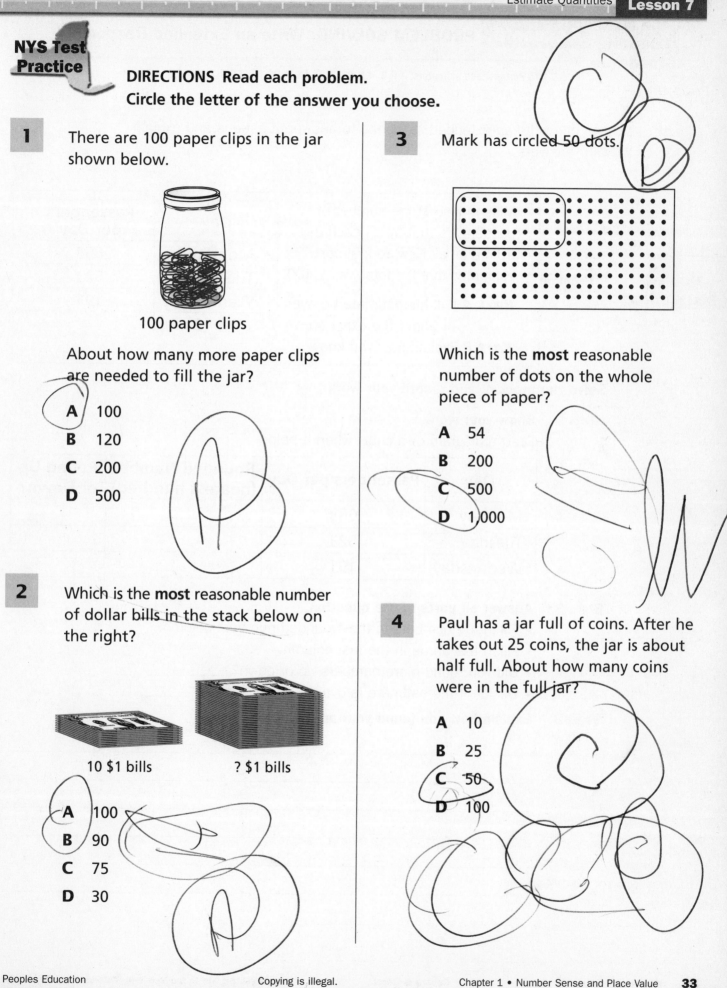

Lesson 8 PROBLEM SOLVING: Write an Extended Response

NYS Performance Indicators: 4.N.3, 4.N.26, 4.PS.14, 4.PS.15, 4.CM.1, 4.CM.3, 4.CM.5

You can write an extended response to answer questions and explain your answers.

Guided Instruction

| Problem |

Mike looked at the number of passengers that travel each day from a small New York airport. He estimated that the total was 1,400.

Part A Will his estimate be over or under the exact sum?

Part B Explain how you know.

Day	Passengers per Day
Monday	663
Tuesday	523
Wednesday	191

Solve the problem and record your work.

Step 1 **Show your work.**

Draw a diagram or a chart when it helps.

Day	Passengers per Day	Rounded Number (nearest hundred)	Round Up or Down?
Monday	663		
Tuesday	523		
Wednesday	191		

Step 2 **Answer all parts of the question.**

• Fill in the numbers in the "rounded number" column.

• Fill in the words in the last column.

• Did you round more numbers up or down? _____

• Decide if the estimate is over or under. _____

Step 3 **Explain how you found your answer.**

_____

_____

_____

_____

_____

_____

Answer each problem. Show your work.

1. Madison and Chris used a chart to estimate the total number of pennies in three jars. Madison rounded to the nearest ten. Chris rounded to the nearest hundred.

Jars	Pennies
Jar A	849
Jar B	212
Jar C	675

Part A

Whose estimate was closer?

Answer _____

Part B

On the lines below, explain how you found your answer.

_____

_____

_____

_____

_____

2. The students at Rockwell School collected newspaper to be recycled. Grade 3 collected 4,389 pounds of newspaper. Grade 4 collected 6,592 pounds, and Grade 5 collected 4,571 pounds of newspaper.

Part A

Which grade collected the **greatest** number of pounds of newspaper? Which grade collected the **least**?

Answer greatest: _____ least: _____

Part B

On the lines below, explain how you found your answer.

_____

_____

_____

_____

NYS Test Practice

DIRECTIONS Read each question carefully before writing your response. Be sure to show your work when asked.

1. Mrs. Lakind owns three delis. She puts out a jar in each deli for people to donate pennies for charity. Her first store collected 5,832 pennies. Her second store collected 5,429 pennies. Her third store collected 6,831 pennies.

Part A

List the number of pennies collected in order from **least** to **greatest**.
Show your work.

Answer _____

Part B

On the lines below, explain how you found your answer.

_____

_____

_____

_____

_____

_____

DIRECTIONS Read each problem.
Circle the letter of the answer you choose.

1 What is another way to write five thousand three hundred nine?

A 5,039

B 5,093

C 5,309

D 5,903

2 What is the value of the underlined digit of 7,831?

A 7   C 700

B 70   **D** 7,000

3 By how much would the value of 4,567 change if the digit 4 were replaced with the digit 3?

A 1   C 1,000

B 3   **D** 3,000

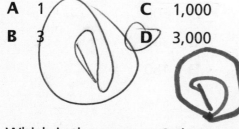

4 Which is the same as 8 thousand?

A 80 tens

B 800 ones

C 8 hundreds

D 80 hundreds

5 Which statement is **not** true?

A 2,356 < 2,365 < 2,536

B 1,345 = 1,345

C 2,367 > 2,365 > 2,356

D 1,345 > 1,435 > 1,465

6 Which is an equivalent form of 5 hundreds 2 tens 9 ones?

A 520 + 9

B 520 + 19

C 530 − 9

D 629 − 10

7 Which of the following statements is true?

A 4,563 < 4,653 < 4,657

B 3,455 = 3,456

C 7,940 > 7,890 > 8,790

D 5,658 < 5,678 < 5,676

8 The table shows the number of books sold at a book store over the course of three years.

BOOKS SOLD

Type of Book	Number of Books
Mystery	5,234
Adventure	5,342
Sports	3,452
Biography	5,432

Which type of book sold more than Mystery but less than Biography?

A Mystery

B Adventure

C Sports

D Biography

9 Which list shows the numbers in order from **greatest** to **least**?

A 1,225; 1,522; 2,152; 2,215

B 1,522; 2,215; 1,225; 2,152

C 2,152; 2,215; 1,225; 1,522

D 2,215; 2,152; 1,522; 1,225

10 Which of these numbers does **not** round to 110 when rounded to the nearest 10?

A 104

B 106

C 113

D 114

11 Which is the **most** reasonable number of marbles in the full jar?

300 marbles

A 6,000

B 600

C 300

D 150

Extended-Response Questions
DIRECTIONS Read each question carefully before writing your response. Be sure to show your work when asked.

12 The students in the fourth grade classes at Little Tor Elementary School had a reading contest. The table shows how many minutes each class read during the month of October.

Classes	Minutes
Mrs. Smith	8,379
Mr. Pollock	9,763
Mr. Strauss	8,717

Part A

Order the number of pages read from **greatest** to **least** using symbols.

Answer *Mr. Pollock Mr. Strauss 9,763, 8,717, 8,379 Mrs. Smith*

Part B

On the lines below, explain how you found your answer.

_____

_____

_____

_____

_____

_____

13 Zachary receives twenty dollars for his birthday. He decides to spend it at the mall. He buys a ball, a game, and some candy. He spends a total of $18.49.

Part A

Zachary hands the clerk a twenty-dollar bill. Circle the bills and coins that he should receive as change. What is his total in change?

Answer $1.51

$$\begin{array}{r} \overset{1}{\cancel{2}}\overset{9}{\cancel{0}}.\overset{9}{\cancel{0}}\,\overset{10}{0} \\ -\;1\,8.\;4\,9 \\ \hline \$1.51 \end{array}$$

Part B

On the lines below, describe how you found your answer.

_____

_____

_____

_____

Chapter 2
Lesson 9   Add Whole Numbers

NYS Performance Indicators: 4.N.14, 4.PS.5

When you add, sometimes you need to **regroup,** or rename a number.
You can regroup 10 ones as 1 ten, 10 tens as 1 hundred, and 10 hundreds
as 1 thousand.

Guided Instruction

Problem   In the month of May, 1,476 books were checked out of the local library. In the month of June the number of books checked out was 1,926. What was the total number of books checked out during May and June?

Add to find the total number of books.

Step 1   Add the ones.

Do you need to regroup? _____

Regroup 12 ones as 1 ten _____ ones.

$$\begin{array}{r} \overset{1}{1,47\mathbf{6}} \\ +\,1,92\mathbf{6} \\ \hline - \end{array}$$

Step 2   Add the tens.

Do you need to regroup? _____

How many tens do you have? _____

Regroup 10 tens as _____ hundred no tens.

$$\begin{array}{r} \overset{1}{1,4\mathbf{7}6} \\ +\,1,9\mathbf{2}6 \\ \hline 2 \end{array}$$

Step 3   Continue to add and regroup as needed.

You only need to regroup when the sum in any column is _____ or more.

$$\begin{array}{r} \overset{1\ 1}{1,\mathbf{4}76} \\ +\,1,\mathbf{9}26 \\ \hline 02 \end{array}$$

Solution   What was the total number of books checked out during May and June? _____

Another Example

You can add three or more numbers the same way that you add two numbers.

$$\begin{array}{r} \overset{1\ 1\ 1}{432} \\ 2,786 \\ 1,528 \\ \hline 4,746 \end{array}$$

Apply the NYS Learning Standards

Find each sum. Regroup when necessary.

1.
```
  349
+ 547
```

2.
```
  2,586
+   398
```

3.
```
  $8.40
+  3.96
```

4.
```
  8,658
+ 5,823
```

5.
```
  4,912
+ 8,416
```

6.
```
  6,743
+ 3,956
```

7.
```
  $2,249
+  3,975
```

8.
```
  3,491
+ 5,629
```

9.
```
  3,492
+ 5,699
```

10.
```
  $31.94
+  12.93
```

11.
```
  777
  111
+ 346
```

12.
```
  349
  141
+ 451
```

Rewrite each addition problem. Then find each sum.

13. 390 + 29 _____

14. 7,393 + 458 _____

15. 9,102 + 89 + 1,201 _____

16. 982 + 1,094 + 87 + 452 _____

Short-Response Question
Solve the problem.

17. Use all the digits in the box at the right to make 2 three-digit numbers that add to the greatest possible sum. Use each digit only once. Explain how you found your answer.

```
8     6
  1     7
    2     4
```

_____

_____

_____

_____

NYS Test Practice

DIRECTIONS Read each problem.
Circle the letter of the answer you choose.

1 The Kaleidoscope Video Games Store sold 78 electronic games in May, 62 games in June, and 53 games in July. How many games did the store sell in all three months?

A 83
B 93
C 183
D 193

2 Yesterday, Brandon scored 728 points on his video game. He improved his score by 386 points today. Which was his score today?

A 1,104
B 1,114
C 1,204
D 1,214

3 Tanya bought a saxophone for $895, a case for $168, and music for $36. Which of the following is true?

A Tanya spent more than $2,000.
B Tanya spent less than $2,000.
C Tanya spent less than $1,000.
D Tanya spent more than $2,500.

4 The Roadrunners Club had 8,508 members in 2004. In 2005, the membership increased by 1,098. How many members were there in 2005?

A 9,596
B 9,606
C 10,596
D 10,606

5 How should the tens be regrouped to find this sum?

4,051
+6,978

A 1 hundred 0 tens
B 1 hundred 1 ten
C 1 hundred 2 tens
D 1 hundred 3 tens

6 Charlie was traveling from New York to California by car. The first day he traveled 378 miles, the second day he traveled 406 miles, and the third day he traveled 397 miles. Which shows how many miles he traveled in three days?

A 1,071
B 1,081
C 1,171
D 1,181

When you subtract, sometimes you need to regroup.

Guided Instruction

Problem

The students at two schools are raising money for a children's hospital. The amount they have raised so far is shown in the table. How much more money has Garden School raised than Park School?

School	Money Raised
Park	$3,935
Garden	$5,024

Subtract to find how much more.

Step 1 Subtract the ones. Do you need to regroup? _____

Regroup 2 tens 4 ones as 1 ten _____ ones.

$$\begin{array}{r} \$5,0\,2\,4 \\ -\ 3,9\,3\,5 \end{array}$$

Step 2 Subtract the tens. Do you need to regroup? _____

There are no hundreds. You must first regroup

5 thousands 0 hundreds as

4 _____ hundreds.

Then regroup 10 hundreds 1 ten as

9 hundreds _____ tens.

$$\begin{array}{r} {\scriptstyle 9\ 11} \\ {\scriptstyle 4\ 10\ 1\ 14} \\ \$5,0\,2\,4 \\ -\ 3,9\,3\,5 \\ \hline 9 \end{array}$$

Step 3 Continue subtracting.
Subtract the hundreds.
Then subtract the thousands.

$$\begin{array}{r} {\scriptstyle 9\ 11} \\ {\scriptstyle 4\ 10\ 1\ 14} \\ \$5,0\,2\,4 \\ -\ 3,9\,3\,5 \\ \hline 8\,9 \end{array}$$

Step 4 Check your answer.
Use addition to check subtraction.

$$\begin{array}{r} {\scriptstyle 9\ 11} \\ {\scriptstyle 4\ 10\ 1\ 14} \\ 5,0\,2\,4 \\ -\ 3,9\,3\,5 \\ \hline 1,0\,8\,9 \end{array} \qquad \begin{array}{r} {\scriptstyle 1\ 1\ 1} \\ 1,0\,8\,9 \\ +\ 3,9\,3\,5 \\ \hline 5,0\,2\,4 \end{array}$$

Solution

How much more money has Garden School raised than Park School? _____

Apply the
NYS
Learning
Standards

Find each difference. Regroup when necessary.

1.   234
        − 154

2.   2,406
        − 398

3. $840
        − 96

4.   8,658
        − 5,823

5.   4,912
        − 416

6. $3,004
        − 1,293

7.   1,349
        − 451

8.   3,491
        − 2,629

9.   3,492
        − 2,699

10.   6,043
         − 3,956

11. $7.77
         − 3.46

12. $6,000
         − 3,975

Subtract. Check each answer by using addition.

13. 390 − 79 =

14. 7,003 − 458 =

15. 9,102 − 1,276 =

16. 1,094 − 79 =

Short-Response Questions
Solve each problem.

17. Use all the digits in the box at the right to make
2 three-digit numbers that have a difference greater
than 600. Use each digit only once. Write the
number sentence.

```
8      6
    1      7
        2      4
```

_____

18. Use all the digits in the box at the right to make
2 three-digit numbers that have a difference less
than 100. Use each digit only once. Write the
number sentence.

```
0      5
    4      8
        7      6
```

_____

NYS Test Practice

DIRECTIONS Read each problem.
Circle the letter of the answer you choose.

1 Tanya and Jacob were in the Super Race. On the first leg of the trip they traveled 894 miles. On the second leg of the trip, they traveled 327 miles. What is the difference in miles traveled?

A 1,221

B 577

C 567

D 467

2 The table shows the number of video games each toy company purchased during the month of May.

Company	Video Games
Mugzee Toys	1,462
Toy Plus	559
Games A Go	1,541
Toys For All	618

How many more games did Mugzee Toys purchase in May than Toys For All?

A 256

B 844

C 846

D 856

3 Ms. Lee finds two used cars that she would like to buy. A mid-sized car costs $9,445, and a compact car costs $6,999. Which shows the difference in cost?

A $1,444

B $1,556

C $2,446

D $2,556

4 Todd and Liliana play a video game. Todd scored 8,946 points, and Liliana scored 5,879 points. Which number shows how much better Todd's score was than Liliana's score?

A 3,067

B 3,133

C 3,163

D 3,167

 5 Which is the missing number?

$$\begin{array}{r} 703 \\ - \ ??? \\ \hline 238 \end{array}$$

A 455

B 465

C 467

D 535

 Measuring Up® to the New York State Learning Standards

You can round numbers to **estimate** when an exact answer is not necessary.

Guided Instruction

Problem	Charla and her family are buying a lantern, tent, and sleeping bag for a camping trip. About how much money will they spend for these supplies?

Supplies	Price
Lantern	$65
Tent	$94
Sleeping Bag	$29

You can round to estimate a sum.

Step 1 Decide what place should be the rounding place.

All the numbers are two-digit numbers, so round to the nearest ten.

Complete the chart.

Look at the digit in the ones place.

Remember: 5 or greater rounds up.

So 6<u>5</u> rounds to 70.

	Rounds to
65	70
94	
29	

Step 2 Add the rounded numbers using mental math.
Hint: You can add numbers in any order.
So look for pairs of numbers that are easy to add.

$$\left.\begin{array}{r} 70 \\ 90 \\ + 30 \end{array}\right\} = 100$$

Solution	About how much money will they spend for these supplies? _____

Another Example

You can round to the nearest hundred to estimate.
Think: 900 − 200 = 700

$$\begin{array}{r} \mathbf{8}81 \longrightarrow \mathbf{9}00 \\ -\mathbf{2}13 \longrightarrow -\mathbf{2}00 \\ \hline 700 \end{array}$$

Apply the NYS Learning Standards

Estimate. Round each number to the nearest ten.

1. 234 + 154

2. 486 + 398

3. $613 − $296

4. 569 − 23

5. 842 + 716

6. 194 − 93

7. 379 − 351

8. 393 − 258

Estimate. Round each number to the nearest hundred.

9. 474 + 627

10. 94 + 679

11. 102 + 276

12. 712 − 259

13. 364
+ 587

14. 638
− 112

15. 724
+ 109

16. 933
− 475

Short-Response Questions
Solve each problem. Use the table for questions 17–18.

17. Meg estimates that she will need to set up 850 chairs for the concert. Is that a reasonable estimate? Explain.

CONCERT TICKET SALES

Adult Tickets Sold	318
Child Tickets Sold	520

18. Joe estimates that at $1 per ticket, they will make $2,000 from the ticket sales. Is that a reasonable estimate? Explain.

NYS Test Practice

DIRECTIONS Read each question.
Circle the letter of the answer you choose.

1 Which of the following is a reasonable **estimate** for the difference of 658 − 324?

  A 100

  B 200

  C 300

  D 400

2 Which shows a way to **estimate** 926 − 415 rounded to the nearest ten?

  A 900 − 406

  B 910 − 420

  C 920 − 410

  D 930 − 420

3 The Star Health Club has 686 members, and the DeWitt Health Club has 522 members. About how many more members belong to the Star Health Club than to the DeWitt Health Club?

  A 100

  B 200

  C 300

  D 1,200

4 Round the numbers 986 and 479 to the nearest hundred. Then add the rounded numbers. Which statement is true about the **estimate**?

  A It is less than the exact answer.

  B It is greater than the exact answer.

  C It is equal to the exact answer.

  D It cannot be found by rounding to the nearest hundred.

5 The sum of two numbers is about 1,100. One number is 743. Which of the following could be the other number?

  A 141   C 402

  B 244   D 519

6 The difference of two numbers is about 500. One number is 589. Which of the following could not be the other number?

  A 98   C 65

  B 89   D 25

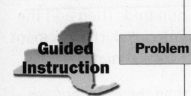
Decide if a solution or an answer is **reasonable** when you solve a problem. You can use the problem-solving guide in the back of the book to help you.

Guided Instruction

Problem

It took Mr. Jackson two days to drive from Ashville to Smithtown. On Saturday he left Ashville and drove 311 miles. On Sunday he arrived in Smithtown after driving 294 more miles. How many miles is it from Ashville to Smithtown?

Understand the problem.

Mr. Jackson drove from Ashville to Smithtown.

He drove _____ miles on Saturday and _____ miles on Sunday.

What do you need to find? _____

_____

Make a plan.

You can use rounding or any other strategy to estimate before solving the problem. Then you can compare your answer to your estimate.

Your answer is reasonable if your answer is close to your estimate.

Solve the problem.

Since both numbers are close to 300, estimate by rounding to the nearest hundred.

311   +   294
 ↓   ↓

_____ + _____ = _____ miles

Add 311 and 294 to find the exact answer.

```
  3 1 1
+ 2 9 4
_____
```

It is _____ miles from Ashville to Smithtown.

Check your answer.

Compare your answer with your estimate.

605 miles is close to the estimate of 600 miles.

So 605 miles is a reasonable answer.

Apply the NYS Learning Standards

Estimate the answer to each problem. Then solve the problem. Show how you found your answers.

Work Space

Solve each problem.

1. LaToya has 719 baseball cards and 583 basketball cards. How many more baseball cards than basketball cards does LaToya have?

Estimate: _____

Exact answer: _____

2. A hotel spent $187 on new towels and $806 on new carpeting. How much did the hotel spend altogether?

Estimate: _____

Exact answer: _____

3. The Music Store sold 833 CDs in April and 197 CDs in May. How many more CDs did the store sell in April than in May?

Estimate: _____

Exact answer: _____

Short-Response Question

4. Ms. Ramirez saved $497 last year, $481 two years ago, and $512 three years ago. How much did she save in the past three years? Tell if your exact answer is reasonable and why.

Estimate: _____

Exact answer: _____

_____

_____

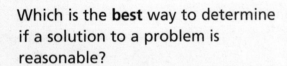

DIRECTIONS Read each problem.
Circle the letter of the answer you choose.

1 Mrs. Chan bought a television set for $775 and a DVD recorder for $209. Which is the **best estimate** of the total cost of both items?

A between $100 and $200

B between $700 and $800

C between $900 and $1,000

D between $1,500 and $2,500

2 Which is the **best** way to determine if a solution to a problem is reasonable?

A Compare your solution to your friend's solution.

B Estimate first. Then see if your solution is close to your estimate.

C Solve the problem. Then look for extra information.

D Make a list. Then solve the problem.

3 Last week about 300 children visited the zoo. Which could not be the number of boys and the number of girls who visited the zoo?

A 279 boys and 130 girls

B 135 boys and 143 girls

C 109 boys and 198 girls

D 74 boys and 230 girls

4 Which describes when you would need to find an exact difference?

A to find how much longer one piece of string is than another

B to find about how many more pages one book has than another

C to find about how much taller one person to than another

D to find about how much more one item costs than another

DIRECTIONS Read each problem.
Circle the letter of the answer you choose.

1 Clark Elementary School had a candy sale. The table shows the results for Grades 3, 4, 5, and 6.

Grade	Candy Bars Sold
3	896
4	429
5	948
6	123

Estimate to the nearest ten how many candy bars were sold in all.

A 2,100

B 2,200

C 2,300

D 2,400

2 Jason scored 2,354 points on Level 1 of a video game. He scored 3,106 points on Level 2 of the same game. How many more points did Jason score on Level 2 than on Level 1?

A 742

B 752

C 842

D 852

3 On Monday, 532 people visited the local zoo. On Tuesday, 428 people visited the zoo. How many people visited the zoo on those two days?

A 860

B 870

C 960

D 970

4 Stephany received a $50 gift certificate for her favorite clothing store. She bought a sweatshirt for $29. Which shows how much change Stephany received?

A −$19

B −$21

C −$30

D −$39

5 The sum of two numbers is about 400. One number is 278.
Which of the following could be the other number?

A 299

B 205

C 175

D 105

6 What is the missing digit in the problem below?

```
  3 8 4
+1 □ 6
───────
  5 3 0
```

A 3

B 4

C 5

D 6

7 Round 454 and 579 to the nearest ten. Then add the rounded numbers to **estimate** the sum. Which statement is true?

A Your estimate is less than the exact sum.

B Your estimate is greater than the exact sum.

C Your estimate is the same as the exact sum.

D Your estimate is less than 1,000.

8 The table shows the number of DVD rentals at Greene's Movie Store during 4 months of this year.

GREENE'S MOVIE STORE

Month	Number of DVD Rentals
May	−596
June	−983
July	2,768
August	1,247

What is the difference between the month with the **greatest** number of DVD rentals and the month with the **least** number of rentals?

A 1,834

B 2,172

C 2,232

D 3,364

9 The height of Mt. Marcy, in New York, is 5,344 feet. The height of Mt. Colvin, in New York, is 4,057 feet. How much higher is Mt. Marcy?

A 4,015

B 3,521

C 1,531

D 1,521

Extended-Response Questions
DIRECTIONS Read each question carefully before writing your response. Be sure to show your work when asked.

10 In a game, Linda and Mike were making subtraction problems. They each have the six cards shown below.

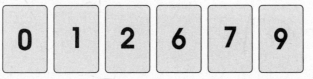

The winner of the game is the person who can make the problem with the greatest difference by making two three-digit numbers.

Linda placed the cards like this:

$$\begin{array}{r} 9\;6\;7 \\ -\;2\;0\;1 \\ \hline 766 \end{array}$$

Mike placed the cards like this:

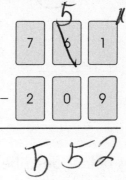

$$\begin{array}{r} 7\;6\;1 \\ -\;2\;0\;9 \\ \hline 552 \end{array}$$

Part A

Who won the game?

Answer _Linda_

Part B

On the lines below, describe how you found if your answer is reasonable.

_____

_____

_____

_____

_____

11 Ben had 975 baseball cards in his collection. He gave his brother, Josh, 448 cards and then collected 99 more cards.

Part A

How many cards are now in Ben's collection?

Show your work.

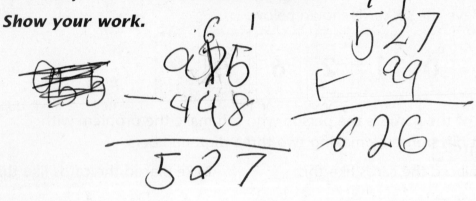

$$\begin{array}{r} \cancel{9}\overset{6}{7}\overset{1}{5} \\ -448 \\ \hline 527 \end{array} \qquad \begin{array}{r} \overset{1}{5}\overset{1}{2}7 \\ +\ 99 \\ \hline 626 \end{array}$$

Answer _626_

Part B

On the lines below, describe how you know your answer is reasonable.

_____

_____

_____

_____

_____

NYS Performance Indicators: 4.N.16, 4.PS.6, 4.PS.7, 4.R.7

Multiplication is an easy way to find the total number of items in equal-sized groups. The numbers you multiply are called **factors**. The answer is called the **product**.
You can use an array to solve a multiplication problem. An **array** is an arrangement of objects in rows and columns.

$$4 \times 6 = 24$$

factor   factor   product

Guided Instruction

Problem

There are 5 boxes of pencils. There are 7 pencils in each box. What is the total number of pencils in the boxes?

| 7 Pencils | 7 Pencils | 7 Pencils | 7 Pencils | 7 Pencils |

An array can help you find the product of two factors.

7 columns

5 rows

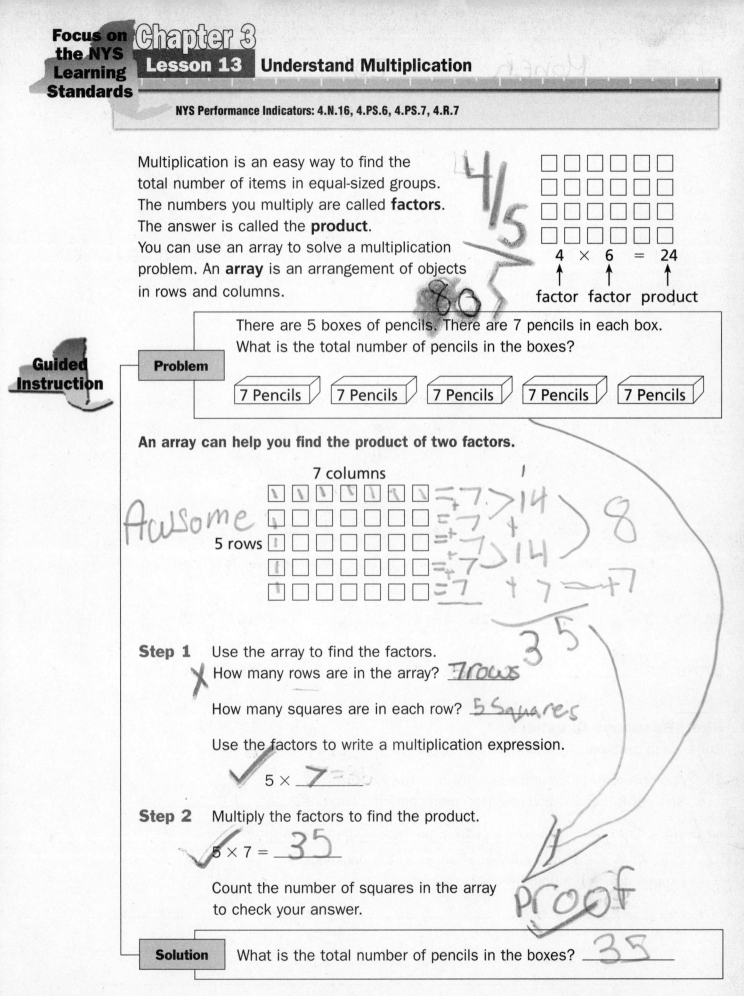

Step 1   Use the array to find the factors.
How many rows are in the array? 7 rows

How many squares are in each row? 5 squares

Use the factors to write a multiplication expression.

$5 \times 7 = 35$

Step 2   Multiply the factors to find the product.

$5 \times 7 = 35$

Count the number of squares in the array to check your answer.

Solution   What is the total number of pencils in the boxes? 35

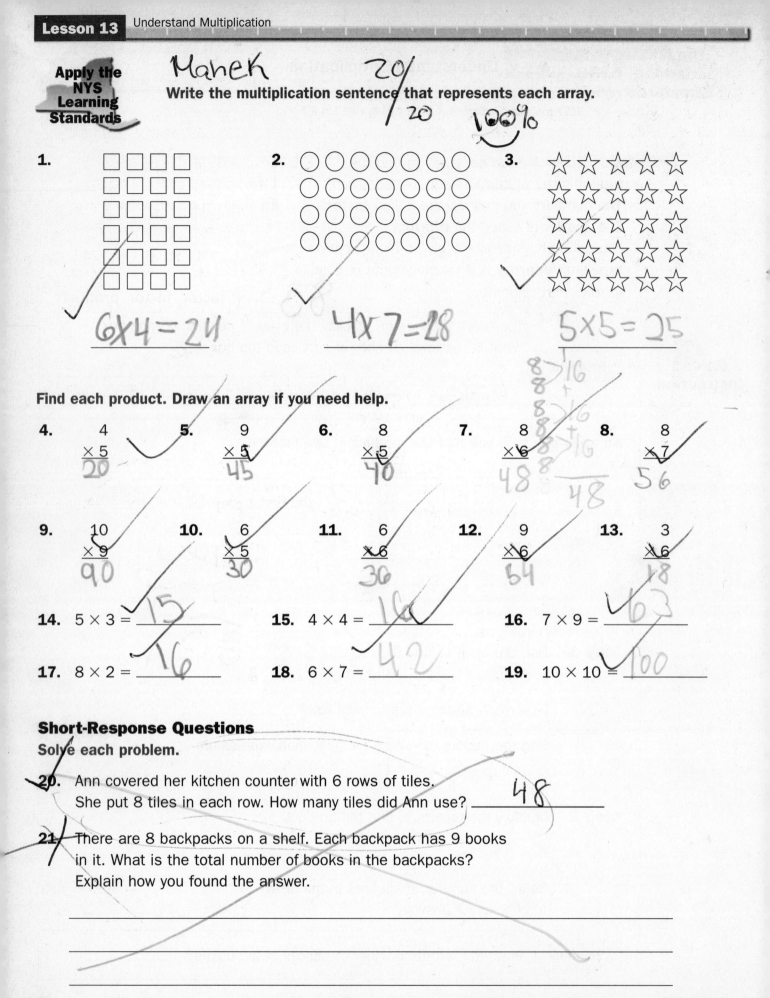

Manek   20/
/20
100%

Write the multiplication sentence that represents each array.

1.

2.

3.

6×4=24

4×7=28

5×5=25

Find each product. Draw an array if you need help.

4. $\begin{array}{r} 4 \\ \times 5 \\ \hline 20 \end{array}$

5. $\begin{array}{r} 9 \\ \times 5 \\ \hline 45 \end{array}$

6. $\begin{array}{r} 8 \\ \times 5 \\ \hline 40 \end{array}$

7. $\begin{array}{r} 8 \\ \times 6 \\ \hline 48 \end{array}$

8. $\begin{array}{r} 8 \\ \times 7 \\ \hline 56 \end{array}$

9. $\begin{array}{r} 10 \\ \times 9 \\ \hline 90 \end{array}$

10. $\begin{array}{r} 6 \\ \times 5 \\ \hline 30 \end{array}$

11. $\begin{array}{r} 6 \\ \times 6 \\ \hline 36 \end{array}$

12. $\begin{array}{r} 9 \\ \times 6 \\ \hline 54 \end{array}$

13. $\begin{array}{r} 3 \\ \times 6 \\ \hline 18 \end{array}$

14. $5 \times 3 = \underline{15}$

15. $4 \times 4 = \underline{16}$

16. $7 \times 9 = \underline{63}$

17. $8 \times 2 = \underline{16}$

18. $6 \times 7 = \underline{42}$

19. $10 \times 10 = \underline{100}$

Short-Response Questions

Solve each problem.

20. Ann covered her kitchen counter with 6 rows of tiles.
She put 8 tiles in each row. How many tiles did Ann use? _____48_____

21. There are 8 backpacks on a shelf. Each backpack has 9 books
in it. What is the total number of books in the backpacks?
Explain how you found the answer.

_____

_____

_____

Measuring Up® to the New York State Learning Standards

DIRECTIONS Read each problem.
Circle the letter of the answer you choose.

1 Which number sentence could you use to find the total number of stars?

☆ ☆ ☆ ☆ ☆ ☆ ☆ ☆
☆ ☆ ☆ ☆ ☆ ☆ ☆ ☆
☆ ☆ ☆ ☆ ☆ ☆ ☆ ☆
☆ ☆ ☆ ☆ ☆ ☆ ☆ ☆
☆ ☆ ☆ ☆ ☆ ☆ ☆ ☆

A $5 + 8 = 13$

B $16 + 16 = 32$

C $5 \times 8 = 40$

D $7 \times 8 = 56$

2 LaToya uses 7 beads to make a necklace. If she makes 6 necklaces, how many beads will she use?

A 42

B 32

C 13

D 3

3 One cabinet has 3 shelves with 4 plates on each shelf. Another cabinet has 2 shelves with 5 plates on each shelf. How many plates are in both cabinets?

A 10

B 14

C 20

D 22

4 The picture below shows the number of stamps Britney has on the first page of her stamp album.

Britney wants to fill 5 pages of her album. How many more stamps does she need?

A 10

B 24

C 48

D 72

Lesson 14 Find Patterns in Multiplication

NYS Performance Indictors: 4.N.13, 4.N.16, 4.RP.8, 4.R.10

You can use patterns to help you multiply.

Guided Instruction

Problem

Jim is 5 times older than his cousin. Jim's age is an odd number. Is Jim's cousin's age an odd or an even number? How do you know?

Use a multiplication table to find patterns.

Step 1 Look across the row for the factor 5. Are the products odd or even when you multiply the factor 5 by an even factor?

_____

_____

Factors

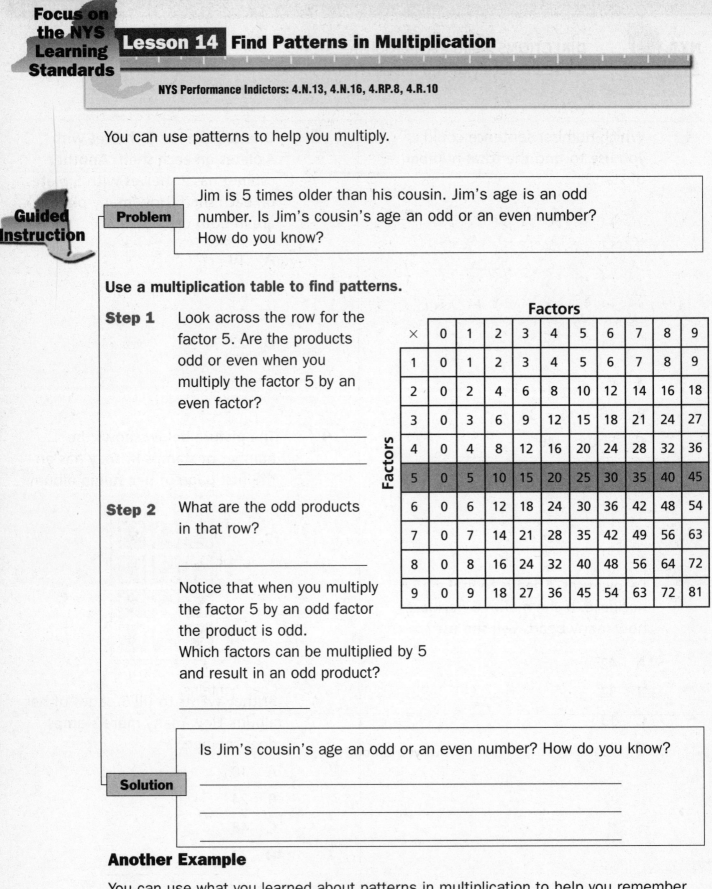

×	0	1	2	3	4	5	6	7	8	9
1	0	1	2	3	4	5	6	7	8	9
2	0	2	4	6	8	10	12	14	16	18
3	0	3	6	9	12	15	18	21	24	27
4	0	4	8	12	16	20	24	28	32	36
5	0	5	10	15	20	25	30	35	40	45
6	0	6	12	18	24	30	36	42	48	54
7	0	7	14	21	28	35	42	49	56	63
8	0	8	16	24	32	40	48	56	64	72
9	0	9	18	27	36	45	54	63	72	81

Step 2 What are the odd products in that row?

_____

Notice that when you multiply the factor 5 by an odd factor the product is odd.
Which factors can be multiplied by 5 and result in an odd product?

_____

Is Jim's cousin's age an odd or an even number? How do you know?

Solution

_____

_____

_____

Another Example

You can use what you learned about patterns in multiplication to help you remember other multiplication facts. What is 6 × 7?
Think: 5 × 7 = 35.
So 6 × 7 = 35 + 7 = 42.

Apply the NYS Learning Standards

Tell whether each product will be *odd* or *even*.

1. 5 × 6 = _30_

2. 6 × 6 = _36_

3. 9 × 9 = _81_

4. 7 × 3 = _21_

5. 2 × 7 = _14_

6. 5 × 1 = _5_

7. odd × odd = _odd_

8. odd × even = _even_

9. even × even = _even_

Find the product. Use patterns if you wish.

10. 4
    × 5
    _20_

11. 5
    × 5
    _25_

12. 8
    × 5
    _40_

13. 8
    × 6
    _48_

14. 8
    × 7
    _56_

15. 10
    × 9
    _90_

16. 6
    × 5
    _30_

17. 6
    × 6
    _36_

18. 9
    × 6
    _54_

19. 9
    × 7
    _63_

20. 7
    × 6
    _42_

21. 9
    × 9
    _81_

22. 4
    × 7
    _28_

23. 9
    × 8
    _72_

24. 6
    × 3
    _18_

Short-Response Questions

Solve each problem.

25. Alice wanted to only have an odd number of marbles. Each bag contains 7 marbles. Should she take 2, 4 or 5 bags of marbles? _____

26. Is there a factor that will always give you an odd product? Explain by giving examples.

_____

_____

_____

_____

NYS Test Practice

DIRECTIONS Read each problem.
Circle the letter of the answer you choose.

1 Look at the multiplication fact below.

$$5 \times ?$$

Which could be the missing factor if the product is odd?

A 2

B 4

C 5

D 8

2 Which number will make the product even?

$$9 \times ?$$

A 5

B 7

C 8

D 9

3 Which is true about the product of an even factor times an even factor?

A It is always odd.

B It is always even.

C It can be odd or even.

D It is never even.

4 Jim paid $40 for CDs. If the cost of each CD is an odd number, what do you know about the number of CDs Jim bought?

A Jim bought an odd number of CDs.

B Jim bought an even number of CDs.

C Jim bought 7 CDs.

D Jim bought 9 CDs.

5 Look at the multiplication fact below.

$$3 \times ?$$

Which could not be the missing factor if the product is even?

A 2

B 4

C 5

D 8

Lesson 15 Properties of Multiplication

NYS Performance Indicators: 4.N.6, 4.N.16, 4.PS.7, 4.PS.23, 4.RP.7, 4.CM.11

The properties of multiplication can help you multiply.

Associative Property	The grouping of the factors does not change the product.	$(7 \times 2) \times 5 = 7 \times (2 \times 5)$ $14 \times 5 = 7 \times 10$ $70 = 70$
Commutative Property	The order of the factors does not change the product.	$3 \times 4 = 4 \times 3$ $12 = 12$
Zero Property	The product of any number and zero is 0.	$7 \times 0 = 0$
Identity Property	The product of 1 and any number is that number.	$1 \times 8 = 8$

Guided Instruction

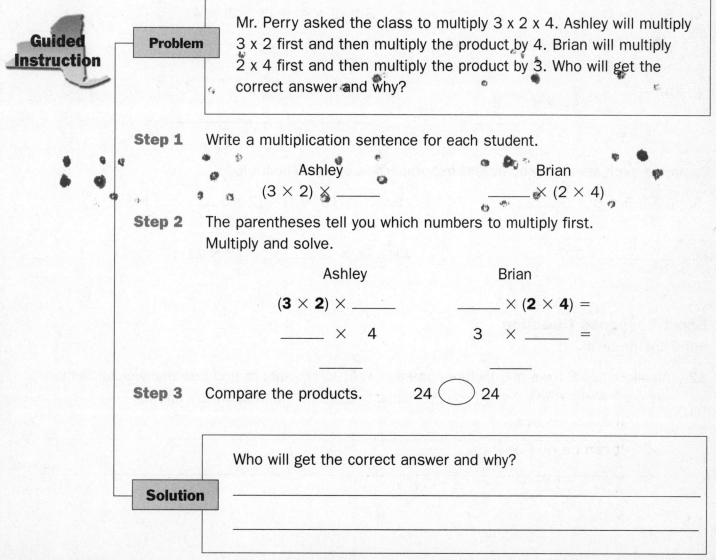

Problem

Mr. Perry asked the class to multiply 3 x 2 x 4. Ashley will multiply 3 x 2 first and then multiply the product by 4. Brian will multiply 2 x 4 first and then multiply the product by 3. Who will get the correct answer and why?

Step 1 Write a multiplication sentence for each student.

Ashley   Brian

$(3 \times 2) \times$ _____   _____ $\times (2 \times 4)$

Step 2 The parentheses tell you which numbers to multiply first. Multiply and solve.

Ashley   Brian

$(3 \times 2) \times$ _____   _____ $\times (2 \times 4) =$

_____ $\times$ 4   3 $\times$ _____ $=$

_____   _____

Step 3 Compare the products.   24 $\bigcirc$ 24

Who will get the correct answer and why?

Solution

_____

_____

Complete the sentences. Write *Zero, Identity, Commutative,* or *Associative.*

1. The _____ Property says that two factors can be multiplied in any order and the product will be the same.

2. The _____ Property says that the product of 1 and any number is that number.

3. The _____ Property says that the way in which factors are grouped does not change the product.

Write the name of the multiplication property that each number sentence shows.

4. $8 \times 0 = 0$

   _____

5. $3 \times (2 \times 4) = (3 \times 2) \times 4$

   _____

6. $9 \times 3 = 3 \times 9$

   _____

7. $1 \times 57 = 57$

   _____

Complete each number sentence, using properties of multiplication.

8. $10 \times 6 = 6 \times$ _____

9. $2 \times (10 \times 1) = (2 \times$ _____$) \times 1$

10. _____ $\times 307 = 0$

11. $21 \times$ _____ $= 73 \times 21$

Short-Response Question

Solve the problem.

12. A gallery has 8 rows of 5 pictures on each wall. John wants to find how many pictures there are on 2 walls. Show 2 ways you can solve this problem and show the answer.

   _____

   _____

NYS Test Practice

DIRECTIONS Read each problem.
Circle the letter of the answer you choose.

1 Which has a product equal to
$9 \times (8 \times 3)$?

A $(9 + 8) \times 3$

B $(9 \times 8) \times 3$

C $9 + (8 \times 3)$

D $(9 \times 8) + (8 \times 3)$

2 Which is equal to 7×8?

A $7 + 8$

B $(4 \times 2) + 7$

C $7 \times (8 \times 1)$

D $7 \times 7 \times 7$

3 Maryanne and Gary each planted
corn in a garden. Maryanne
planted four rows with ten plants
in each row. Gary planted five rows
with four plants in each row. Who
planted more corn?

A Gary

B Maryanne

C They both have the same.

D not enough information

4 Which number makes the number
sentence below true?

$4 \times (4 \times 2) = \underline{\hspace{1cm}} \times 2$

A 4   **C** 16

B 8   **D** 32

5 Which property of multiplication
does the number sentence
below show?

$2 \times (8 \times 3) = (2 \times 8) \times 3$

A Identity Property

B Commutative Property

C Associative Property

D Zero Property

6 Ria and Kim each found the value
of $6 \times 4 \times 8$. Ria multiplied 6×4
first and then multiplied the
product by 8. Kim multiplied 4×8
first and then multiplied the product
by 6. Who got the correct product?

A Only Ria got the correct
product.

B Only Kim got the correct
product.

C Both Ria and Kim got the
correct product.

D Neither Ria nor Kim got the
correct product.

The **Distributive Property** of multiplication says that to multiply a sum by a number you can multiply each addend by the number and then add the products.

$$6 \times \mathbf{12} = 6 \times (\mathbf{10} + \mathbf{2})$$
$$= (6 \times \mathbf{10}) + (6 \times \mathbf{2})$$
$$= \quad 60 \quad + \quad 12$$
$$6 \times 12 = 72$$

Guided Instruction

Problem

Ali is planting a vegetable garden. She wants to plant 8 rows of vegetables with 15 vegetables in each row. How many vegetables will Ali have in her garden?

You can use a grid and the Distributive Property to solve the problem.

Step 1 Use a grid to model the factors from the problem. Then separate the grid into 2 parts.

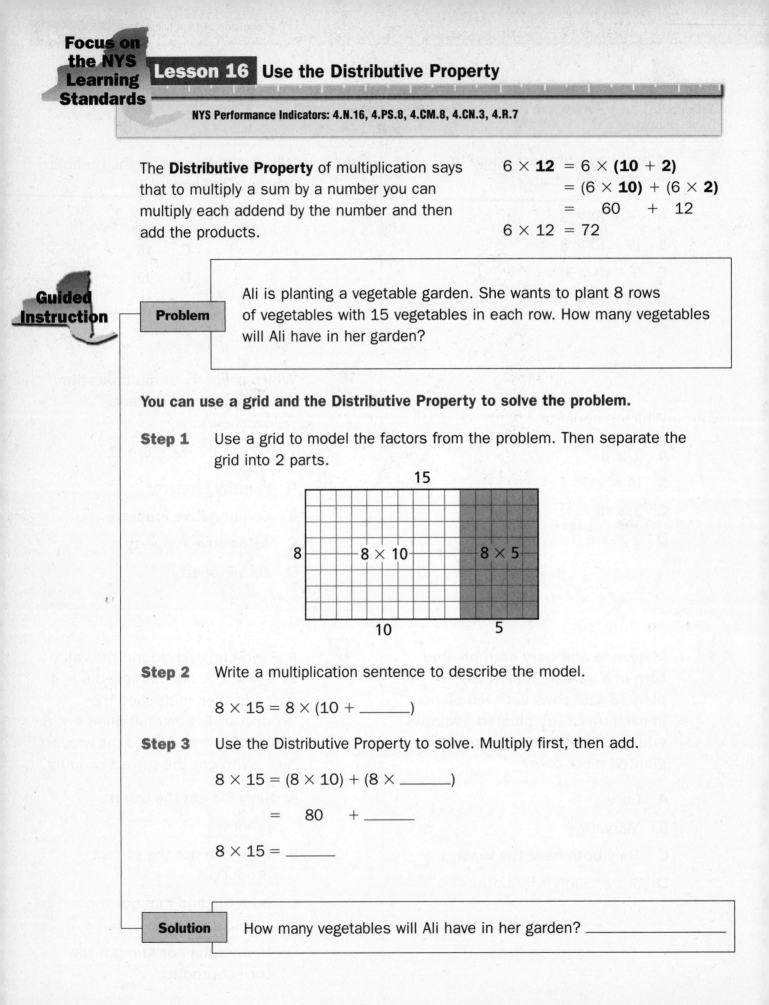

Step 2 Write a multiplication sentence to describe the model.

$8 \times 15 = 8 \times (10 + \underline{\hspace{1cm}})$

Step 3 Use the Distributive Property to solve. Multiply first, then add.

$8 \times 15 = (8 \times 10) + (8 \times \underline{\hspace{1cm}})$

$= \quad 80 \quad + \underline{\hspace{1cm}}$

$8 \times 15 = \underline{\hspace{1cm}}$

Solution How many vegetables will Ali have in her garden? \underline{\hspace{3cm}}

Apply the NYS Learning Standards

Use the Distributive Property to solve each problem.

1. 5 × 15 = 5 × (10 + 5)

   = (5 × 10) + (5 × _____)

   =   50   +   _____

5 × 15 = _____

2. 6 × 17 = 6 × (10 + 7)

   = (6 × _____) + (6 × 7)

   =   60   + _____

6 × 17 = _____

3. 8 × 13 = 8 × (10 + 3)

   = (8 × 10) + (8 × _____)

   =   80   +   _____

8 × 13 = _____

4. 3 × 15 = 3 × (_____ + 5)

   = (_____ × 10) + (_____ × _____)

   =   _____   +   _____

3 × 15 = _____

5. 7 × 14 = _____

6. 3 × 12 = _____

7. 9 × 19 = _____

8. 5 × 13 = _____

9. 4 × 17 = _____

10. 8 × 16 = _____

Short-Response Questions

Solve each problem.

11. There are 8 hot dog rolls in a package. How many are in 15 packages?

Anita said (8 × 15) = (8 × 10) + (8 × 5)

Ron said 15 × 8 means

8 + 8 + 8 + 8 + 8 + 8 + 8 + 8 + 8 + 8 + 8 + 8 + 8 + 8 + 8.

Find out how many hotdog rolls there are in 15 packages using one of the methods. _____

Which method did you use? Why? _____

_____

_____

12. Chan tiled his floor. He put down 9 rows of tiles with 18 tiles in each row. How many tiles did Chan use in all? Explain how you found your answer.

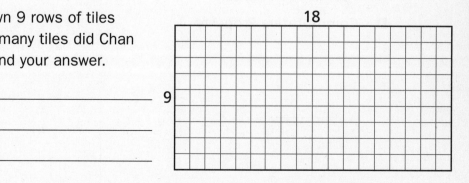

_____

_____

_____

NYS Test Practice

DIRECTIONS Read each problem.
Circle the letter of the answer you choose.

1 Which has a product of 36?

   A $3 \times (10 \times 2)$

   B $3 \times (10 + 2)$

   C $6 \times (6 \times 2)$

   D 0×36

2 Which number makes the number sentence below true?

$$5 \times 23 = 5 \times (\square + 3)$$

   A 23

   B 20

   C 3

   D 0

3 Which property of multiplication would you use if you wanted to change a factor into 2 addends?

   A Distributive Property

   B Zero Property

   C Associative Property

   D Commutative Property

4 Which does not give a product of 48?

   A 48×0

   B $4 \times (10 + 2)$

   C $(4 \times 5) + (4 \times 7)$

   D 4×12

5 Billy's team is raising money for caps. There are 8 players and 1 coach. Each cap costs $15. Which of the following problems can simplify figuring out how much money they have to raise for each player and the coach to have a cap?

   A $10 + 8 + 8 + 8 + 8 + 1$

   B $(9 + 15) \times 10$

   C $(8 \times 1) + (8 \times 15)$

   D $(9 \times 10) + (9 \times 5)$

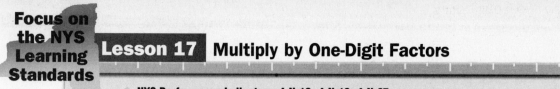

Focus on the NYS Learning Standards

Lesson 17 Multiply by One-Digit Factors

NYS Performance Indicators: 4.N.16, 4.N.18, 4.N.27

You can use multiplication facts to help you multiply two-digit numbers. When you multiply you may need to regroup. **Regroup** means to rename a number, such as 10 ones regrouped as 1 ten and 0 ones.

Guided Instruction

Problem

At a warehouse store, Mr. Thorsen bought hot dog rolls for the concession stand. He bought 6 packages of 18. How many rolls did he buy?

Use multiplication to find how many rolls were bought.

Step 1 Multiply the ones.

6 × 8 = _____ ones

Regroup the ones as

_____ tens _____ ones.

$$\begin{array}{r} \overline{}\\ 18 \\ \times\ 6 \\ \hline \overline{} \end{array}$$

Step 2 Multiply the tens.

6 × 1 = _____

Add the regrouped tens.

6 tens + _____ regrouped tens = _____ tens

Regroup 10 tens as _____ hundred _____ tens.

$$\begin{array}{r} {}^{4}\\ 18 \\ \times\ 6 \\ \hline \underline{}\ 8 \end{array}$$

Step 3 Estimate to see if your answer is reasonable.

18 rounds to _____

20 × 6 = _____

Is 108 close to 120? _____

Solution How many rolls did Mr. Thorsen buy? _____

Apply the NYS Learning Standards

Find each product.

1. 21 × 9	**2.** 78 × 5	**3.** 14 × 6	**4.** 55 × 8	**5.** 92 × 4
6. 72 × 5	**7.** 51 × 7	**8.** 23 × 4	**9.** 93 × 2	**10.** 78 × 6
11. 85 × 3	**12.** 25 × 8	**13.** 81 × 6	**14.** 20 × 3	**15.** 48 × 7

Short-Response Questions

Fill in the numbers in the table.

Use the table to answer problems 16–18.

Type of Model	Number in Carton	Price per Model	Number × Price = Cost per Carton
Submarine	18	$ 9	18 × ____ = $162
Aircraft Carrier	9	$18	9 × $18 =
Sailboat	24	$ 8	____ × $ 8 = $192
Yacht	30	$ ____	30 × $ 6 =

16. Why is the total cost of submarines the same as the aircraft carriers?

_____

17. If the sailboat models are packed in one layer of rows and columns in the box, name two ways the boats could be packed.

_____

18. How much money would it cost to buy 6 sailboats and 4 submarines? Explain how you found your answer.

_____

_____

NYS Test Practice

**DIRECTIONS Read each problem.
Circle the letter of the answer you choose.**

1 Look at the number sentence below.

$$5 \times \square = 10 \times 9$$

Which number makes the number sentence true?

A 14   C 85

B 18   D 90

2 Scott's family traveled 98 miles a day for 6 days. How many miles did they travel?

A 92

B 104

C 588

D 624

3 Machell put together a scrapbook. She completed 49 pages. Each page had 4 pictures. She solved to find how many pictures she has in her scrapbook so far. Which can she use to check the reasonableness of her answer?

A 50×40

B 490×4

C 49×40

D 50×4

4 The students in fourth grade are rewarded with points each time they raise money for charity. Each dollar is worth 6 points. When a class reaches 500 points, they will have a party.

MONEY RAISED FOR CHARITY

Room Number	Money Raised
201	$78
202	$97
203	$76
204	$81

Which classroom reached 500 points first?

A 201

B 202

C 203

D 204

5 There are 15 rows of tables in the cafeteria. Each row has 8 tables. What is the total number of tables in the cafeteria?

A 23

B 120

C 320

D 360

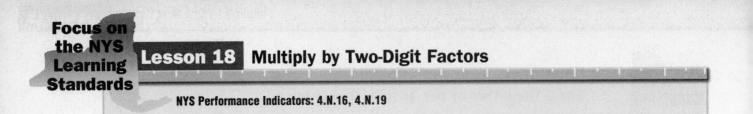
You can use multiplication facts to help you multiply by greater numbers.

Guided Instruction

Problem

Superintendent Lee ordered new desks for his schools. He ordered 25 desks for each of the 65 classrooms. How many desks have been ordered?

Multiply to find how many desks have been ordered.

Step 1 Multiply by the ones.

$5 \times 5 =$ _____ ones

Regroup 25 ones as

_____ tens _____ ones.

Remember to add the regrouped ones.

What is the partial product? _____

$$\begin{array}{r} \bar{} \\ 65 \\ \times\ 25 \\ \hline \end{array}$$

Step 2 Multiply by the tens.

Use a zero in the ones place as a placeholder.

What is the partial product? _____

$$\begin{array}{r} 2 \\ 65 \\ \times\ 25 \\ \hline 325 \\ 0 \end{array}$$

Step 3 Add the partial products.

Remember to use a comma between the hundreds and thousands places in the product.

$$\begin{array}{r} 1 \\ 2 \\ 65 \\ \times\ 25 \\ \hline 325 \\ \mathbf{1,300} \end{array}$$

Solution How many desks have been ordered? _____

Apply the NYS Learning Standards

Find each product.

1.	56 × 13	2.	56 × 11	3.	13 × 36	4.	45 × 29	5.	78 × 11

6.	23 × 19	7.	14 × 26	8.	55 × 38	9.	17 × 35	10.	52 × 22

11.	32 × 40	12.	93 × 22	13.	45 × 13	14.	25 × 42	15.	81 × 16

16. $28 \times 10 =$ _____

17. $95 \times 10 =$ _____

18. $34 \times 20 =$ _____

19. $25 \times 30 =$ _____

Short-Response Questions

Solve each problem.

20. Look at problems 16–19. What can you do when using a factor that is a multiple of ten to make finding the product easier?

_____

_____

Use the table to solve problems 21–22.

21. Ms. Sullivan's class got 24 new chairs. What was the total cost of the chairs? _____

22. Ms. Sullivan's class also got new desks. How can you find the cost of 24 desks without multiplying 24×60? Explain how you found your answer.

Hint: What is the cost of a desk compared to the cost of a chair?

_____

_____

CLASSROOM FURNITURE

Student Chair	$30
Student Desk	$60

NYS Test Practice

DIRECTIONS Read each problem.
Circle the letter of the answer you choose.

1 The students and teachers in Lincoln Elementary School went on a picnic at the State Park. There were 38 people on each of 12 buses. How many people went to the picnic?

A 50

B 243

C 386

D 456

2 Dan is driving to his uncle's house. His van has a 28-gallon tank and goes 29 miles for every gallon of gasoline. How many miles can Dan go on a full tank of gas?

A 812

B 792

C 252

D 57

3 A store has 87 boxes of dolls. There are 25 dolls in each box. How many dolls are there in all? Which number sentence would you use to solve this problem?

A $87 + 25 = \Box$

B $87 \times 20 + 5 = \Box$

C $87 \times 25 = \Box$

D $87 - 25 = \Box$

4 Ms. Conley bought 36 rolls of film. She can take 24 pictures with each roll of film. What is the total number of pictures she can take with 36 rolls of film?

A 314

B 634

C 864

D 1,844

5 There are 24 hours in a day. How many hours are in 2 weeks?

A 48

B 130

C 328

D 336

6 Each athletic team at Maria's school practices 14 hours weekly. How many total hours does each athletic team practice in 17 weeks?

A 218

B 238

C 298

D 301

You can use patterns to multiply by multiples of 10 and 100.

A multiplication **equation** is a number sentence with an equal sign.

Guided Instruction

Problem 1   Each ticket for the school play costs $10. Mr. Vega buys 6 tickets. What is the total cost of the tickets?

You can use a pattern to multiply.

Step 1   Write an equation, or number sentence, that describes this problem.

_____ × 6 = ☐

Step 2   Use a pattern to multiply by 10.

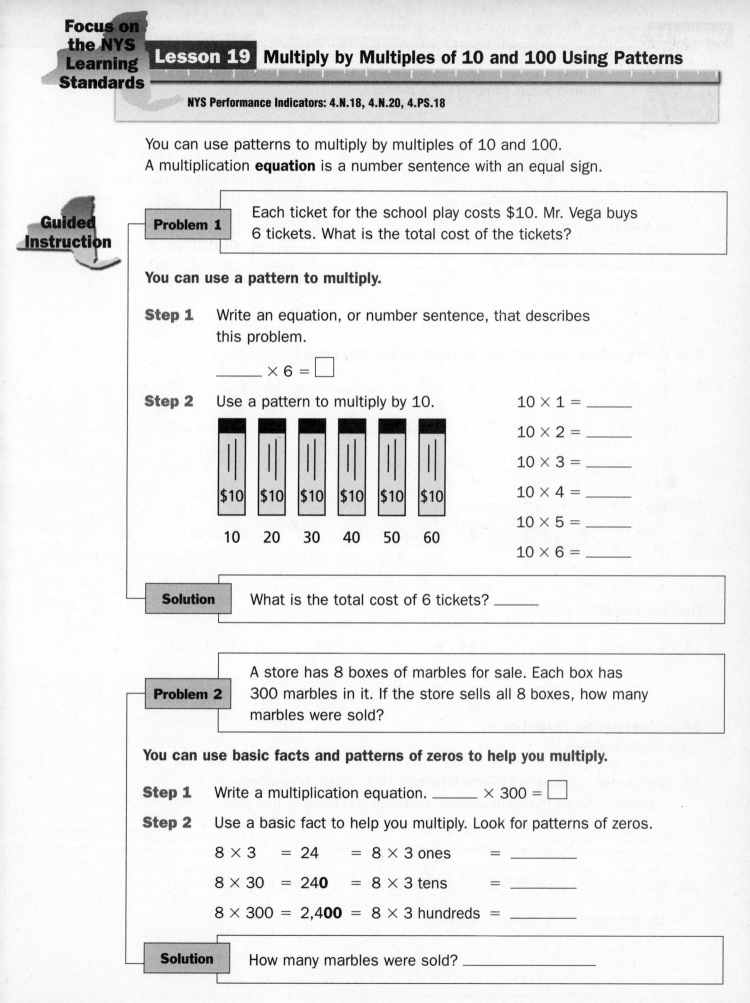

10   20   30   40   50   60

10 × 1 = _____

10 × 2 = _____

10 × 3 = _____

10 × 4 = _____

10 × 5 = _____

10 × 6 = _____

Solution   What is the total cost of 6 tickets? _____

Problem 2   A store has 8 boxes of marbles for sale. Each box has 300 marbles in it. If the store sells all 8 boxes, how many marbles were sold?

You can use basic facts and patterns of zeros to help you multiply.

Step 1   Write a multiplication equation. _____ × 300 = ☐

Step 2   Use a basic fact to help you multiply. Look for patterns of zeros.

8 × 3   = 24   = 8 × 3 ones   = _____

8 × 30   = 24**0**   = 8 × 3 tens   = _____

8 × 300 = 2,4**00** = 8 × 3 hundreds = _____

Solution   How many marbles were sold? _____

Apply the NYS Learning Standards

Multiply and complete the pattern.

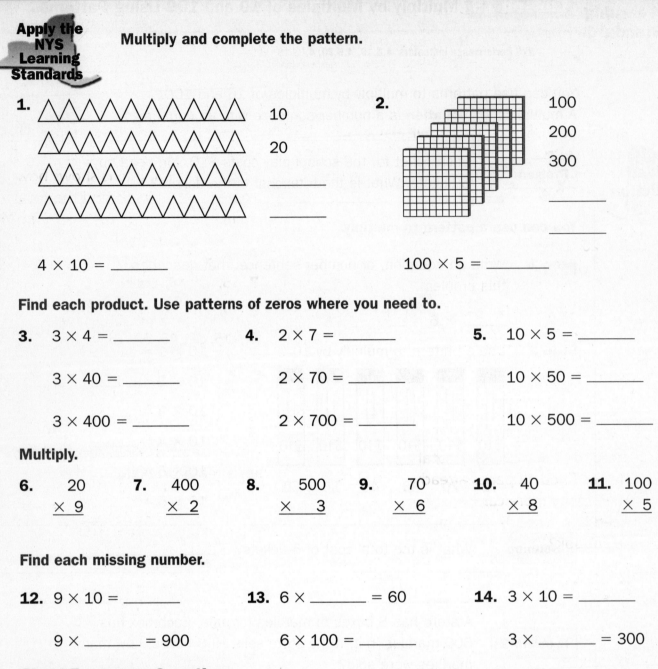

1.   10
                                    20
                                    _____
                                    _____

    4 × 10 = _____

2.   100
                                    200
                                    300
                                    _____
                                    _____

    100 × 5 = _____

Find each product. Use patterns of zeros where you need to.

3. 3 × 4 = _____

    3 × 40 = _____

    3 × 400 = _____

4. 2 × 7 = _____

    2 × 70 = _____

    2 × 700 = _____

5. 10 × 5 = _____

    10 × 50 = _____

    10 × 500 = _____

Multiply.

6.   20
     × 9

7.   400
     × 2

8.   500
     × 3

9.   70
     × 6

10.   40
     × 8

11.   100
     × 5

Find each missing number.

12. 9 × 10 = _____

    9 × _____ = 900

13. 6 × _____ = 60

    6 × 100 = _____

14. 3 × 10 = _____

    3 × _____ = 300

Short-Response Questions

Solve each problem.

15. One meter is equal to 100 centimeters. How many centimeters are in
    7 meters? Show the multiplication equation you used to find your answer.

    _____

16. You know that 15 × 1 = 15. Use this fact to find the product of 15 × 10.

    Explain how you found your answer.

    _____

    _____

NYS Test Practice

DIRECTIONS Read each problem.
Circle the letter of the answer you choose.

1 Which number makes this number sentence true?

$$6 \times \underline{\hspace{1.5cm}} = 1,200$$

A 2

B 20

C 200

D 2,000

2 Each page in Henry's scrapbook holds 20 baseball cards. Henry's scrapbook has 20 pages total and he has filled 12 pages already. How many more cards will he need in order to fill the rest of the scrapbook?

A 16

B 80

C 160

D 400

3 In one flower bed, a gardener planted 5 rows of 10 seeds each. Which list of numbers shows how you would count to find the total number of seeds in the flower bed?

A 4, 8, 12, 16, 20

B 5, 10, 15, 20, 25

C 10, 20, 30, 40, 50

D 15, 30, 45, 60, 75

4 Aisha uses the blocks shown below for a math problem.

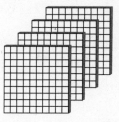

Which problem below is Aisha most likely solving?

A $10 \times 4 = 40$

B $100 + 4 = 104$

C $100 + 40 = 140$

D $100 \times 4 = 400$

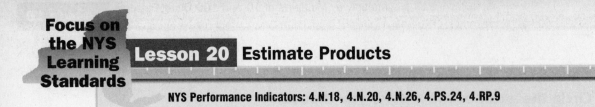

Focus on the NYS Learning Standards

Lesson 20 Estimate Products

NYS Performance Indicators: 4.N.18, 4.N.20, 4.N.26, 4.PS.24, 4.RP.9

You can use **rounding** and basic facts to estimate an answer to a multiplication problem.

Guided Instruction

Problem

There are 6 cartons of books in a warehouse. Each carton contains 295 books. About how many books are in the warehouse?

Round the greater factor to estimate the product.

Step 1   Round 295 to the nearest hundred.

295 rounds to _____.

Step 2   Multiply using patterns and basic facts.

6 × 3 = _____, so

6 × 3**00** = _____

Step 3   Estimate the answer.

6 × 295 is about _____.

Solution

About how many books are in the warehouse?

_____

Apply the NYS Learning Standards

Estimate each product. Use rounding to estimate.

1. 62
× 4

2. 37
× 7

3. 91
× 8

4. 55
× 5

5. 34
× 3

6. 91
× 7

7. 34
× 6

8. 75
× 8

9. 62
× 9

10. 64
× 6

11. 138
× 6

12. 204
× 3

13. 571
× 2

14. 337
× 9

15. 809
× 5

Choose two factors from the box for each estimated product.

2	5	
	7	9
231	577	
	728	802

16. 1,200 _____

17. 3,500 _____

18. 5,600 _____

19. 1,800 _____

Short-Response Questions
Solve each problem.

20. Alan has a 78-page album. He puts 8 baseball cards on each page of the album. About how many baseball cards does he use in all?

_____

21. Ms. Ramirez earned $389 in each of 4 weeks. She said she earned between $1,900 and $2,000 altogether. Do you agree or disagree? How much did Ms. Ramirez actually earn? Explain how you know.

_____

_____

_____

_____

NYS Test Practice

DIRECTIONS Read each problem.
Circle the letter of the answer you choose.

1 Stan bought 3 pairs of jeans for $18 each. About how much did Stan spend on jeans?

A $20

B $40

C $60

D $80

2 Tamara estimated the product of the expression below.

$$7 \times 391$$

Which statement about the estimated product is true?

A It is less than 7.

B It is less than 391.

C It is equal to 391.

D It is greater than 391.

3 The table below shows the prices of different size plants.

PLANT PRICES

Plant Size	Price
small	$9
medium	$18
large	$29

Marlee bought some plants. She spent about $60. What did Marlee buy?

A 2 small plants

B 3 small plants

C 3 medium plants

D 4 large plants

4 Jack bought five gallons of paint. Each gallon cost $28. About how much did he spend?

A between $10 and $15

B between $50 and $60

C between $100 and $110

D between $140 and $150

 Measuring Up® to the New York State Learning Standards

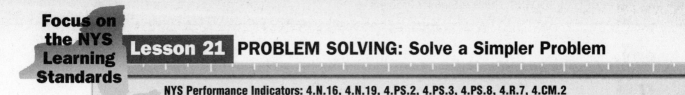

Lesson 21 | PROBLEM SOLVING: Solve a Simpler Problem

NYS Performance Indicators: 4.N.16, 4.N.19, 4.PS.2, 4.PS.3, 4.PS.8, 4.R.7, 4.CM.2

You can use the properties of numbers to make a problem simpler to solve. You can use the problem-solving guide in the back of the book to help you.

Guided Instruction

Problem	There are 75 sheets of computer paper in a box. Jack bought 4 boxes of paper. How many sheets of computer paper did Jack buy?

Understand the problem.

There are _____ sheets of paper in one box.

Jack bought _____ boxes.

What do you need to find?

_____

Make a plan.

You can use the Distributive Property to make the numbers easier to multiply.

Solve the problem.

Write 75 in expanded form.

70 + _____

Multiply each number by 4.

4 × 70 = _____

4 × 5 = _____

Add the products.

280 + _____ = _____

Jack bought _____ sheets of computer paper.

Check your answer.

Use repeated addition.

75 + _____ + _____ + _____ = _____

Solve each problem by writing a simpler problem.

Work Space

1. A restaurant manager bought 40 new plates.
    Each plate cost $19. What was the total cost of the plates?

    The plates cost $760

    $$\begin{array}{r} 40 \\ \times 19 \\ \hline 360 \\ + 40 \times \\ \hline \$760 \end{array}$$

2. A principal wants to give each fourth-grade student in
    her school 20 colored markers. There are 73 fourth
    graders in her school. How many colored markers does
    the principal need to buy?

3. A stamp collector has a 30-page album. There are
    18 stamps on each page of the album. How many
    stamps are in the album?

Short-Response Question

4. A gardener bought 15 packs of seeds. There were
    50 seeds in each pack. How many seeds is this in all?
    Explain how you found your answer.

     Measuring Up® to the New York State Learning Standards

NYS Test Practice

DIRECTIONS Read each problem.
Circle the letter of the answer you choose.

1 A theater has 80 rows. There are 24 seats in each row. Which could you use to find how many seats are in the theater?

A $(80 \times 20) - (80 \times 4)$

B $(80 \times 20) + (80 \times 4)$

C $(80 \times 20) + (24 \times 24)$

D $(80 \times 24) + (24 \times 24)$

2 There are 30 apples in each bag. How many apples are there in 18 bags?

A 60

B 78

C 540

D 1,000

3 Which could you use to find the product 90×68?

A (90×60)

B $(90 \times 60) + (90 \times 800)$

C $(90 \times 60) + (90 \times 8)$

D $(900 \times 60) + (900 \times 8)$

4 Jacob wrote the following to help solve a multiplication problem.

$(20 \times 70) + (20 \times 4)$

Which problem was Jacob solving?

A How many stickers are on 70 sheets if there are 20 stickers on each sheet?

B How many stickers are on 74 sheets if there are 20 stickers on each sheet?

C How many stickers are on 20 sheets if there are 70 stickers on each sheet?

D How many stickers are on 4 sheets if there are 74 stickers on each sheet?

5 Which could you use to find the product 18×70?

A $(70 \times 10) + (70 \times 8)$

B $(70 \times 10) - (70 \times 8)$

C $(70 \times 10) + (18 \times 18)$

D $(70 + 10) \times (70 + 8)$

DIRECTIONS Read each problem.
Circle the letter of the answer you choose.

1 Coach Linda went to a shop to buy sweatshirts for her school team. Each sweatshirt cost $26. There are 23 girls on the team. How much will the sweatshirts cost?

A $578

B $588

C $598

D $618

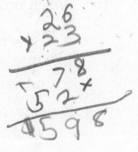

2 John and Katie want to put postcards on the wall. They have planned out how the postcards will look. Which sentence shows how many postcards will be on the wall?

A   4 + 7 = 11

B   7 × 7 = 49

C   4 × 4 = 16

D   4 × 7 = 28

3 Each day that Matteo runs, he runs 5 kilometers. Matteo ran on 26 days last month. How many kilometers did he run?

A   650

B   130

C   500

D   331

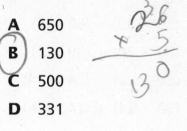

4 Sadie wants to have a product that is odd. Which types of factors can she use?

A   odd × odd

B   even × even

C   even × odd

D   odd × even

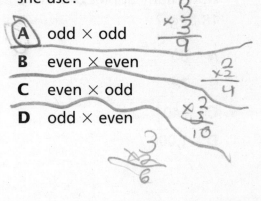

5 Which is equal to (6 × 7) × 4?

A   (6 × 7) + (7 × 4)

B   6 × (7 + 4)

C   6 + (7 + 4)

D   6 × (7 × 4)

6 Travis arranged his 36 photographs on his wall in an array. Which could not have been an array he used?

A 4 by 9

B 3 by 12

C 2 by 16

D 6 by 6

7 Syria used the model below to check her answer to a multiplication problem.

Which problem did Syria want to check?

A 55 × 1 = ☐

B 55 × 3 = ☐

C 54 × 3 = ☐

D 45 × 4 = ☐

8 One calculator costs $28. How much do 5 calculators cost?

A $150   C $104

B $140   D $100

9 There is a downpour at the parade. Everyone huddles under the closest overhang he or she can find. There are 38 overhangs, with 16 people under each. How many people are under the overhangs?

A 54   C 608

B 438   D 624

10 One video game costs $47. About how much do 5 video games cost?

A $200   C $280

B $250   D $300

11 Billy's basketball team is raising money for uniforms. There are 14 players and each uniform costs $25. Which could you use to find how much they have to raise?

A (25 × 10) + (25 × 4)

B (14 × 2) + (14 × 5)

C (25 + 14) × 10

D 10 + 25 + 25 + 25 + 25

Extended-Response Questions
DIRECTIONS Read each question carefully before writing your response.
Be sure to show your work when asked.

12 Gina has a carton of crayons. There are 200 boxes of crayons in the carton. Each box has 6 crayons.

Part A

How many crayons are in the carton?

Show your work.

$6 \times 2 = 12$
$6 \times 20 = 120$
$6 \times 200 = 1,200$

200
× 6
1,200

Answer ___1,200___

Part B

On the lines below, explain how you can solve this problem if you **only** know basic facts.

If you only know your basic facts you can do $6 \times 2 = 12$, $6 \times 20 = 120$ and $6 \times 200 = 1,200$.

13. Christopher lives in New York City. His apartment building has 7 floors. There are 18 apartments on each floor in the building.

Part A

How many apartments are in Christopher's building?

Show your work.

$$\begin{array}{r} {}^5\,18 \\ \times\ 7 \\ \hline 126 \end{array}$$

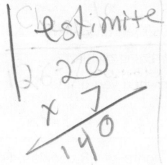

estimite

$$\begin{array}{r} 20 \\ \times\ 7 \\ \hline 140 \end{array}$$

14

Answer _____126_____

Part B

On the lines below, show how your answer is reasonable by using an estimate.

A estimite can be 20 x 7 because the answer is 140 and it is 14 away from 126.

You can use division to separate a number into equal groups, find the number of groups, or find the number of things in each group.

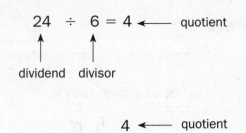

$24 \div 6 = 4$ ← quotient

dividend   divisor

A **divisor** is the number you are dividing by.

A **dividend** is the number being divided.

A **quotient** is the answer when you divide.

divisor → $6\overline{)24}$

4 ← quotient

dividend

Guided Instruction

| Problem | A package contains 28 cookies. Four friends decide to share them equally. How many cookies will each friend get? |

You can use models to help you divide.

Step 1   Use counters to show cookies.

Start with _____ rows for the 4 friends.
Put 1 counter in each row.

Step 2   Put another counter in each row.
Draw the counters.
Continue until 28 counters have been placed in an array and drawn.

Step 3   Circle each row. Count. There are _____ rows.

How many are in each row? _____

Step 4   Complete the division sentence to show how many are in each equal group.

$28 \div 4 =$ _____

| Solution | How many cookies will each friend get? _____ |

Apply the
NYS
Learning
Standards

Use the picture to complete each division sentence.

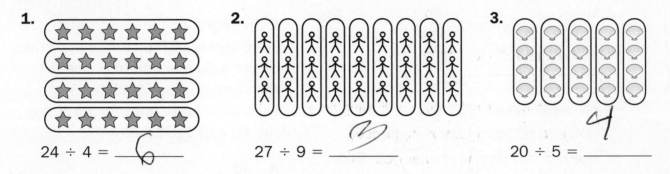

1.
24 ÷ 4 = _6_

2.
27 ÷ 9 = _3_

3.
20 ÷ 5 = _4_

Write each division sentence under the correct picture. Then solve.

| 32 ÷ 1 = | 32 ÷ 8 = | 32 ÷ 4 = |

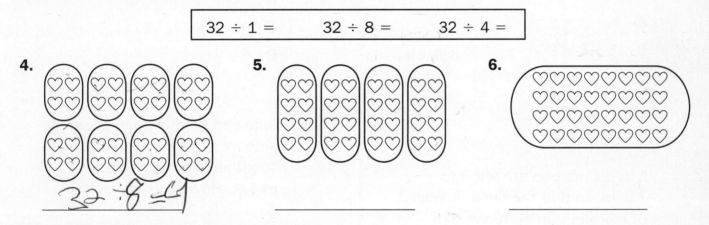

4.
32 ÷ 8 = 4

5.
_____

6.
_____

Solve each problem. Use models if you want to.

7. 25 ÷ 5 = _____

8. 18 ÷ 3 = _____

9. 50 ÷ 10 = _____

10. 10 ÷ 5 = _____

11. 21 ÷ 3 = _____

12. 20 ÷ 2 = _____

13. 36 ÷ 4 = _____

14. 35 ÷ 7 = _____

15. 12 ÷ 3 = _____

Short-Response Questions

Solve each problem.

16. Linda had 30 pieces of silverware. She used them
all by placing 3 pieces at each place. How many places
did she set? _____

17. Thirty-six people are coming to a team dinner. What is one way Coach
Al can divide them to have an equal number at each table? Is there
another way he can divide them? Explain.

_____

_____

_____

NYS Test Practice

DIRECTIONS Read each problem.
Circle the letter of the answer you choose.

1 Which number sentence shows how many there are in each group?

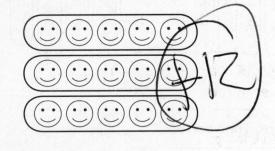

A 5 + 3 = 8

B 3 + 5 = 8

C 15 ÷ 5 = 3

(D) 15 ÷ 3 = 5

2 Fifty-six marbles are put into 7 bags, so that the same number of marbles is in each bag. Sari got 3 bags. How many marbles did she get?

A 392

B 32

C 24

D 21

3 Each helicopter has 6 blades. We see 36 blades. How many helicopters are there?

A 6

B 9

C 30

D 42

4 A photographer took a total of 36 pictures. Each picture was of one of the 4 Cooper children. She took the same number of pictures of each child. How many pictures did she take of each child?

A 40

B 32

C 12

D 9

5 Julie and Heidi earned an equal amount of money babysitting. Together they earned a total of $24. How much did each girl receive?

A $12

B $22

C $26

D $48

6 Julio has 42 rocks in his rock collection. He has 6 boxes. Each box has an equal number of rocks. How many rocks are in each box?

A 48

B 36

C 8

D 7

 Measuring Up® to the New York State Learning Standards

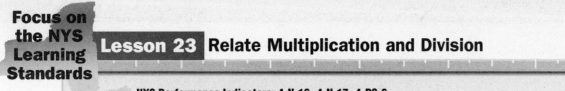

Lesson 23 Relate Multiplication and Division

NYS Performance Indicators: 4.N.16, 4.N.17, 4.PS.6

You can use what you know about arrays to relate multiplication and division. **Related facts** are facts that are in the same fact family. A **fact family** is a group of related facts that use the same numbers.

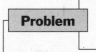
Guided Instruction

Problem Some fourth graders will put 35 chairs in 5 equal rows. How many chairs will be in each row?

Use multiplication facts to solve this division problem.

Step 1 How many chairs are there in all? _____

How many rows will there be? _____

Draw an array to show the problem.

How many columns did you draw? _____

Step 2 What multiplication facts use the numbers 35, 5, and 7?

_____

Step 3 What division facts use the numbers 35, 5, and 7?

_____

Step 4 Write the fact family for 35, 5, and 7.

_____   _____

_____   _____

So 35 ÷ 5 = _____

Solution How many chairs will be in each row? _____

Apply the NYS Learning Standards

Complete each fact family.

1. $3 \times 9 = \underline{27}$
   $9 \times 3 = \underline{27}$
   $27 \div 3 = \underline{9}$
   $27 \div 9 = \underline{3}$

2. $6 \times 5 = \underline{30}$
   $5 \times 6 = \underline{30}$
   $30 \div 6 = \underline{5}$
   $30 \div 5 = \underline{6}$

3. $4 \times 5 = \underline{20}$
   $5 \times 4 = \underline{20}$
   $20 \div 5 = \underline{4}$
   $20 \div 4 = \underline{5}$

4. $7 \times 8 = \underline{56}$
   $8 \times 7 = \underline{56}$
   $56 \div 8 = \underline{7}$
   $56 \div 7 = \underline{8}$

5. $2 \times 8 = \underline{16}$
   $8 \times 2 = \underline{16}$
   $16 \div 2 = \underline{8}$
   $16 \div 8 = \underline{2}$

6. $9 \times 6 = \underline{54}$
   $6 \times 9 = \underline{54}$
   $54 \div 6 = \underline{9}$
   $54 \div 9 = \underline{6}$

Complete each division fact. Write a related multiplication fact to help you.

7. $48 \div 6 = \underline{\hspace{2cm}}$

8. $42 \div 7 = \underline{\hspace{2cm}}$

9. $63 \div 9 = \underline{\hspace{2cm}}$

10. $35 \div 7 = \underline{\hspace{2cm}}$

11. $36 \div 4 = \underline{\hspace{2cm}}$

12. $24 \div 3 = \underline{\hspace{2cm}}$

Write the fact family for the array.

13. _____ _____
    _____ _____

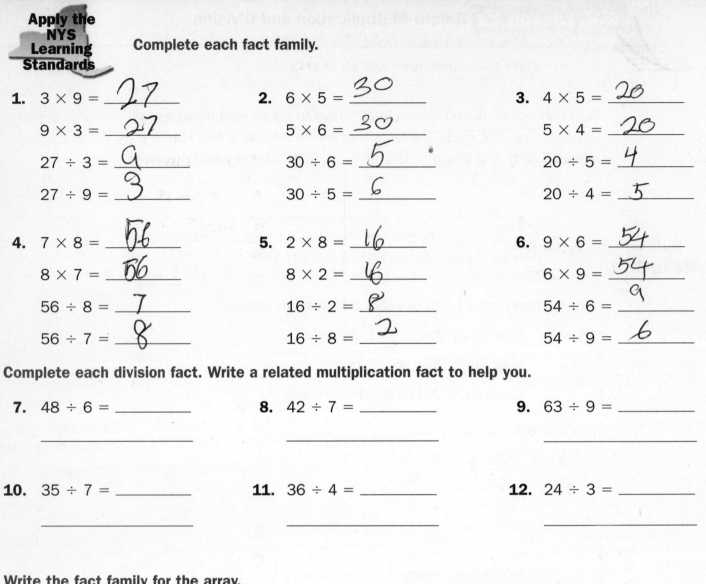

Short Response Question

Solve the problem.

14. Write the fact family for the array.
    Explain how and why it is different from other fact families.

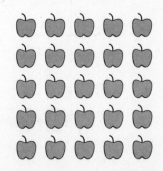

NYS Test Practice

DIRECTIONS Read each problem.
Circle the letter of the answer you choose.

1 Frank is writing the fact family that includes 72 ÷ 9 = 8. Which is not a member of this fact family?

A 8 × 9 = 72

B 72 ÷ 3 = 24

C 72 ÷ 8 = 9

D 9 × 8 = 72

2 Which number completes the fact family?

$$\square \times 8 = 48$$
$$48 \div \square = 8$$
$$8 \times \square = 48$$
$$48 \div 8 = \square$$

A 3

B 6

C 7

D 8

3 Which of the numbers will have a fact family with **only** 2 facts?

A 2, 3, 6

B 3, 4, 12

C 4, 4, 16

D 4, 5, 20

4 Sam thinks that 56 ÷ 7 = 8. Which number sentence could he use to check his answer?

A 8 + 7 = 15

B 56 − 7 = 49

C 8 × 7 = 56

D 56 ÷ 2 = 28

5 Darleen passes out 27 pieces of paper. She gives 3 pieces of paper to each student. Which of the following could be used to find out how many students there were?

A 27 + 3 = 30

B 27 × 3 = 81

C 27 ÷ 3 = 9

D 27 − 3 = 24

6 Which fact is missing from this fact family?

$$7 \times 9 = 63$$
$$9 \times 7 = 63$$
$$63 \div 7 = 9$$

A 9 + 7 = 16

B 63 ÷ 3 = 21

C 63 − 9 = 54

D 63 ÷ 9 = 7

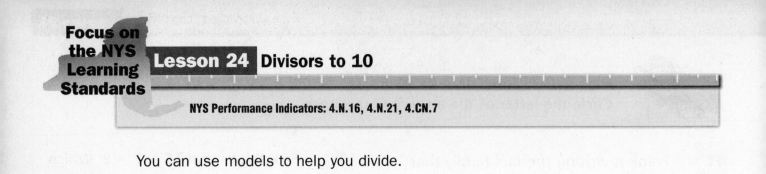
You can use models to help you divide.

Guided Instruction

Problem There are 72 wheels on the tricycles in Mr. Scott's bicycle store. How many tricycles are there in all?

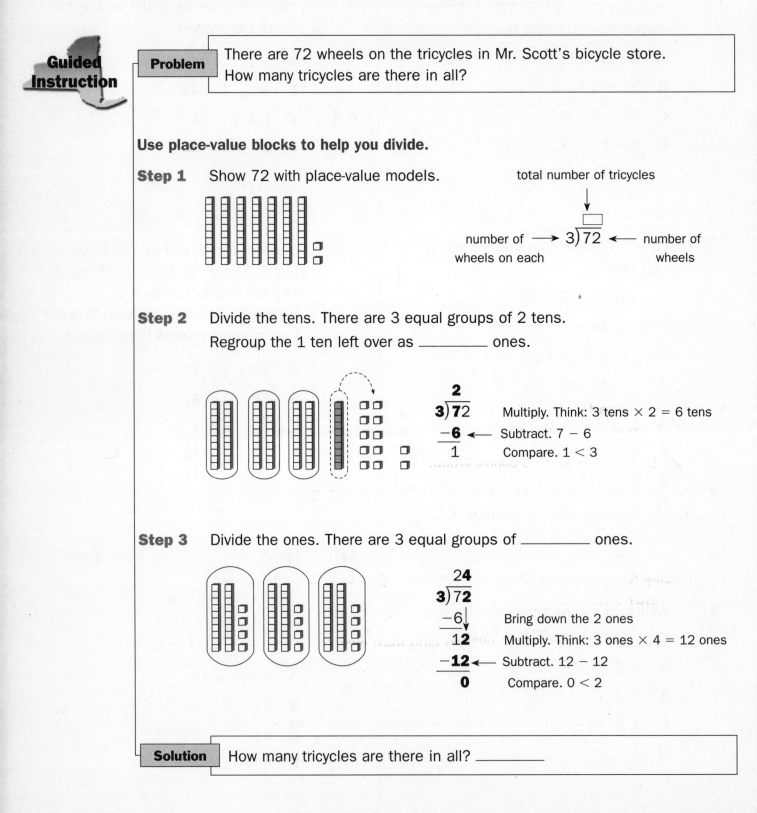

Use place-value blocks to help you divide.

Step 1 Show 72 with place-value models.

total number of tricycles

number of → 3)72 ← number of
wheels on each   wheels

Step 2 Divide the tens. There are 3 equal groups of 2 tens.

Regroup the 1 ten left over as _____ ones.

$$\begin{array}{r} 2 \\ 3)\overline{72} \\ -6 \\ \hline 1 \end{array}$$

Multiply. Think: 3 tens × 2 = 6 tens
Subtract. 7 − 6
Compare. 1 < 3

Step 3 Divide the ones. There are 3 equal groups of _____ ones.

$$\begin{array}{r} 24 \\ 3)\overline{72} \\ -6\downarrow \\ \hline 12 \\ -12 \\ \hline 0 \end{array}$$

Bring down the 2 ones
Multiply. Think: 3 ones × 4 = 12 ones
Subtract. 12 − 12
Compare. 0 < 2

Solution How many tricycles are there in all? _____

Apply the NYS Learning Standards

Find each quotient.

1. 7)77   **2.** 6)78   **3.** 9)90   **4.** 4)80

5. 3)54   **6.** 7)42   **7.** 4)72   **8.** 5)60

9. 5)25   **10.** 6)84   **11.** 2)48   **12.** 3)81

13. $90 \div 5 = $ ____   **14.** $36 \div 9 = $ ____   **15.** $60 \div 4 = $ ____   **16.** $91 \div 7 = $ ____

Short-Response Questions

Solve each problem. Use the information below to answer questions 17–19.

There are 36 girls in Melody's choral group.

17. The group will have an end-of-the-year dinner. If all the girls come, how many tables of 6 will there be? _____

18. When Melody's choral group sings, they arrange themselves in equal rows with 9 in each row. How many rows of girls are there? _____

19. For last week's performance, only 30 girls were able to perform. They arranged themselves in 3 equal rows. How many girls were in each row? Explain how you found your answer.

_____

_____

_____

DIRECTIONS Read each problem.
Circle the letter of the answer you choose.

1 Farmer Mary went to the barn and saw 24 legs under the stall. Each animal has 4 legs. Which number sentence could you use to find how many animals there were?

A $24 \div 4 = 6$

B $4 \times 4 = 16$

C $24 - 4 = 20$

D $4 \times 5 = 20$

2 Six friends want to share 42 cookies equally. How many cookies will each person get?

A 6

B 7

C 8

D 12

3 Which shows the quotient for $63 \div 7$?

A 6

B 7

C 8

D 9

4 Jeff has 24 tires in his store. He puts all the tires on cars in the shop. How many cars in the shop did he put tires on?

A 7

B 6

C 5

D 4

5 Sharon had a box with 32 pieces of candy. She used all the candy by giving her friends and herself 4 pieces of candy each. How many friends did she share her candy with?

A 5

B 7

C 8

D 16

6 Which number sentence will not help you find the missing number in the division sentence?

$$80 \div ? = 8$$

A $80 \times 1 = 80$

B $8 \times 10 = 80$

C $10 \times 8 = 80$

D $80 \div 8 = 10$

Copying is illegal. Measuring Up® to the New York State Learning Standards

Lesson 25 Interpret and Apply Remainders

NYS Performance Indicators: 4.N.16, 4.N.21, 4.N.22, 4.PS.1, 4.CN.2, 4.R.9

A **remainder** is an amount left over when a whole number cannot be divided evenly.

There are 3 ways to interpret a remainder, depending on the question: drop the remainder, increase the quotient, or use the remainder as the answer.

Guided Instruction

Problem | There are 76 club members going on an outing. 6 members can fit into each van. How many vans will be needed to bring all the members?

Divide to find out how many vans will be needed.

Step 1 Divide 76 club members into groups of 6.

$$\begin{array}{r} 12 \text{ R4} \\ 6\overline{)76} \\ -6 \\ \hline 16 \\ -12 \\ \hline 4 \end{array}$$

Step 2 Interpret the remainder.

There will be 12 vans filled.

How many members will be left over? __4__

Is another van needed? __yes__

Solution | How many vans will be needed to bring all the members? __13__

Another Example

There are 97 students signing up for 8 art classes. Each class can only have 12 students. How many students will not get into a class?

The remainder is the answer.

1 student will not get into a class.

$$\begin{array}{r} 12 \text{ R1} \\ 8\overline{)97} \\ -8 \\ \hline 17 \\ -16 \\ \hline 1 \end{array}$$

Apply the NYS Learning Standards

Divide.

1. $7\overline{)89}$
2. $4\overline{)39}$
3. $6\overline{)75}$
4. $2\overline{)55}$

5. $83 \div 5 =$ _____
6. $97 \div 4 =$ _____
7. $82 \div 3 =$ _____
8. $25 \div 8 =$ _____

9. $50 \div 9 =$ _____
10. $22 \div 6 =$ _____
11. $75 \div 7 =$ _____
12. $97 \div 5 =$ _____

Short-Response Questions
Solve each problem.

incree the qution

$50 \div 8 = 6 r 2 = 7$ pages

13. Ari has 50 stickers. He can fit 8 stickers on each page of an album. How many pages will he need for all his stickers? _7 pages_

14. Marlon is making muffins. Each muffin uses 3 ounces of flour. How many muffins can Marlon make with 25 ounces of flour? _8 muffins_

$25 \div 3 = 8 r 1$ ignore the reminder

15. The 75 students of Lakeview School are having a picnic. Each picnic table holds 6 students. How many tables are needed for all the students? Explain how you found your answer.

$75 \div 6 = 12 R 3 = 13$ incree the Remainder

13 tables will be needed because if there 12 tables 3 students won't have a seat so you have to increes the qoution and get 13 tables.

16. Jennifer has 85 sports cards. She wants to put them into packs of 9. Does Jennifer have enough cards to make 10 full packs? Explain how you know.

NO

$9\overline{)85}$

$85 \div 9 = 9 r 4$

Measuring Up® to the New York State Learning Standards

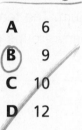

NYS Test Practice

DIRECTIONS Read each problem.
Circle the letter of the answer you choose.

1 A manager has 27 bats. He put the same number of bats in each of 3 bags. What was the greatest number he could have put in each bag?

A   6

B   9

C   10

D   12

$27 \div 3 = 9$

2 Sarah has 37 beads. She put the same number of beads on 5 bracelets using as many beads as she could. How many beads are left over?

A   4

B   3

C   2

D   1

$37 \div 5 = 7 \, r2$

3 Ms. Collins works at a toy factory. She puts 4 wheels on each toy car. She **only** has 35 wheels today. What is the **greatest** number of 4-wheeled cars she can make today?

A   4

B   6

C   8

D   9

$35 \div 4 = 8$

4 Bridget collects baseball cards. She puts them into stacks of 7 cards each. She has 49 cards. Which number sentence can be used to tell how many stacks of cards she has?

A $49 + 7 = 56$

B $49 - 7 = 42$

C $49 \div 7 = 7$

D $49 \times 7 = 343$

5 Sandi has 26 pens. For a party, she puts 4 pens in each goodie bag. How many more pens will she need if she wants to fill one more bag than she can fill with 26 pens?

A   4

B   3

C   2

D   1

6 Colton has 59 action figures. He tries to divide them evenly among 8 bags. What is the **greatest** number he can put in each bag? How many will he have left over?

A   7 in each bag with 3 left over

B   7 in each bag with 2 left over

C   6 in each bag with 7 left over

D   6 in each bag with 9 left over

You can use basic facts and patterns to find quotients.

dividend		divisor		quotient
9	÷	3	=	3
90	÷	3	=	30
900	÷	3	=	300

Guided Instruction

Problem

A total of 800 students went to the Hayden Planetarium. The teachers want to put them into groups of 4 students. How many groups of students will there be?

Use basic facts and patterns of zero to solve the problem.

Step 1 Find a basic fact that could help solve this problem.

$$800 ÷ 4 = \square$$

basic fact: 8 ÷ 4 = _____

Step 2 Divide the basic fact.
Then look for a pattern.

As the number of zeros in the dividend increases, does the number of zeros in the quotient increase or decrease?

_____

8 ÷ 4 = 2

80 ÷ 4 = 20

800 ÷ 4 = 200

Solution How many groups of students will there be? _____

Another Example

Divide. 1,000 ÷ 5

Think of a basic fact.
Extend the pattern.
Since the basic fact already has one zero, there will be 1 more zero in the dividend than the quotient.

10 ÷ 5 = 2

100 ÷ 5 = 20

1,000 ÷ 5 = 200

Apply the NYS Learning Standards

Divide.

1.　6 ÷ 3 = _____

60 ÷ 3 = _____

600 ÷ 3 = _____

2.　15 ÷ 5 = _____

150 ÷ 5 = _____

1,500 ÷ 5 = _____

3.　24 ÷ 6 = _____

240 ÷ 6 = _____

2,400 ÷ 6 = _____

Divide. Write the basic division fact and the quotient.

4. 180 ÷ 9

_____

5. 250 ÷ 5

_____

6. 800 ÷ 8

_____

7. 810 ÷ 9

_____

8. 300 ÷ 6

_____

9. 120 ÷ 6

_____

10. 640 ÷ 8

_____

11. 350 ÷ 7

_____

12. 210 ÷ 3

_____

13. 480 ÷ 6

_____

14. 320 ÷ 4

_____

15. 560 ÷ 8

_____

Short-Response Questions

Solve each problem.

16. Kenny burned 1,000 calories while rock climbing. He climbed for 2 hours.

How many calories did Kenny burn each hour? _____

17. There are 250 pages in a book. While on vacation, Vince wants to read the same number of pages each day for 5 days. How many pages will Vince have to read each day? Explain how you found your answer.

_____

_____

_____

NYS Test Practice

DIRECTIONS Read each problem. Circle the letter of the answer you choose.

1 Amber made 7 necklaces. Each necklace has the same number of seed beads. If Amber used a total of 280 seed beads, how many seed beads are on each necklace?

A 28

B 35

C 40

D 70

2 A craft store has 270 beads in stock. The beads come in packages of 3. How many packages of beads does the store have?

A 70

B 80

C 90

D 100

3 The coach is ordering T-shirts for her team. The T-shirts cost $8 each. The coach spends $240 to buy a T-shirt for herself and for each student on the track team. How many students are on the track team?

A 29

B 30

C 31

D 32

4 A music store displays 90 CDs in groups of 10. Which basic fact can help you find how many groups of CDs there are?

A $90 - 10 = 80$

B $9 + 1 = 10$

C $9 \div 1 = 9$

D $10 \div 1 = 10$

 Measuring Up® to the New York State Learning Standards

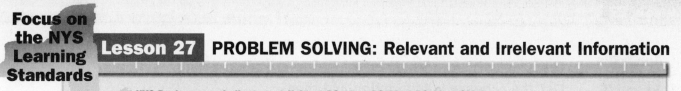

Lesson 27 **PROBLEM SOLVING: Relevant and Irrelevant Information**

NYS Performance Indicators: 4.N.21, 4.PS.17, 4.PS.20, 4.PS.23, 4.CM.2

You can decide which information is relevant or needed to solve a problem and which information is irrelevant or not needed. You can use the problem-solving guide in the back of the book to help you.

Guided Instruction

Problem

> There are 6 rows of desks in class. 3 rows have used desks and 3 rows have new desks. Each row has the same number of desks. There are a total of 78 desks. How many desks are in each row?

Understand the problem.

What do you want to find?

_____

Make a plan.

Figure out what information is needed to solve the problem.
Figure out what information is not needed to solve the problem.

Solve the problem.

What information is needed to answer the question?

_____

_____

What information is not needed to answer the question?

_____

Use division to find how many desks are in each row.

How many desks are in each row? _____ $6\overline{)78}$

Check your answer.

Use multiplication. Multiply the number of desks in each row by the number of rows.
The product is the total number of desks.

$13 \times 6 =$ _____

Apply the NYS Learning Standards

Cross out the unnecessary information in each problem. List the necessary information and then solve each problem.

Work Space

1. Mr. Pine has 60 slices of cake for the picnic. Each person at the picnic will get 2 slices. He cut each cake into 5 slices. How many cakes did Mr. Pine cut into slices?

_____

_____

2. Mia has a board 96 centimeters long. She saws the board into 8 equal pieces. Each piece is 16 centimeters wide. How long is each piece?

_____

_____

3. A baker has 48 pounds of flour. He uses 3 pounds of flour each day. He uses 1 pound each day for muffins and 2 pounds each day for bread. How many days will the supply of flour last?

_____

_____

Short-Response Question

4. Andrew spent 84 minutes on homework last week. He spent 50 minutes on math and 34 minutes on science. He spent the same amount of time on homework each day. Andrew worked on homework 3 days last week. How much time did Andrew spend on homework each day? Explain how you found your answer.

_____

_____

_____

Measuring Up® to the New York State Learning Standards

NYS Test Practice

DIRECTIONS Read each problem.
Circle the letter of the answer you choose.

1 Jenna has 99 marbles in her collection. Exactly 15 marbles are large, and 43 marbles are small. She stores them in 9 bags. Each bag has the same number of marbles. How many marbles are in each bag?

Which information is not needed to solve this problem?

A   Jenna has 15 large marbles.

B   Jenna has 99 marbles in all.

C   Jenna has 9 bags of marbles.

D   Each bag has the same number of marbles.

2 The school store has 75 pencils. The store manager divided the pencils into packs that contain 5 pencils each. One pack of pencils cost $0.40. How many packs of pencils did the manager make?

A   18

B   17

C   16

D   15

3 Carlos works 8-hour shifts. He worked a total of 32 hours last week. He earned $11 per hour. How many shifts did Carlos work last week?

Which information is needed to solve this problem?

A   Carlos works 8-hour shifts. He worked a total of 32 hours last week.

B   Carlos works 8-hour shifts. He earned $11 per hour.

C   Carlos earned $11 per hour. He worked a total of 32 hours last week.

D   Carlos is paid $11 per hour.

4 Sonia is making bows for decorations. She has 28 feet of ribbon. She has 12 feet of red ribbon and 16 feet of blue ribbon. She needs 4 feet of ribbon for each bow. How many blue bows can Sonia make?

A   3

B   4

C   7

D   8

Building Stamina®

DIRECTIONS Read each problem.
Circle the letter of the answer you choose.

1 Dawn has 72 craft sticks. She needs 8 craft sticks to make a frame. How many frames can she make using her craft sticks?

A   7

B   8

C   9

D   10

2 What is the quotient for 1,000 ÷ 5?

A   2

B   20

C   200

D   2,000

3 There are 81 baseball cards arranged in 3 stacks. The same number of cards are in each stack. How many baseball cards are in each of the 3 stacks?

A   36

B   27

C   18

D   9

4 Alex has 63 collector cards. 20 of the cards are in mint condition. He has them all on 9 pages in an album. Each page has the same number of cards. How many cards are in on each page?

Which information is not needed to solve this problem?

A   Alex has 63 collector cards.

B   20 of the cards are in mint condition.

C   He has them all on 9 pages in an album.

D   Each page has the same number of cards.

5 Which of the numbers will have a fact family with **only** 2 facts?

A   3, 4, 12

B   4, 5, 20

C   6, 7, 42

D   7, 7, 49

6 There are 72 books on 9 shelves. The same number of books are on each shelf. Which number sentence would you use to find out how many books are on each shelf?

A $72 \div 9 = 8$

B $72 \times 9 = 648$

C $72 - 9 = 63$

D $72 + 9 = 81$

 7 Farmer Connie saw a total of 18 legs in the barnyard. Some of the animals had 4 legs and some had 2 legs. Which of the following is possible in Farmer Connie's yard?

A 1 four-legged animal and 7 two-legged animals

B 4 four-legged animals and 2 two-legged animals

C 3 four-legged animals and 5 two-legged animals

D 4 four-legged animals and 4 two-legged animals

8 What is the missing number?

$\square \div 8 = 6$

A 2   **C** 48

B 14   **D** 68

9 Donna works at a bike shop. She has 57 tires to put on tricycles. What is the greatest number of tricycles that will get tires?

A 18

B 19

C 20

D 21

10 Pete needs to buy paper plates for 78 people. There are 8 plates in each package. How many packages does he need to buy?

A 9   **C** 11

B 10   **D** 12

11 Which number sentence shows how many there are in each group?

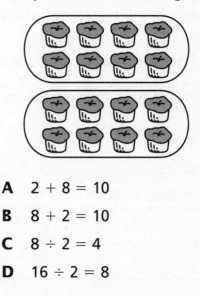

A $2 + 8 = 10$

B $8 + 2 = 10$

C $8 \div 2 = 4$

D $16 \div 2 = 8$

Extended-Response Questions
DIRECTIONS Read each question carefully before writing your response. Be sure to show your work when asked.

12 Mateo has to read a book that is 96 pages long. He wants to read an equal number of pages each day.

Part A

How many pages per day would he need to read if he wants to read the entire book in 2 days? In 3 days?

Show your work.

2 days _____ pages

3 days _____ pages

Part B

If Mateo wants to read 9 pages at most each day, what is the **fewest** number of days it will take him to finish his 96-page book?

Answer _____ days

On the lines below, explain how you found your answer.

_____

_____

_____

_____

13 Jesse went to Sport City to buy tennis balls. They were having a sale: "Buy two cans and get the third can free." Each can had 3 tennis balls in it. When Jesse got home, he counted 18 tennis balls.

Part A

How many of the tennis balls did Jesse get for free?

Show your work.

Answer _____ tennis balls

Part B

How many cans would he have to pay for to get 12 free balls?

Answer _____ cans

On the lines below, explain how you found your answer.

_____

_____

_____

_____

_____

You can describe, extend, and create numerical and geometric patterns.

Guided Instruction

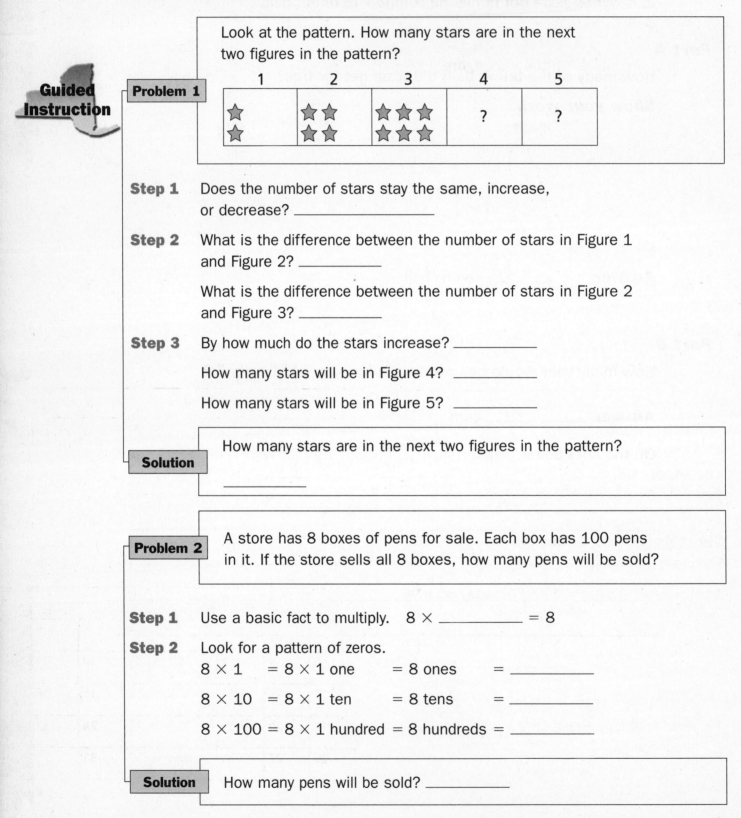

Problem 1

Look at the pattern. How many stars are in the next two figures in the pattern?

1	2	3	4	5
★ ★	★ ★ ★ ★	★ ★ ★ ★ ★ ★	?	?

Step 1 Does the number of stars stay the same, increase, or decrease? _____

Step 2 What is the difference between the number of stars in Figure 1 and Figure 2? _____

What is the difference between the number of stars in Figure 2 and Figure 3? _____

Step 3 By how much do the stars increase? _____

How many stars will be in Figure 4? _____

How many stars will be in Figure 5? _____

Solution

How many stars are in the next two figures in the pattern?

_____

Problem 2

A store has 8 boxes of pens for sale. Each box has 100 pens in it. If the store sells all 8 boxes, how many pens will be sold?

Step 1 Use a basic fact to multiply. $8 \times$ _____ $= 8$

Step 2 Look for a pattern of zeros.

8×1 $= 8 \times 1$ one $= 8$ ones $=$ _____

8×10 $= 8 \times 1$ ten $= 8$ tens $=$ _____

$8 \times 100 = 8 \times 1$ hundred $= 8$ hundreds $=$ _____

Solution How many pens will be sold? _____

Measuring Up® to the New York State Learning Standards

Look for a pattern. Write the next two numbers.

1. 97, 92, 87, 82, _____, _____   2. 50, 60, 70, 80, _____, _____

3. 2, 4, 8, 16, _____, _____   4. 1, 10, 100 _____, _____

Look for a pattern. Draw the next figure.

5.

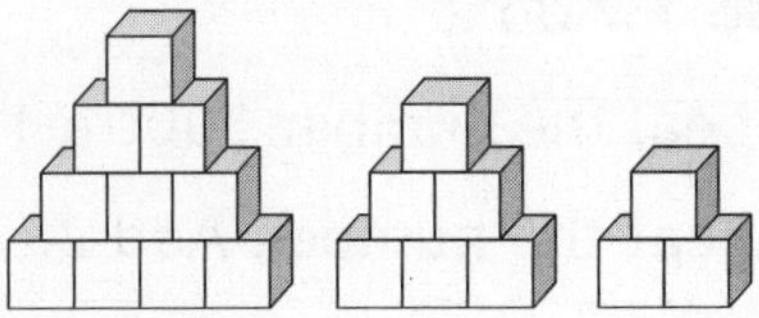

6. □ ◇ △ ▷ □ ◇ △ ▷ □ ◇ △ ▷

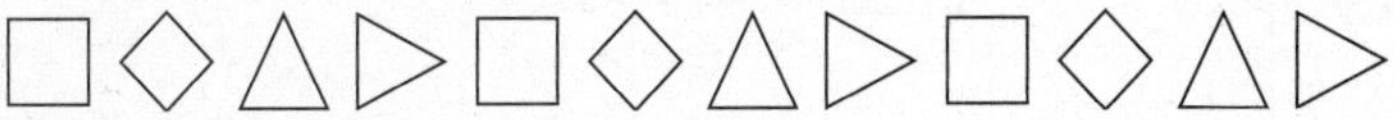

Describe each pattern.

7. ■ ■ ● ▲ ▲ ● ■ ■ ● ▲ ▲ ●

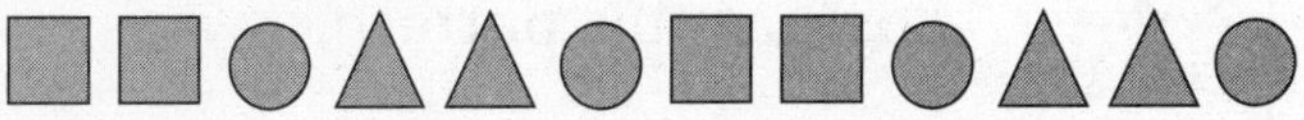

_____

_____

8.

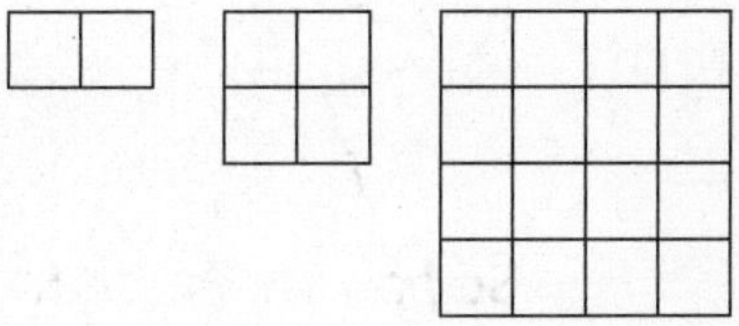

_____

_____

9. 94, 80, 66, 52, 38 _____

10. 1, 4, 16, 64, 256 _____

Short-Response Questions

Solve each problem.

11. Describe a pattern in the Tuesday column.

_____

_____

_____

12. Find another pattern on the calendar. Describe it.

_____

_____

MARCH 2006						
Sunday	Monday	Tuesday	Wednesday	Thursday	Friday	Saturday
			1	2	3	4
5	6	7	8	9	10	11
12	13	14	15	16	17	18
19	20	21	22	23	24	25
26	27	28	29	30	31	

NYS Test Practice

DIRECTIONS Read each problem.
Circle the letter of the answer you choose.

1 Look at the pattern below. Each figure is made with toothpicks.

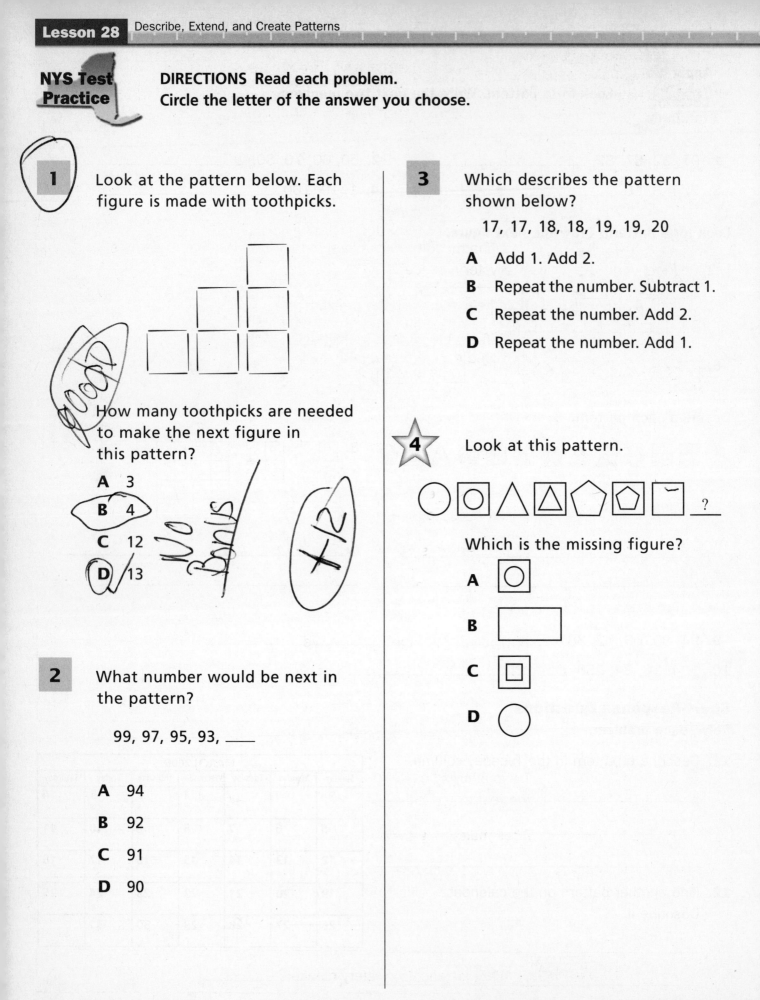

How many toothpicks are needed to make the next figure in this pattern?

A 3

B 4

C 12

D 13

2 What number would be next in the pattern?

99, 97, 95, 93, ____

A 94

B 92

C 91

D 90

3 Which describes the pattern shown below?

17, 17, 18, 18, 19, 19, 20

A Add 1. Add 2.

B Repeat the number. Subtract 1.

C Repeat the number. Add 2.

D Repeat the number. Add 1.

4 Look at this pattern.

Which is the missing figure?

A

B

C

D

Lesson 29 Analyze Patterns and Functions

NYS Performance Indicators: 4.A.5, 4.PS.16, 4.PS.18, 4.CM.5, 4.R.1

You can find the rule for an input/output table by looking for a pattern. The **rule** tells you how the numbers in a pattern change.

Guided Instruction

Problem Jenna made the input/output table below. What is Jenna's mystery number?

Find the rule to help you solve the problem.

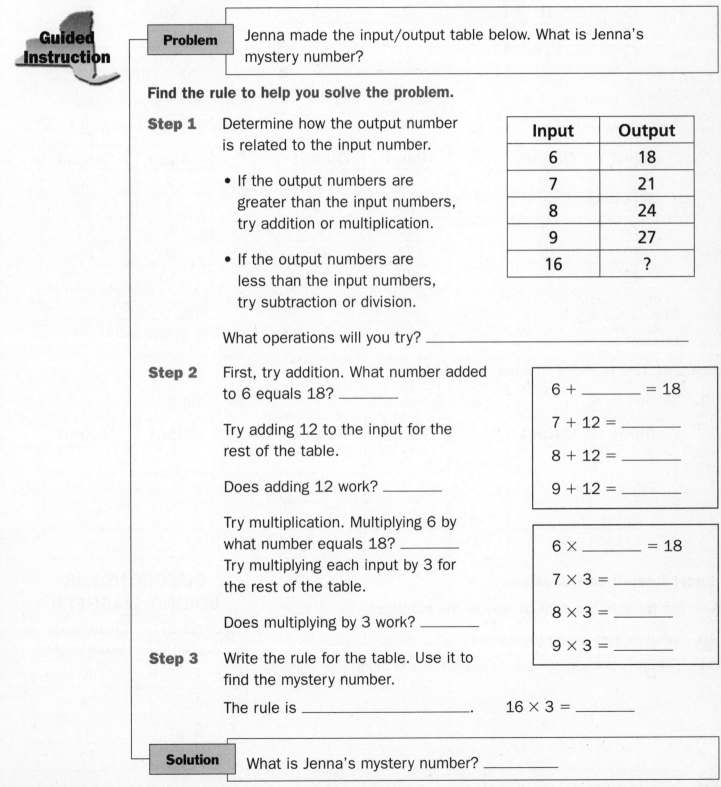

Step 1 Determine how the output number is related to the input number.

- If the output numbers are greater than the input numbers, try addition or multiplication.

- If the output numbers are less than the input numbers, try subtraction or division.

Input	Output
6	18
7	21
8	24
9	27
16	?

What operations will you try? _____

Step 2 First, try addition. What number added to 6 equals 18? _____

Try adding 12 to the input for the rest of the table.

Does adding 12 work? _____

$6 + \underline{\hspace{1cm}} = 18$

$7 + 12 = \underline{\hspace{1cm}}$

$8 + 12 = \underline{\hspace{1cm}}$

$9 + 12 = \underline{\hspace{1cm}}$

Try multiplication. Multiplying 6 by what number equals 18? _____
Try multiplying each input by 3 for the rest of the table.

Does multiplying by 3 work? _____

$6 \times \underline{\hspace{1cm}} = 18$

$7 \times 3 = \underline{\hspace{1cm}}$

$8 \times 3 = \underline{\hspace{1cm}}$

$9 \times 3 = \underline{\hspace{1cm}}$

Step 3 Write the rule for the table. Use it to find the mystery number.

The rule is _____. $16 \times 3 = \underline{\hspace{1cm}}$

Solution What is Jenna's mystery number? _____

Find each rule. Then use the rule to find the missing number.

1.

Input	Output
6	12
10	16
15	21
16	22
18	?

Rule _____

Number _____

2.

Input	Output
2	18
5	45
7	63
10	?
11	99

Rule _____

Number _____

3.

Input	Output
10	5
25	?
40	35
65	60
90	85

Rule _____

Number _____

4.

Input	Output
8	4
12	6
22	11
30	15
42	?

Rule _____

Number _____

5.

Input	Output
15	0
25	10
30	?
33	18
40	25

Rule _____

Number _____

6.

Input	Output
2	20
4	40
6	60
8	80
10	?

Rule _____

Number _____

Use each rule to make an input/output table.

7. Multiply by 5.

Input	Output

8. Subtract 2.

Input	Output

9. Add 3.

Input	Output

Short-Response Questions

Use the table to the right to answer the problems.

10. What is the rule for this table? _____

11. Find the missing number. Explain how you found this number.

_____

_____

_____

DIRECTIONS FOR BOILING SPAGHETTI

Quarts of Water	Ounces of Spaghetti
2	8
4	16
6	?
8	32

 Measuring Up® to the New York State Learning Standards

NYS Test Practice

DIRECTIONS Read each problem.
Circle the letter of the answer you choose.

1 What is the rule for this input/output table?

Input	Output
12	10
14	12
16	14
18	16
22	20

A Add 2.

B Subtract 2.

C Multiply by 2.

D Divide by 2.

2 What is the missing number?

Input	Output
6	12
7	14
8	16
12	?
16	32

A 17

B 18

C 19

D 24

3 Which explains how you find a rule for an input/output table?

A Look at the input values only.

B Look at the output values only.

C Find the relationship between the input values and the output values.

D Find the relationship among all of the input values.

4 Mrs. Graham is baking cookies for a holiday party. It has taken her one hour to complete two dozen cookies.

Time (in hours)	1 h	2 h	3 h	4 h	5 h
Number of Cookies	24	48	72	96	?

How many cookies will Mrs. Graham have after 5 hours of baking?

A 100

B 120

C 144

D 150

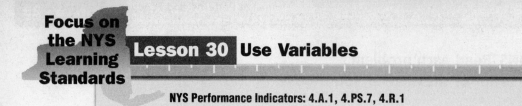
A **variable** is a letter or symbol that stands for an unknown number. You can use a variable in an expression or in an equation. An **expression** can use numbers, variables, and operations. An **equation** is a number sentence with an equal sign.

You can use a variable to stand for a number in an equation. Then you can use models to find the value of the variable.

Guided Instruction

Problem

Mark picked 8 yellow flowers and some red flowers. He picked 12 flowers in all. How many red flowers did Mark pick?

$$8 + r = 12$$

You can use models or counters to show the equation.

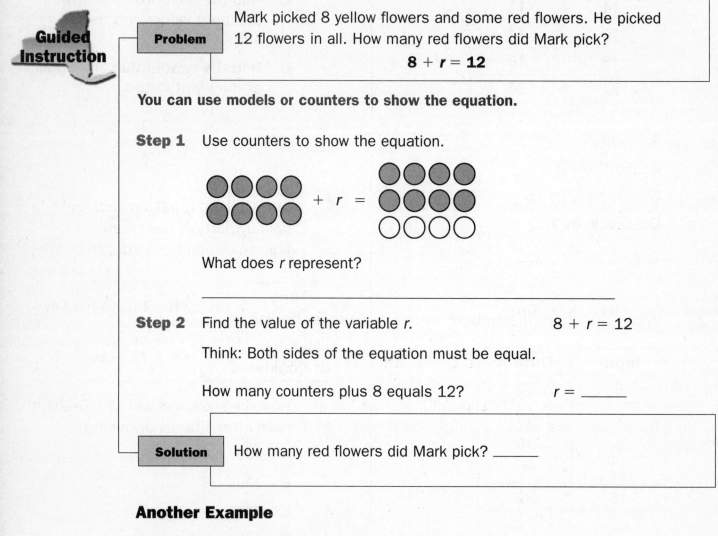

Step 1 Use counters to show the equation.

What does r represent?

_____

Step 2 Find the value of the variable r. $8 + r = 12$

Think: Both sides of the equation must be equal.

How many counters plus 8 equals 12? $r =$ _____

Solution How many red flowers did Mark pick? _____

Another Example

What is the value of the expression $7 + n$, if $n = 2$?

Replace n with _____.

The value of $7 + 2$ is _____.

If $n = 2$, then $7 + n =$ _____.

Apply the NYS Learning Standards

Find the number represented by each variable. Use counters if you want to.

1. $n + 3 = 5$

$n = $ _2_

2. $4 - \square = 3$

$\square = $ _1_

3. $s \times 2 = 8$

$s = $ _4_

4. $5 \times a = 30$

$a = $ _6_

5. $12 \div x = 4$

$x = $ _3_

6. $9 + \square = 12$

$\square = $ _3_

7. $\square + 4 = 10$

$\square = $ _6_

8. $6 \times p = 84$

$p = $ _____

9. $11 - c = 4$

$c = $ _____

Find the value of each expression.

10. $7 + f$, if $f = 3$ _____

11. $15 - s$, if $s = 2$ _____

12. $5 - d$, if $d = 1$ _____

13. $28 \div \triangle$, if $\triangle = 4$ _____

14. $7 \times \triangle$, if $\triangle = 10$ _____

15. $g + 5$, if $g = 20$ _____

Short-Response Questions
Solve each problem.

16. Mark and Josie each have stickers. Mark has 15 more stickers than Josie. Write a number sentence to show that Mark has 15 more stickers than Josie. Let j stand for the number of stickers Josie has. Let m stand for the number of stickers Mark has. Explain how you found your answer.

_____

_____

_____

17. If Josie has 6 stickers, how many stickers does Mark have? Explain how you solved the problem.

_____

_____

_____

NYS Test Practice

DIRECTIONS Read each problem.
Circle the letter of the answer you choose.

1 Which number is represented by f?

$$12 + f = 22$$

- **A** 1
- **B** 10
- **C** 12
- **D** 34

2 Lee and Susan have cards. Lee has 2 **fewer** cards than Susan. Let l stand for the number of cards that Lee has. Let s stand for the number of cards that Susan has. Which number sentence correctly shows their cards?

- **A** $s + 2 = l$
- **B** $s + l = 2$
- **C** $l - 2 = s$
- **D** $s - 2 = l$

3 The letters a and b stand for numbers. If $a - 10 = b - 10$, which statement is true?

- **A** $a = b$
- **B** $a < b$
- **C** $a = b + 10$
- **D** $a > b + 10$

4 Look at the equation below.

$$\triangle = 8 - p$$

If $p = 6$, what is $\triangle$?

- **A** 14
- **B** 10
- **C** 8
- **D** 2

5 Rita and Ian have pens. Rita has 8 more pens than Ian. Let r stand for the number of pens that Rita has. Let i stand for the number of pens that Ian has. Which number sentence correctly shows their pens?

- **A** $r + i = 8$
- **B** $r + 8 = i$
- **C** $i + 8 = r$
- **D** $i - 8 = r$

6 Which number is represented by m?

$$7 \times m = 28$$

- **A** 4
- **B** 3
- **C** 2
- **D** 1

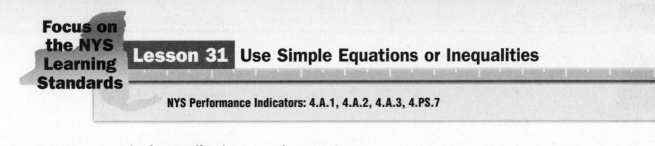
An **inequality** is a number sentence that uses one of these symbols: $<$, $>$, $\neq$.

	Symbol	Words
$17 = 17$	$=$	is equal to
$17 > 13$	$>$	is greater than
$13 < 17$	$<$	is less than
$13 \neq 17$	$\neq$	is not equal to

Guided Instruction

Problem
Marti and Steve both have pet fish. Marti has fewer pet fish than Steve. Steve has 6 fish and Marti has m fish. How many pet fish might Marti have?

Use a number line to help you.

Step 1 How many pet fish does Steve have? _____ Circle that number on the number line.

Step 2 Write an inequality to show how many fish Marti has. Marti has fewer fish than Steve, so $m < 6$.

Step 3 Which numbers on the number line are less than 6?

_____

Draw a box around those numbers on the number line.

number of pet fish less than 6

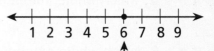

1 2 3 4 5 6 7 8 9

↑ number of pet fish Steve has

Solution How many pet fish might Marti have? _____

Another Example

Solve the equation $7 + y = 16$.
Think: How many counters plus 7 equal 16?
$7 + \mathbf{9} = 16$
$y = 9$

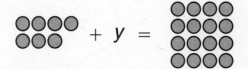

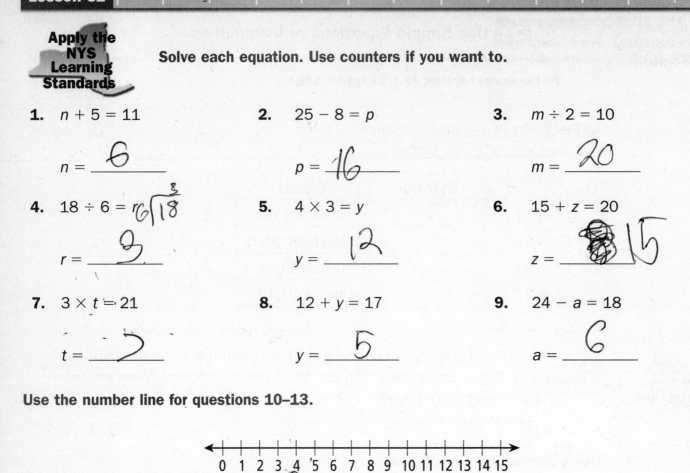

Apply the NYS Learning Standards

Solve each equation. Use counters if you want to.

1. $n + 5 = 11$

$n = $ _6_

2. $25 - 8 = p$

$p = $ _16_

3. $m \div 2 = 10$

$m = $ _20_

4. $18 \div 6 = r$ $6\overline{)18}$

$r = $ _3_

5. $4 \times 3 = y$

$y = $ _12_

6. $15 + z = 20$

$z = $ _15_

7. $3 \times t = 21$

$t = $ _2_

8. $12 + y = 17$

$y = $ _5_

9. $24 - a = 18$

$a = $ _6_

Use the number line for questions 10–13.

0 1 2 3 4 5 6 7 8 9 10 11 12 13 14 15

10. If $n < 2$, which whole number or numbers could n be? _1 and 0_

11. If $x > 8$, which whole numbers from 1 to 10 could x be? _9 and 10_

12. If $y \neq 4$, which whole numbers could y be? _4/2_

13. If $p = 7$, which whole numbers from 1 to 15 could p be? _4_

Short-Response Question

Solve the problem.

14. Sally gave 15 sports cards to 3 friends. She divided the cards equally among them. Let c represent the number of cards Sally gave to each friend. Solve the equation $15 \div c = 3$ to find how many cards each friend received. Explain how you found your answer.

_____

_____

_____

   Measuring Up® to the New York State Learning Standards

NYS Test Practice

DIRECTIONS Read each problem.
Circle the letter of the answer you choose.

1 Donna put the same number of marbles into 7 bags. If the total number of marbles is 35, which equation could you use to find how many marbles, m, are in each bag?

A $35 + 7 = m$

B $35 - m = 7$

C $35 \div m = 7$

D $35 \times 7 = m$

2 If $y > 4$, which whole numbers from 1 to 6 could y be?

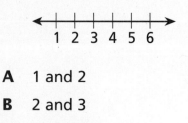

A 1 and 2

B 2 and 3

C 4, 5, and 6

D 5 and 6

3 Which equation or inequality is true?

A $35 \neq 35$

B $56 + 4 > 65$

C $78 + 7 < 87$

D $23 = 15 + 12$

4 Which number belongs in the box to make the number sentence below true?

$$\square > 9 + 7$$

A 12

B 14

C 16

D 18

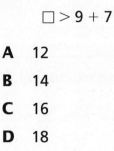

5 Carlos packed 24 CDs into boxes. He divided the CDs equally among the boxes. He packed a total of 4 boxes. Let the variable n represent the number of CDs in 1 box.

$$24 \div n = 4$$

How many CDs did Carlos pack in two boxes?

A 6

B 8

C 12

D 18

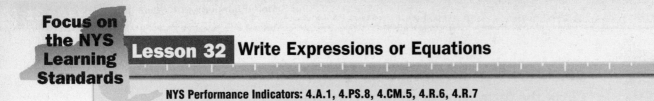
You can write an expression or an equation to describe a word problem.

Guided Instruction

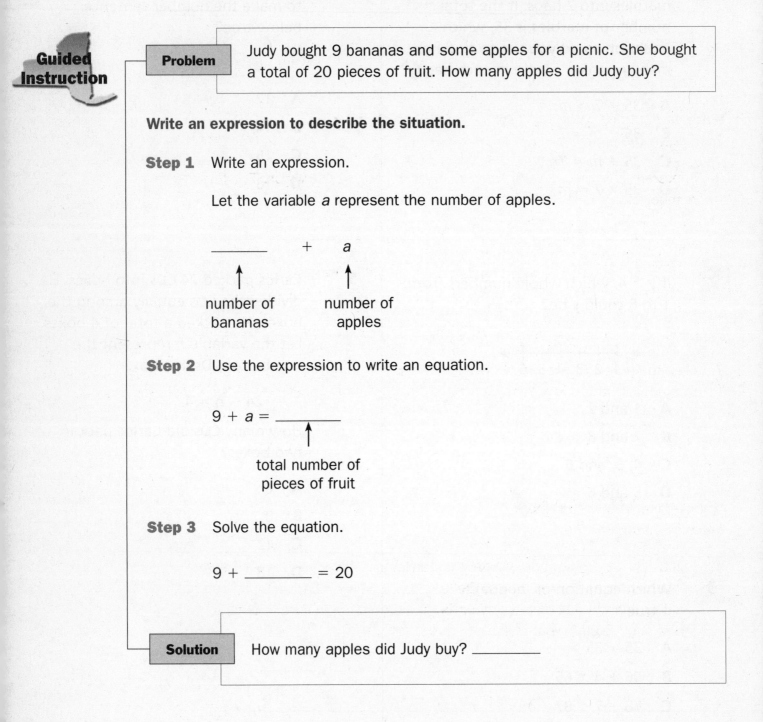

Problem   Judy bought 9 bananas and some apples for a picnic. She bought a total of 20 pieces of fruit. How many apples did Judy buy?

Write an expression to describe the situation.

Step 1   Write an expression.

Let the variable *a* represent the number of apples.

_____   +   *a*

↑   ↑

number of   number of
bananas   apples

Step 2   Use the expression to write an equation.

9 + *a* = _____

↑

total number of
pieces of fruit

Step 3   Solve the equation.

9 + _____ = 20

Solution   How many apples did Judy buy? _____

Apply the NYS Learning Standards

Match each expression to a situation.

1. 5 more dollars than Jim _____

2. 6 fewer crayons than Mia _____

3. 4 times as many books as papers _____

4. cards put into 3 equal groups _____

a. $d - 6$

b. $d + 5$

c. $d \div 3$

d. $4 \times d$

**Write an equation using the variable *n* for each situation.
Then solve the equation.**

5. There are 9 boxes with the same number of books in each box. The total number of books is 45. How many books are in each box?

   _____

6. Marcos drew 8 pictures in art class. He gave some pictures to his teacher. He has 6 pictures left. How many pictures did he give to his teacher?

   _____

7. George burned 4 CDs. Each CD holds the same number of minutes of music. He burned 280 minutes of music on the CDs. How many minutes of music does each CD hold?

   _____

Short-Response Question

Solve the problem.

8. Elena and her friend rode different distances in the bike-a-thon. The sum of the distances was 32 miles. Elena rode 17 miles. What equation can be used to find the distance that Elena's friend rode? How far did Elena's friend ride? Explain your answer.

   _____

   _____

   _____

NYS Test Practice

DIRECTIONS Read each problem.
Circle the letter of the answer you choose.

1 Danny has twice as many cards as Richard has. Danny has 100 cards. Let *c* represent the number of Richard's cards. Which equation can be used to find the number of cards that Richard has?

A $c + 2 = 100$

B $c = 100 \times 2$

(C) $2 \times c = 100$

D $c \div 2 = 100$

2 Brad is 2 inches shorter than Alex. Brad is 5 feet tall. Let *h* represent Alex's height. Which of the following could you use to find Alex's height in inches?

A $h - 2 = 5$

B $h - 2 = 60$

(C) $h \times 2 = 5$

D $h \div 2 = 60$

3 LaToya bought 3 of the same books at a total cost of $39. Let *n* represent the cost of 1 book. Which of the following represents the cost of 1 book?

A $n = 39 - 3$

B $n = 39 + 3$

(C) $n = 39 \times 3$

D $n = 39 \div 3$

4 Della scored 6 more points than Sue this basketball season. Sue scored 48 points. Let *p* represent Della's points. Which represents how many points Della scored this season?

(A) $p = 48 + 6$

B $p = 48 \times 6$

C $p = 48 \div 6$

D $p = 48 - 6$

5 There were about 10 times as many sunny days as there were rainy days last year. Let *r* represent the number of rainy days. Which expression represents the number of sunny days?

A $r + 10$

B $r - 10$

(C) $10 \times r$

D $10 \div r$

6 Elaine has half as many books as Linda has. Let *b* represent the number of books that Elaine has. Which expression represents the number of books that Linda has?

A $b + 2$

B $b - 2$

C $2 \times b$

(D) $b \div 2$

Lesson 33 **PROBLEM SOLVING: Make a Table**

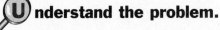

NYS Performance Indicators: 4.A.5, 4.PS.3, 4.PS.15, 4.PS.16, 4.PS.18, 4.R.1, 4.R.7

Tables can help you organize information to make a problem easier to read. You can use the problem-solving guide in the back of the book to help you.

Guided Instruction

Problem

Ben made a machine that changes numbers. When he puts 2 in, 6 comes out. When he puts 5 in, 9 comes out. When he puts 7 in, 11 comes out. When he puts 10 in, 14 comes out. What number comes out when Ben puts 16 into his machine?

Understand the problem.

When 2 goes into the machine, _____ comes out.

When 5 goes into the machine, _____ comes out.

When 7 goes into the machine, _____ comes out.

When 10 goes into the machine, _____ comes out.

Input	Output
x	*y*
2	6
5	9
7	11
10	14
16	?

Make a plan.

Make a table to organize the information.

Solve the problem.

Use the table to find a rule.

Each output number is _____ more than the input number.

So the rule is add _____.

Write an equation to show the rule.

$$x + 4 = y$$

input   output

Use the equation to find the output number for 16.

16 + 4 = _____

So _____ comes out of the machine when Ben puts 16 in.

Check your answer.

Start with the output number.

Subtract 4. You will get the input number.

20 − 4 = 16

Apply the NYS Learning Standards

Make a table to solve each problem.

1. When Stacey puts 1 into her number machine, 10 comes out. When she puts 2 in, 11 comes out. When she puts 3 in, 12 comes out. When she puts 4 in, 13 comes out. What equation shows the rule for Stacey's machine?

   _____

Input	Output
x	y

2. When Andrew puts 8 into his number machine, 5 comes out. When he puts 12 in, 9 comes out. When he puts 16 in, 13 comes out. When he puts 21 in, 18 comes out. What number comes out when Andrew puts 30 into his machine?

   _____

Input	Output
a	b

3. If it takes 2 quarts of water to boil 8 ounces of spaghetti, 4 quarts of water to boil 16 ounces of spaghetti, and 6 quarts of water to boil 24 ounces of spaghetti, how many quarts of water are needed to boil 32 ounces of spaghetti?

   _____

Quarts of Water	Ounces of Spaghetti

Short-Response Question

Solve the problem.

4. It took Ken 2 minutes to read 1 page of his book, 6 minutes to read 3 pages, 14 minutes to read 7 pages, and 24 minutes to read 12 pages. How many pages of his book did Ken read in 30 minutes? What is the rule?

   _____

Time (in minutes)	Number of Pages

 Measuring Up® to the New York State Learning Standards

DIRECTIONS Read each problem.
Circle the letter of the answer you choose.

1 Which equation shows the rule for this table?

Input	Output
x	y
3	13
6	16
19	29
24	34
38	48

A $x + 10 = y$

B $x - y = 10$

C $x + y = 10$

D $x - 10 = y$

100%

2 What is the missing number in this table?

Input	Output
2	6
3	9
4	12
5	?
10	30

A 13

B 14

C 15

D 20

3 Julio is playing a video game. Each day, his score goes up by 15 points. Which table could show his scores?

A

Day	1	2	3	4
Score	0	5	10	15

B

Day	1	2	3	4
Score	45	55	65	75

C

Day	1	2	3	4
Score	100	115	130	145

D

Day	1	2	3	4
Score	15	15	15	15

4 Sara used this rule for her number machine.

$$2 \times x + 4 = y$$

If she puts 5 into the machine, what number will come out?

A 10   **C** 16

B 14   **D** 20

Building Stamina®

DIRECTIONS Read each problem.
Circle the letter of the answer you choose.

1 What is the relationship between the variables in the table below?

r	1	2	3	4
s	3	4	5	6

A r and s increase by different amounts.

B When r increases, s decreases.

C When s increases, r decreases.

D When r increases, s increases.

2 What is the rule for the table?

x	2	3	4	5
y	4	6	8	10

A $x + 2 = y$

B $x \times 2 = y$

C $x - 2 = y$

D $x \div 2 = y$

3 Which number does not make this a true number sentence?

$$257 + n > 398$$

A 200

B 145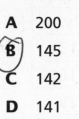

C 142

D 141

4 If this pattern continues, which numbers would complete the table?

Input	Output
0	8
1	11
2	14
3	17
4	?
5	?
6	?

A 18, 19, 20

B 20, 22, 24

C 20, 23, 26

D 20, 23, 26

5 Which describes the pattern below?

♡○○□ ♡○○□ ♡○○□

A   heart, circle, square

(B) heart, 2 circles, square

C   heart, 2 circles, square, circle

D   2 hearts, 2 circles, square

6 Tony has 80 books. He puts the same number of books on each shelf. He uses 8 shelves. Which equation shows how you can find how many books are on each shelf?

A $80 - 8 = \square$

B $80 + \square = 8$

(C) $80 \div 8 = \square$

D $80 \times \square = 8$

7 Which number makes this number sentence true?

$569 + \square < 1{,}403$

A   823

B   834

C   856

D   946

8 Look at the numbers below. Which rule describes the pattern?

89, 85, 81, 77, 73

A   Add 3.

B   Subtract 3.

C   Add 4.

D   Subtract 4.

9 Which number is missing in the pattern?

1, 3, 6, 10, ?, 21

A   14

B   15

C   20

D   40

10 If $33 \times 5 = 165$, then $33 \times 50 = \triangle$. What does $\triangle$ represent?

A   165

B   1,650

C   16,500

D   160,500

Extended-Response Questions
DIRECTIONS Read each question carefully before writing your response. Be sure to show your work when asked.

⭐**11** Candy is making a pattern using tiles. Here are the first four designs in her pattern. She will continue using the same pattern.

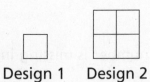

Design 1   Design 2   Design 3   Design 4   Design 5

Part A

Draw Design 5 in the pattern above.

How many tiles are in Design 5?

Show your work.

Answer _____

Part B

On the lines below, explain how you found your answer.

_____

_____

_____

_____

_____

12 Tamara can walk a mile in 15 minutes.

Time (*t*)	15				
Miles (*m*)	1	2			

Steven can run a mile in 12 minutes.

Time (*t*)	12	24			
Miles (*m*)	1				

Part A

Complete the tables. Write an equation using variables that will show how long it will take Tamara to walk 4 miles. Then solve.

Answer _____

Write an equation using variables that will show how many miles Steven will run in 48 minutes. Then solve.

Answer _____

Show your work.

Part B

Tamara will walk and Steven will run from the same spot. They are going to a store that is 5 miles away. How much earlier does Tamara have to leave in order to arrive at the same time as Steven?

Answer _____

On the lines below, explain how you found your answer.

_____

_____

_____

_____

_____

Part 1 Building Stamina®

DIRECTIONS Read each problem.
Circle the letter of the answer you choose.

1 Which expression is **reasonable** to use to check your answer for 493 − 218?

A 400 − 100
B 400 − 200
C 500 − 200
D 500 − 500

2 Jonathan earns $95 each day. How much will he earn in 18 days?

A $855
B $1,610
C $1,710
D $1,720

3 The picture below shows how many stickers are on each page of Rodney's sticker book.

Rodney has 180 stickers in his book. How many pages are filled?

A 10   C 20
B 15   D 25

4 Five students saved their money and put it in their bank savings account. The amounts they saved are shown below.

MONEY SAVED

Name	Amount Saved
Jared	$1,956
Mia	$1,793
Jen	$1,865
Alex	$1,892
Dan	$1,990

Who saved the **most** money?

A Dan
B Jared
C Jen
D Mia

5 The sum of two numbers is about 500. One number is 325. Which of the following could be the other number?

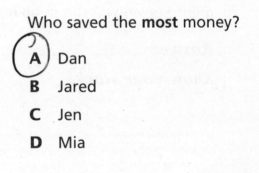

A 305
B 270
C 255
D 170

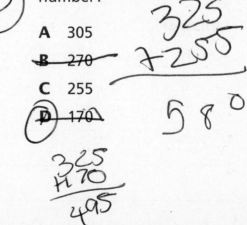

Copying is illegal.   Measuring Up® to the New York State Learning Standards

6 Which form is not equivalent to any of the others?

   A $100 + 300 + 50 + 6$

   B $900 + 400 + 50 + 6$

   C 1 thousand 3 hundreds 56 ones

   D $1,360 - 4$

C / D

7 Maria has a total of 60 cards. She has three times as many baseball cards as basketball cards. How many basketball cards does she have?

   A 5

   B 15

   C 25

   D 45

8 A room has 28 rows of chairs with 14 chairs in each row. Which number sentence will help to find how many chairs there are in all?

   A $28 \div 14 = 2$

   B $28 + 14 = 42$

   C $28 - 14 = 14$

   D $28 \times 14 = 392$

9 Which fact is related to this fact?

     $6 \times 4 = 24$

   A $24 \div 2 = 12$

   B $24 \div 4 = 6$

   C $36 \div 6 = 6$

   D $42 \div 7 = 6$

10 Which of these is an array that models 3×5?

   A

   B

   C

   D

11 Tito is making fundraising calls for his school. He makes a total of 45 calls. He makes the same number of calls each day, for 5 days. Which equation can you use to find out how many calls Tito makes each day?

   A $25 \div 5 = 5$

   B $35 \div 5 = 7$

   C $50 \div 5 = 10$

   D $45 \div 5 = 9$

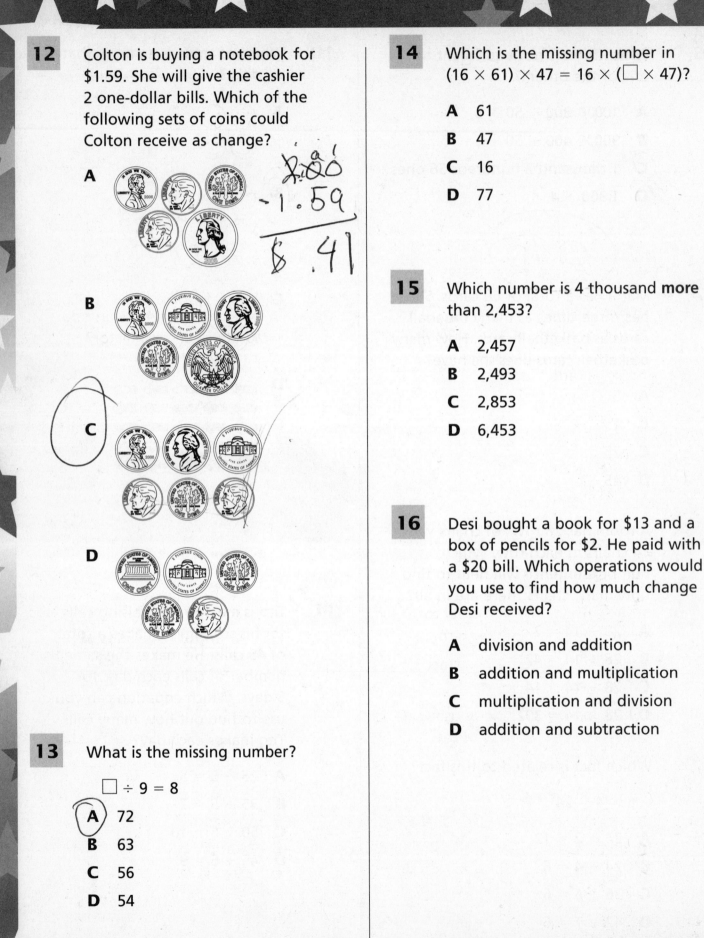

12 Colton is buying a notebook for $1.59. She will give the cashier 2 one-dollar bills. Which of the following sets of coins could Colton receive as change?

A

B

C

D

13 What is the missing number?

$\square \div 9 = 8$

A 72

B 63

C 56

D 54

14 Which is the missing number in $(16 \times 61) \times 47 = 16 \times (\square \times 47)$?

A 61

B 47

C 16

D 77

15 Which number is 4 thousand **more** than 2,453?

A 2,457

B 2,493

C 2,853

D 6,453

16 Desi bought a book for $13 and a box of pencils for $2. He paid with a $20 bill. Which operations would you use to find how much change Desi received?

A division and addition

B addition and multiplication

C multiplication and division

D addition and subtraction

Copying is illegal.

17 Which is not equal to 60 hundreds?

A   6,000 tens

B   6,000 ones

C   6 thousands

D   600 tens

18 All the students in the fourth grade line up in rows of 8. There are no students left over. Which could be the number of fourth-grade students?

A   70

B   85

C   88

D   90

19 Joslyn wrote the rule below to describe her number pattern.

subtract 3, subtract 1, subtract 3, subtract 1

Which pattern was made using Joslyn's rule starting with the number 35?

A   35, 32, 29, 28, 27

B   35, 32, 31, 30, 27

C   35, 34, 31, 30, 27

D   35, 32, 31, 28, 27

20 Which number belongs in the box to make the number sentence below true?

$\square < 50 - 18$

A   68

B   42

C   32

D   30

21 What is the product of an odd factor times an odd factor?

A   always even

B   always odd

C   even or odd

D   never odd

22 What is the rule for this input/output table?

Input	Output
2	10
4	20
6	30
8	40
12	60

A   Add 8.

B   Divide by 5.

C   Multiply by 5.

D   Add 12.

Short-Response Questions
DIRECTIONS Read each question carefully before writing your response. Be sure to show your work when asked.

23 Robin has twice as many books as Julio. Let *b* represent the number of books Julio has.

Part A

Write an expression to represent the number of books Robin has.

_____

Part B

If Julio has 8 books, how many books does Robin have?

Show your work.

_____ books

24 Matt had 127 trading cards. He divided them equally among 10 friends and gave those left over to his younger brother Mark. How many cards did Mark get?

_____ cards

25 What is the missing number in the table?

Input	Output
21	7
30	10
45	15
60	20
75	?

_____

   Measuring Up® to the New York State Learning Standards

26 What is the difference between the greatest four-digit number you can make with the digits 1, 2, 3, and 4 and the least four-digit number you can make with those same digits? (Each number can only use a digit once.)

Show your work.

_____

27 Draw the next two figures in the pattern below.

28 Brittany has a collection of rocks. She puts them in 23 rows. 14 of the rocks are mica. She has 8 rocks in each row. How many rocks does Brittany have in all?

Part A

Cross out any information that is not needed.

Part B

How many rocks does Brittany have in all?

Show your work.

Answer _____ rocks

Extended-Response Questions
DIRECTIONS Read each question carefully before writing your response. Be sure to show your work when asked.

29 The after-school club was taking a field trip to a museum. There are 38 children in the club. Each van holds 5 children.

Part A

How many vans will they need to use to bring all the children to the museum?

Show your work.

Answer _____

Part B

On the lines below, explain how you found your answer.

_____

_____

_____

_____

_____

30   Mr. Santo has a store. His store sold 6,384 CDs last month.
Mrs. Ferrara sold 7,238 CDs in her store last month.

Part A

How many **more** CDs did Mrs. Ferrara sell than Mr. Santo?

Show your work.

Answer _____ CDs

Part B

Ms. Books also has a store and sells CDs. The number of CDs her
store sold last week has 1 more thousand than Mr. Santos, 3 more
hundreds than Mrs. Ferrara, 1 less ten than Mr. Santo, and 3 less ones
than Mrs. Ferrara. How many CDs did Ms. Books' store sell?

thousands	hundreds	tens	ones

Answer _____ CDs

On the lines below, explain how you found your answer.

_____

_____

_____

_____

_____

Chapter 6 Fractions

In Chapter 6, you will study and practice:

- understanding fractions;
- modeling equivalent fractions;
- comparing and ordering fractions;
- adding fractions;
- subtracting fractions;
- using a picture to solve problems.

★ **Building Stamina**® This section gives you a chance to sharpen your skills in fractions while strengthening your test-taking skills.

Chapter 7 Decimals

In Chapter 7, you will study and practice:

- understanding decimal place value;
- relating fractions and decimals;
- comparing and ordering fractions;
- using models to add fractions;
- using models to subtract fractions;
- making a picture to solve problems.

★ **Building Stamina**® This section gives you a chance to sharpen your skills in decimals while strengthening your test-taking skills.

Chapter 8 Geometry

In Chapter 8, you will study and practice:

- understanding points, lines, and planes;
- analyzing and describing polygons;
- analyzing three-dimensional shapes;
- using nets to solve problems.

★ **Building Stamina**® This section gives you a chance to sharpen your skills in geometry while strengthening your test-taking skills.

Chapter 9 Measurement

In Chapter 9, you will study and practice:

- measuring length using customary and metric units;
- estimating and measuring mass;
- estimating and measuring capacity;
- finding elapsed time;
- finding perimeter;
- finding area;
- determining if an exact or estimated solution is needed to solve problems.

★ **Building Stamina**® This section gives you a chance to sharpen your skills in measurement while strengthening your test-taking skills.

Chapter 10 Data Analysis

In Chapter 10, you will study and practice:

- collecting, organizing, and displaying and data;
- making and interpreting bar graphs;
- interpreting line graphs;
- recording data from experiments;
- using a graph to solve problems.

★ **Building Stamina**® This section gives you a chance to sharpen your skills in data analysis while strengthening your test-taking skills.

A **fraction** is a number that names part of a whole or part of a group.

The first model shows a whole with 6 equal parts.
The second model shows a group with 6 equal parts.
The fraction $\frac{2}{6}$ names the shaded part of each model.

The **numerator** tells the number of equal parts shaded.
The **denominator** tells the total number of equal parts.

The arrow points to the location of the fraction $\frac{2}{6}$ on the number line.

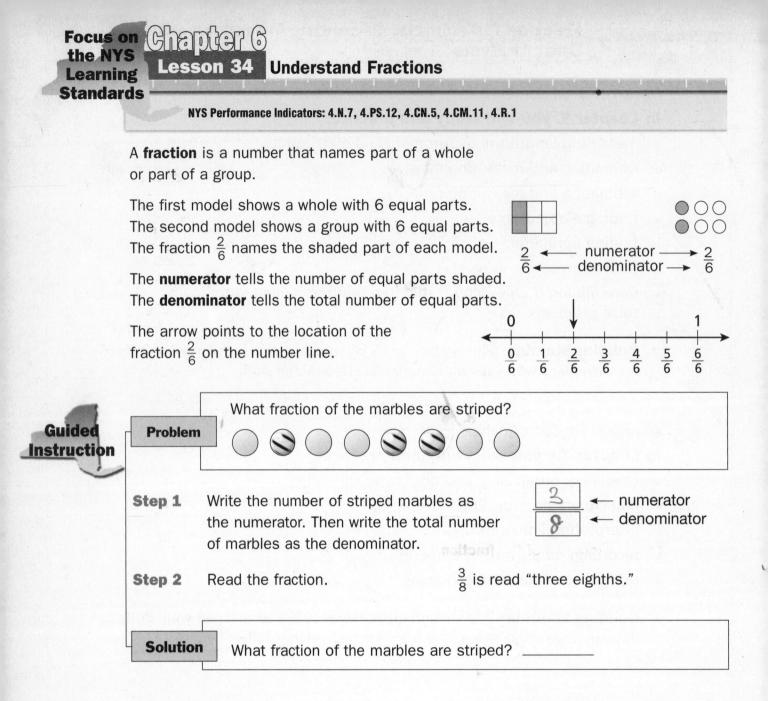

$\frac{2}{6}$ ← numerator → $\frac{2}{6}$
← denominator →

Guided Instruction

Problem What fraction of the marbles are striped?

Step 1 Write the number of striped marbles as the numerator. Then write the total number of marbles as the denominator.

$\frac{3}{8}$ ← numerator
← denominator

Step 2 Read the fraction. $\frac{3}{8}$ is read "three eighths."

Solution What fraction of the marbles are striped? _____

Another Example

You can use models to find $\frac{1}{2}$ of 10.

The denominator, 2, tells you to separate the 10 counters into 2 equal groups.

2 groups

The numerator, 1, tells you to count the number in 1 group.

$\frac{1}{2}$ of 10 is 5.

Apply the NYS Learning Standards

Write a fraction for the shaded part. Then write a fraction for the part that is not shaded.

1.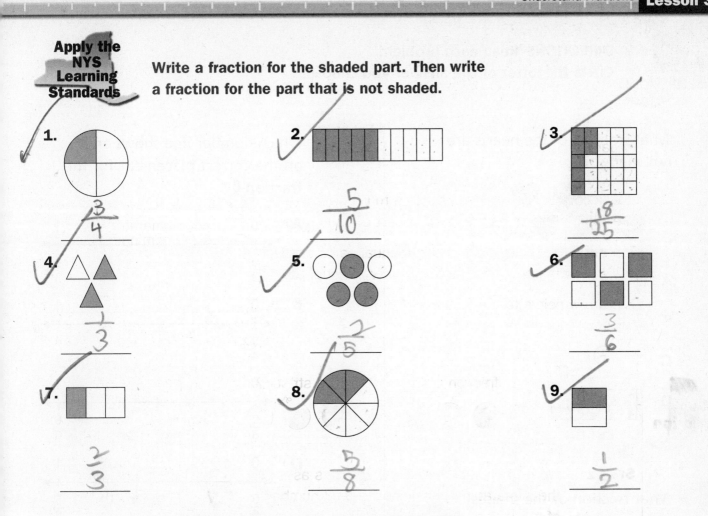

$\dfrac{3}{4}$

2.

$\dfrac{5}{10}$

3.

$\dfrac{18}{25}$

4.

$\dfrac{1}{3}$

5.

$\dfrac{2}{5}$

6.

$\dfrac{3}{6}$

7.

$\dfrac{2}{3}$

8.

$\dfrac{5}{8}$

9.

$\dfrac{1}{2}$

Mark an *X* for the location of the fraction on the number line.

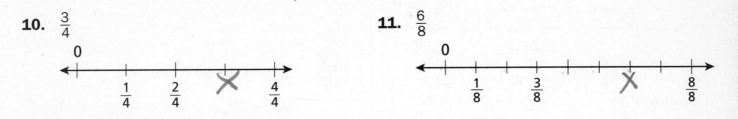

10. $\dfrac{3}{4}$

0

$\dfrac{1}{4}$ $\dfrac{2}{4}$ X $\dfrac{4}{4}$

11. $\dfrac{6}{8}$

0

$\dfrac{1}{8}$ $\dfrac{3}{8}$ X $\dfrac{8}{8}$

Short-Response Question

Solve the problem. You may use 2-color counters to help you if you want to.

12. Carmine has 20 cars on his car lot. 9 of the cars are used. The rest of the cars are new. What fraction of the cars are new? Explain how you found your answer.

$\dfrac{11}{20}$

$\dfrac{11}{20}$

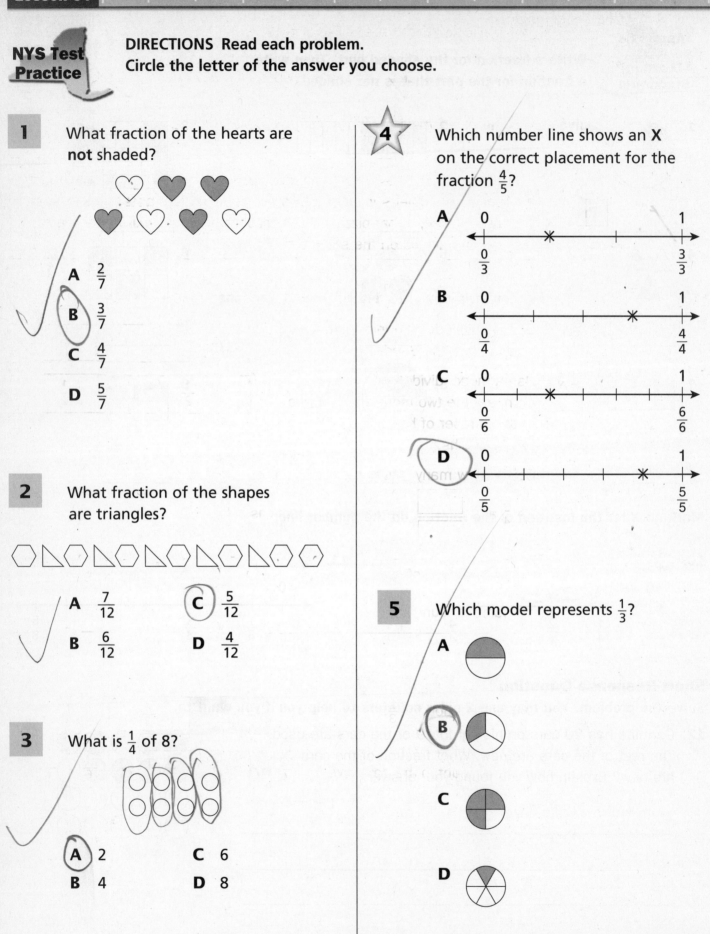

NYS Test Practice

DIRECTIONS Read each problem.
Circle the letter of the answer you choose.

1 What fraction of the hearts are **not** shaded?

A $\frac{2}{7}$

B $\frac{3}{7}$

C $\frac{4}{7}$

D $\frac{5}{7}$

2 What fraction of the shapes are triangles?

A $\frac{7}{12}$ C $\frac{5}{12}$

B $\frac{6}{12}$ D $\frac{4}{12}$

3 What is $\frac{1}{4}$ of 8?

A 2 C 6

B 4 D 8

4 Which number line shows an **X** on the correct placement for the fraction $\frac{4}{5}$?

A 0 .... 1 $\frac{0}{3}$ ... $\frac{3}{3}$

B 0 .... 1 $\frac{0}{4}$ ... $\frac{4}{4}$

C 0 .... 1 $\frac{0}{6}$ ... $\frac{6}{6}$

D 0 .... 1 $\frac{0}{5}$ ... $\frac{5}{5}$

5 Which model represents $\frac{1}{3}$?

A

B

C

D

Copying is illegal. Measuring Up® to the New York State Learning Standards

Equivalent fractions are fractions that name the same amount.

Guided Instruction

Problem

Kim and Tyler have the same size pizzas. Kim's is cut into four equal slices and Tyler's is cut into two equal slices. Kim eats two slices, or two fourths, of her pizza. What fraction of his pizza will Tyler have to eat to have eaten the same amount as Kim?

Use the fraction strip model to find equivalent fractions.

Step 1 Use a model divided into fourths. Start at the left. Shade $\frac{2}{4}$.

| $\frac{1}{4}$ | $\frac{1}{4}$ | $\frac{1}{4}$ | $\frac{1}{4}$ |

Step 2 Use a model divided into halves. Compare the two models and shade in the number of halves equal to two-fourths.

| $\frac{1}{2}$ | $\frac{1}{2}$ |

Step 3 Count. How many halves did you shade? _____

So $\frac{2}{4}$ and $\boxed{}$ are equivalent fractions.

Solution

What fraction of his pizza will Tyler have to eat to have eaten the same amount as Kim? _____

Another Example

Find an equivalent fraction for $\frac{1}{3}$.

Shade $\frac{1}{3}$.

Shade the same amount in the next row.

$\frac{1}{3} = \frac{2}{6}$

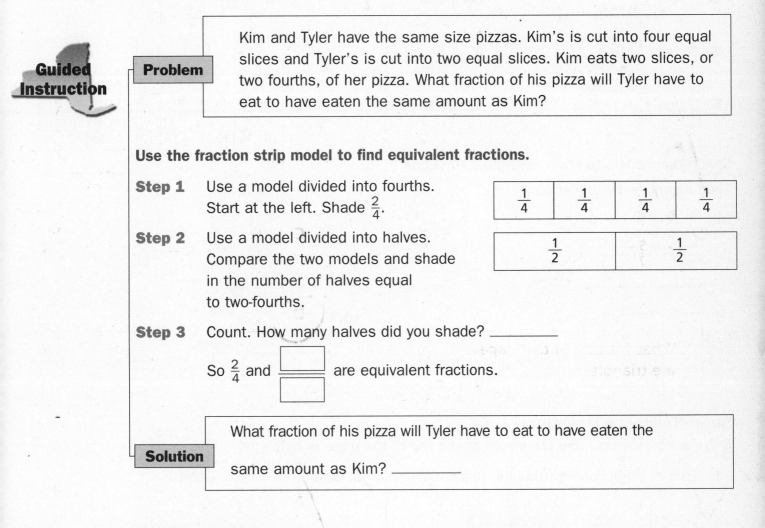

Apply the NYS Learning Standards

Use the fraction strip model to tell whether each pair of fractions is equivalent. Write *yes* or *no*.

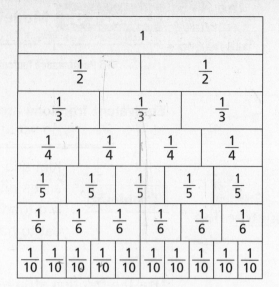

1. $\frac{2}{3}$ and $\frac{4}{6}$ _yes_

2. $\frac{3}{4}$ and $\frac{1}{2}$ _no_

3. $\frac{10}{10}$ and $\frac{6}{6}$ _yes_

4. $\frac{1}{4}$ and $\frac{5}{6}$ _no_

5. $\frac{2}{4}$ and $\frac{6}{10}$ _no_

6. $\frac{4}{10}$ and $\frac{2}{5}$ _yes_

Shade the models to show equivalent fractions. Then complete the equation.

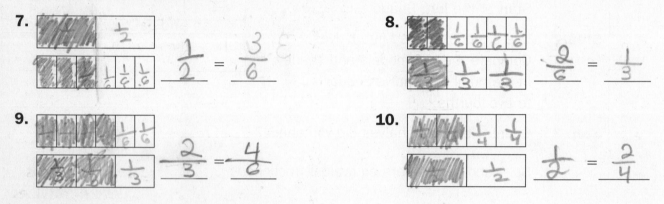

7. $\frac{1}{2} = \frac{3}{6}$

8. $\frac{2}{6} = \frac{1}{3}$

9. $\frac{2}{3} = \frac{4}{6}$

10. $\frac{2}{2} = \frac{2}{4}$

Short-Response Questions

Solve each problem. Use the model at the top of the page to help you.

11. Look at the following fractions. Circle each one that is equivalent to one-half.

$\frac{3}{4}$ $\frac{2}{4}$ $\frac{5}{10}$ $\frac{2}{3}$ $\frac{2}{6}$ $\frac{3}{6}$

12. If you did not have a model, could you still tell which fraction was equivalent to one-half? Explain.

numarter is half of the denomapitor

13. How many twelfths are equal to $\frac{1}{2}$? $\frac{6}{12}$

How do you know? _____

Copying is illegal.   Measuring Up® to the New York State Learning Standards

NYS Test Practice

DIRECTIONS Read each problem.
Circle the letter of the answer you choose.

1 Which fraction is equivalent to $\frac{1}{2}$?
Use the model to help you answer
the problem.

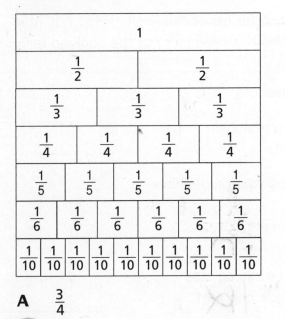

A	$\frac{3}{4}$
B	$\frac{3}{6}$
C	$\frac{4}{10}$
D	$\frac{8}{10}$

2 Which fraction is equivalent to $\frac{2}{6}$?

A $\frac{1}{3}$

B $\frac{2}{3}$

C $\frac{4}{5}$

D $\frac{7}{10}$

3 Bryan has mowed two sixths of his
lawn. Sally has mowed one third
of her same-sized lawn. Which
statement is true?

A   Bryan has mowed less
than Sally.

B   Bryan has mowed more
than Sally.

C   Sally has mowed less
than Bryan.

D   Bryan and Sally have mowed
the same amount.

4 Sandy is following a recipe. It says
to use $\frac{2}{3}$ of a cup of sugar. She does
not have a $\frac{1}{3}$ measuring cup. Which
measuring cup would help her the
most to use the correct amount
of sugar?

A $\frac{1}{2}$ C $\frac{1}{6}$

B $\frac{1}{4}$ D $\frac{1}{10}$

5 Which fraction is equivalent to $\frac{5}{5}$?

A $\frac{8}{8}$ C $\frac{5}{10}$

B $\frac{1}{2}$ D $\frac{5}{12}$

Lesson 36   Compare and Order Fractions

NYS Performance Indicators: 4.N.9, 4.A.2, 4.PS.4, 4.RP.5, 4.CM.7, 4.CM.11

Models can help you to compare and order fractions.

Guided Instruction

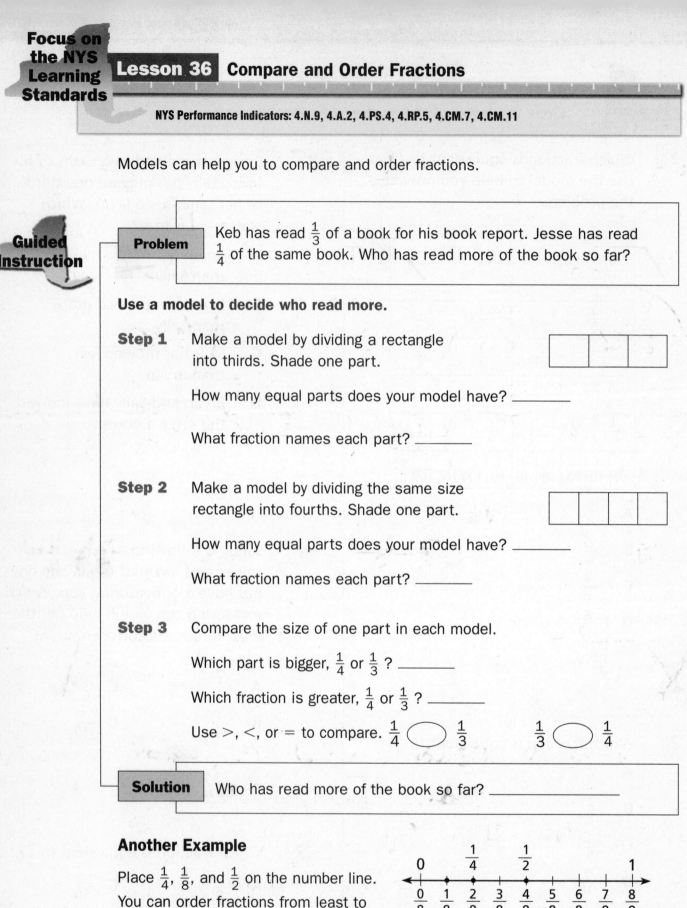

Problem   Keb has read $\frac{1}{3}$ of a book for his book report. Jesse has read $\frac{1}{4}$ of the same book. Who has read more of the book so far?

Use a model to decide who read more.

Step 1   Make a model by dividing a rectangle into thirds. Shade one part.

How many equal parts does your model have? _____

What fraction names each part? _____

Step 2   Make a model by dividing the same size rectangle into fourths. Shade one part.

How many equal parts does your model have? _____

What fraction names each part? _____

Step 3   Compare the size of one part in each model.

Which part is bigger, $\frac{1}{4}$ or $\frac{1}{3}$? _____

Which fraction is greater, $\frac{1}{4}$ or $\frac{1}{3}$? _____

Use >, <, or = to compare. $\frac{1}{4}$ ◯ $\frac{1}{3}$ $\frac{1}{3}$ ◯ $\frac{1}{4}$

Solution   Who has read more of the book so far? _____

Another Example

Place $\frac{1}{4}$, $\frac{1}{8}$, and $\frac{1}{2}$ on the number line.
You can order fractions from least to greatest by reading the fractions from left to right: $\frac{1}{8}$, $\frac{1}{4}$, $\frac{1}{2}$.

Apply the NYS Learning Standards

Use the models to compare the fractions.
Write >, <, ≠ or =.

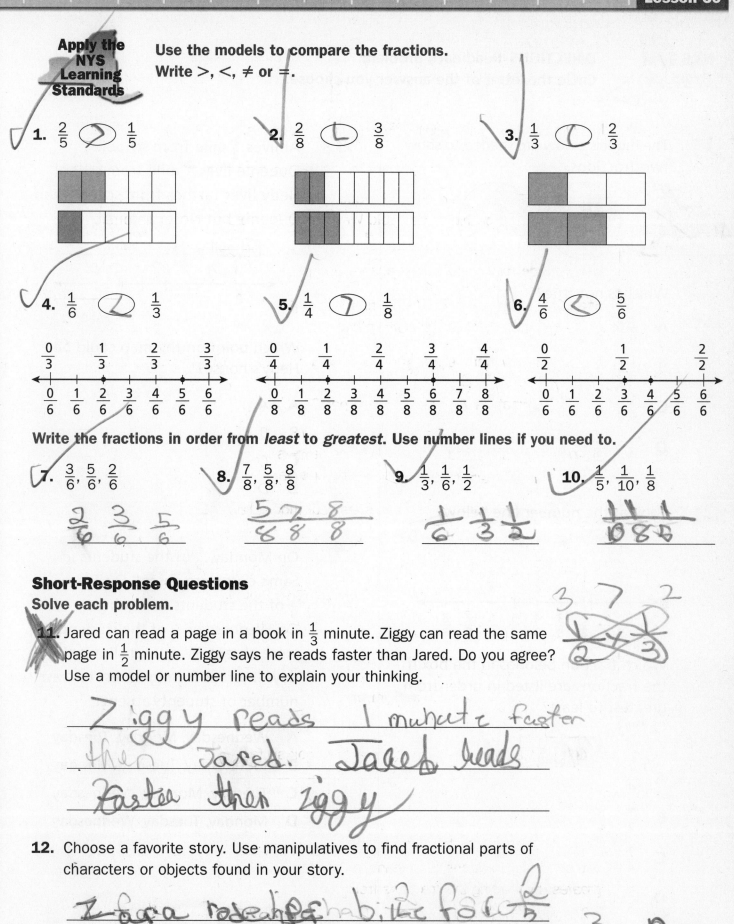

1. $\frac{2}{5}$ ⊘ $\frac{1}{5}$

2. $\frac{2}{8}$ ⊂ $\frac{3}{8}$

3. $\frac{1}{3}$ ⊂ $\frac{2}{3}$

4. $\frac{1}{6}$ ⊂ $\frac{1}{3}$

5. $\frac{1}{4}$ ⊃ $\frac{1}{8}$

6. $\frac{4}{6}$ ⊂ $\frac{5}{6}$

Write the fractions in order from *least* to *greatest*. Use number lines if you need to.

7. $\frac{3}{6}, \frac{5}{6}, \frac{2}{6}$

$\frac{2}{6} \quad \frac{3}{6} \quad \frac{5}{6}$

8. $\frac{7}{8}, \frac{5}{8}, \frac{8}{8}$

$\frac{5}{8} \quad \frac{7}{8} \quad \frac{8}{8}$

9. $\frac{1}{3}, \frac{1}{6}, \frac{1}{2}$

$\frac{1}{6} \quad \frac{1}{3} \quad \frac{1}{2}$

10. $\frac{1}{5}, \frac{1}{10}, \frac{1}{8}$

$\frac{1}{10} \quad \frac{1}{8} \quad \frac{1}{5}$

Short-Response Questions

Solve each problem.

11. Jared can read a page in a book in $\frac{1}{3}$ minute. Ziggy can read the same page in $\frac{1}{2}$ minute. Ziggy says he reads faster than Jared. Do you agree? Use a model or number line to explain your thinking.

Ziggy reads 1 muhcte faster then Jared. Jared reads faster then ziggy

12. Choose a favorite story. Use manipulatives to find fractional parts of characters or objects found in your story.

Zara rode her a bike for $\frac{2}{3}$ miles and Bob rode his bike for $\frac{3}{9}$. Dose Bob or Zara ride more then Zara.

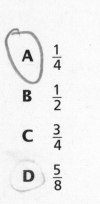

NYS Test Practice

DIRECTIONS Read each problem.
Circle the letter of the answer you choose.

1 The models below are shaded to show two fractions.

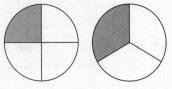

Which is not true?

A $\frac{1}{4} > \frac{1}{3}$

B $\frac{1}{3} > \frac{1}{4}$

C $\frac{1}{4} < \frac{1}{3}$

D $\frac{1}{4} \neq \frac{1}{3}$

2 Look at the number line below.

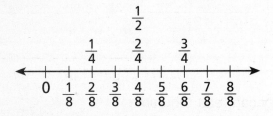

Which fraction belongs in the box if the fractions are listed in order from greatest to least?

$$\frac{3}{8}, \boxed{}, \frac{1}{8}$$

A $\frac{1}{4}$

B $\frac{1}{2}$

C $\frac{3}{4}$

D $\frac{5}{8}$

3 Al lives $\frac{2}{3}$ mile from school. Queenie lives $\frac{2}{6}$ mile from school. Hedy lives farther from school than Queenie but closer than Al.

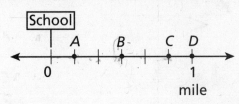

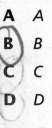

Which point on the map could be Hedy's house?

A A

B B

C C

D D

4 On Monday, $\frac{1}{5}$ of the students in Sam's class were absent. On Tuesday, $\frac{1}{3}$ of the students were absent. On Wednesday, $\frac{1}{8}$ of the students were absent. Which list shows days in order from greatest to least number of students absent?

A Wednesday, Monday, Tuesday

B Wednesday, Tuesday, Monday

C Tuesday, Monday, Wednesday

D Monday, Tuesday, Wednesday

       Measuring Up® to the New York State Learning Standards

You can add fractions with like denominators by adding the numerators. The denominator stays the same.

Guided Instruction

Problem

Sam has two fishbowls. Each holds $\frac{3}{8}$ gallon of water. How much water does Sam need to fill both fishbowls?

Use a model to add $\frac{3}{8} + \frac{3}{8}$.

Step 1   Shade the first 3 parts of the model below. Then shade the next 3 parts.

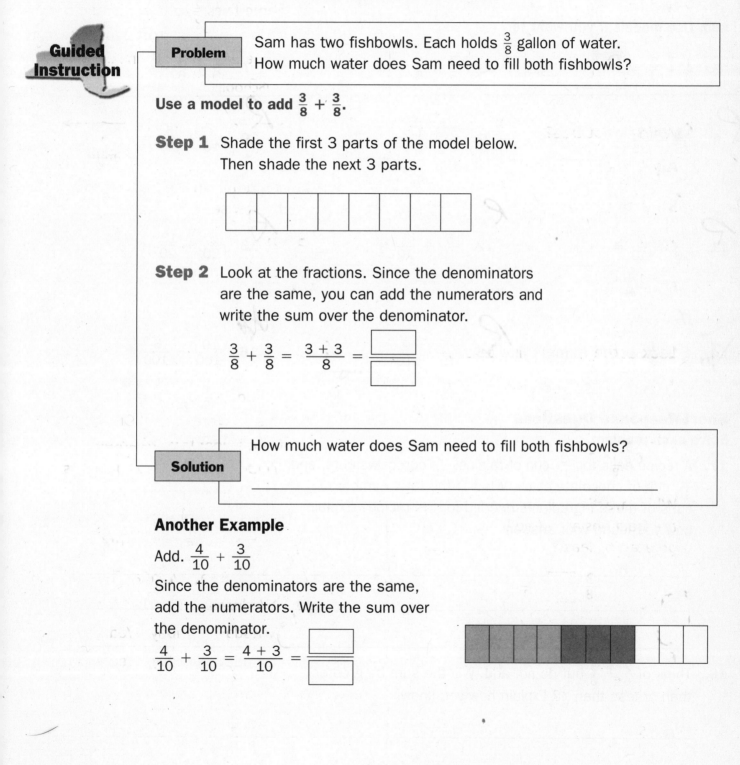

Step 2   Look at the fractions. Since the denominators are the same, you can add the numerators and write the sum over the denominator.

$$\frac{3}{8} + \frac{3}{8} = \frac{3+3}{8} = \frac{\boxed{}}{\boxed{}}$$

Solution

How much water does Sam need to fill both fishbowls?

_____

Another Example

Add. $\frac{4}{10} + \frac{3}{10}$

Since the denominators are the same, add the numerators. Write the sum over the denominator.

$$\frac{4}{10} + \frac{3}{10} = \frac{4+3}{10} = \frac{\boxed{}}{\boxed{}}$$

Apply the NYS Learning Standards

Add. Use the model if you want to.

$$\overset{0}{\vert} \quad \vert \quad \vert \quad \vert \quad \vert \quad \vert \quad \vert \quad \overset{1}{\vert}$$
$$\frac{0}{8} \quad \frac{1}{8} \quad \frac{2}{8} \quad \frac{3}{8} \quad \frac{4}{8} \quad \frac{5}{8} \quad \frac{6}{8} \quad \frac{7}{8} \quad \frac{8}{8}$$

1. $\frac{1}{8} + \frac{3}{8} = \frac{1}{2}$

2. $\frac{3}{8} + \frac{5}{8} = \frac{8}{8}$

3. $\frac{2}{8} + \frac{5}{8} = \frac{7}{8}$

4. $\frac{4}{8} + \frac{2}{8} = \frac{6}{8} \frac{3}{4}$

Add. Use models if you want to.

5. $\frac{1}{4} + \frac{2}{4} = \frac{3}{4}$

6. $\frac{3}{5} + \frac{1}{5} = \frac{4}{5}$

7. $\frac{2}{6} + \frac{3}{6} = \frac{5}{6}$

8. $\frac{12}{25} + \frac{8}{25} = \frac{20 \div 5}{25 \div 5} = \frac{4}{5}$

9. $\frac{5}{6} + \frac{1}{6} = \frac{6}{6}$ 1

10. $\frac{3}{10} + \frac{5}{10} = \frac{8 \div 2}{10 \div 2} \frac{4}{5}$

11. $\frac{1}{10} + \frac{7}{10} = \frac{8 \div 2}{10 \div 2} = \frac{4}{5}$

12. $\frac{5}{12} + \frac{4}{12} = \frac{9 \div 3}{12 \div 3} \frac{3}{4}$

13. $\frac{2}{20} + \frac{13}{20} = \frac{15 \div 5}{20 \div 5} \frac{3}{4}$

14. $\frac{1}{2} + \frac{1}{2} = \frac{2}{2}$

15. $\frac{4}{10} + \frac{2}{10} = \frac{6 \div 2}{10 \div 2} \frac{3}{5}$

16. $\frac{10}{100} + \frac{5}{100} = \frac{15}{100}$

Short-Response Questions
Solve each problem.

$\frac{3 + 2 + 4}{10 \ 10 \ 10} = \frac{9}{10}$

17. A recipe calls for $\frac{3}{10}$ cup of raisins, $\frac{2}{10}$ cup of walnuts, and $\frac{4}{10}$ cup of chocolate chips. What is the total number of cups of these ingredients needed for the recipe? Explain how you found your answer.

9/10 Because I add 3/10 + 2/10 + 4/10 and got 9/10.

18. Think of $\frac{2}{6} + \frac{3}{6}$ but do not add. Will the sum be greater than or less than $\frac{3}{6}$? Explain how you know.

The sam will be grater then 3/6 because the answer will be 5/6.

NYS Test Practice

DIRECTIONS Read each problem.
Circle the letter of the answer you choose.

1 The first act of the play lasted $\frac{2}{6}$ of an hour. The second act was just as long as the first act. The third act lasted $\frac{1}{6}$ of an hour. How many hours long was the play?

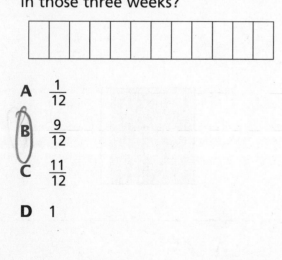

A $\frac{10}{12}$

B $\frac{3}{6}$

C $\frac{5}{6}$

D 1

2 Stella's class grew plants as part of an experiment. Stella's plant grew $\frac{1}{12}$ inch in the first week, $\frac{3}{12}$ of an inch in the second week, and $\frac{5}{12}$ of an inch in the third week. How many inches did Stella's plant grow in those three weeks?

A $\frac{1}{12}$

B $\frac{9}{12}$

C $\frac{11}{12}$

D 1

3 Which is the **best** prediction of the sum below?

$$\frac{1}{8} + \frac{4}{8} = ?$$

A less than $\frac{3}{8}$

B between $\frac{1}{8}$ and $\frac{4}{8}$

C more than $\frac{4}{8}$

D less than $\frac{4}{8}$

4 The chart shows how far Ronnie jogged in the first week of her program.

Day	Miles
Monday	$\frac{3}{10}$
Tuesday	$\frac{4}{10}$
Wednesday	$\frac{5}{10}$
Thursday	$\frac{6}{10}$
Friday	$\frac{7}{10}$

How many miles did Ronnie jog on Monday and Thursday combined?

A $\frac{9}{20}$

B $\frac{7}{10}$

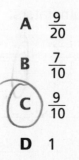

C $\frac{9}{10}$

D 1

You can subtract fractions with like denominators by subtracting the numerators. The denominator remains the same.

Guided Instruction

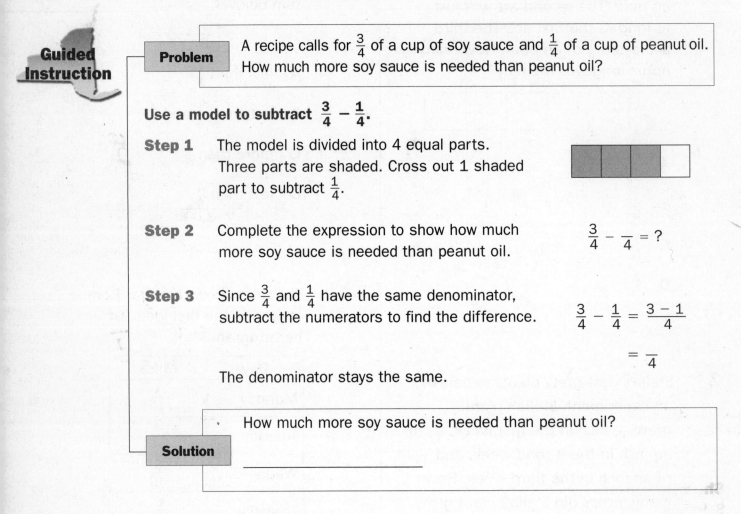

Problem

A recipe calls for $\frac{3}{4}$ of a cup of soy sauce and $\frac{1}{4}$ of a cup of peanut oil. How much more soy sauce is needed than peanut oil?

Use a model to subtract $\frac{3}{4} - \frac{1}{4}$.

Step 1 The model is divided into 4 equal parts. Three parts are shaded. Cross out 1 shaded part to subtract $\frac{1}{4}$.

Step 2 Complete the expression to show how much more soy sauce is needed than peanut oil.

$$\frac{3}{4} - \frac{}{4} = ?$$

Step 3 Since $\frac{3}{4}$ and $\frac{1}{4}$ have the same denominator, subtract the numerators to find the difference.

$$\frac{3}{4} - \frac{1}{4} = \frac{3-1}{4}$$

$$= \frac{}{4}$$

The denominator stays the same.

Solution

How much more soy sauce is needed than peanut oil?

_____

Another Example

Subtract. $\frac{9}{10} - \frac{4}{10}$

Since the denominators are the same, subtract the numerators.

$$\frac{9}{10} - \frac{4}{10} = \frac{9-4}{10} = \frac{\boxed{}}{\boxed{}}$$

Measuring Up® to the New York State Learning Standards

Apply the NYS Learning Standards

Write the subtraction sentence that each model represents. The Xs show what is being subtracted.

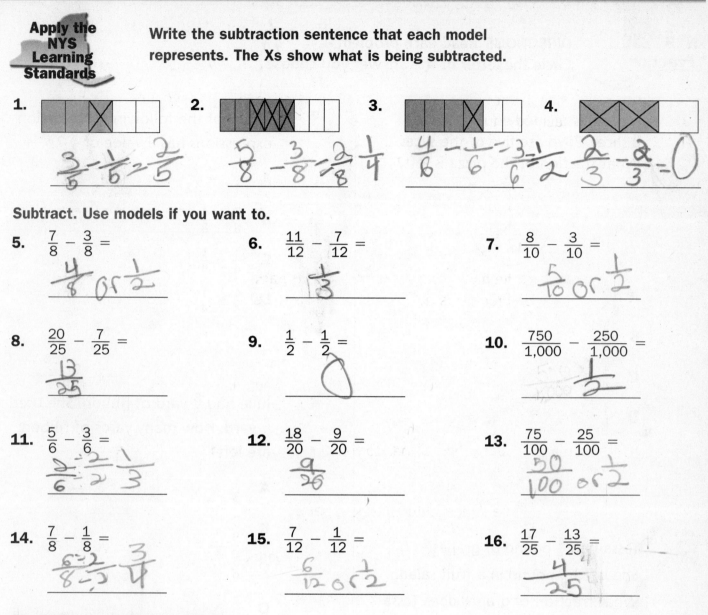

1. $\frac{3}{5} - \frac{1}{6} = \frac{2}{5}$

2. $\frac{5}{8} - \frac{3}{8} = \frac{2}{8} \quad \frac{1}{4}$

3. $\frac{4}{6} - \frac{1}{6} = \frac{3}{6} \frac{1}{2}$

4. $\frac{2}{3} - \frac{2}{3} = 0$

Subtract. Use models if you want to.

5. $\frac{7}{8} - \frac{3}{8} = $

$\frac{4}{8} \; or \; \frac{1}{2}$

6. $\frac{11}{12} - \frac{7}{12} = $

$\frac{1}{3}$

7. $\frac{8}{10} - \frac{3}{10} = $

$\frac{5}{10} \; or \; \frac{1}{2}$

8. $\frac{20}{25} - \frac{7}{25} = $

$\frac{13}{25}$

9. $\frac{1}{2} - \frac{1}{2} = $

0

10. $\frac{750}{1,000} - \frac{250}{1,000} = $

$\frac{1}{2}$

11. $\frac{5}{6} - \frac{3}{6} = $

$\frac{2}{6} = \frac{2}{2} \frac{1}{3}$

12. $\frac{18}{20} - \frac{9}{20} = $

$\frac{9}{20}$

13. $\frac{75}{100} - \frac{25}{100} = $

$\frac{50}{100} \; or \; \frac{1}{2}$

14. $\frac{7}{8} - \frac{1}{8} = $

$\frac{6 \div 2}{8 \div 2} \frac{3}{4}$

15. $\frac{7}{12} - \frac{1}{12} = $

$\frac{6}{12} \; or \; \frac{1}{2}$

16. $\frac{17}{25} - \frac{13}{25} = $

$\frac{4}{25}$

Short-Response Questions

Solve each problem.

17. In Adan's city, it rained 11 out of 20 days. In Luis's city, it rained 16 out of 20 days. What is the difference between the fraction of days it rained in Adan's city and the fraction of days it rained in Luis's city? Explain how you found your answer.

$11/20 - 16/20 = 5/20$ 4. t rined

18. Think of $\frac{7}{12} - \frac{4}{12}$ but do not subtract. Will the difference be greater than or less than $\frac{7}{12}$? Explain your answer.

It will be less then 7/12 because the answer is 3/12.

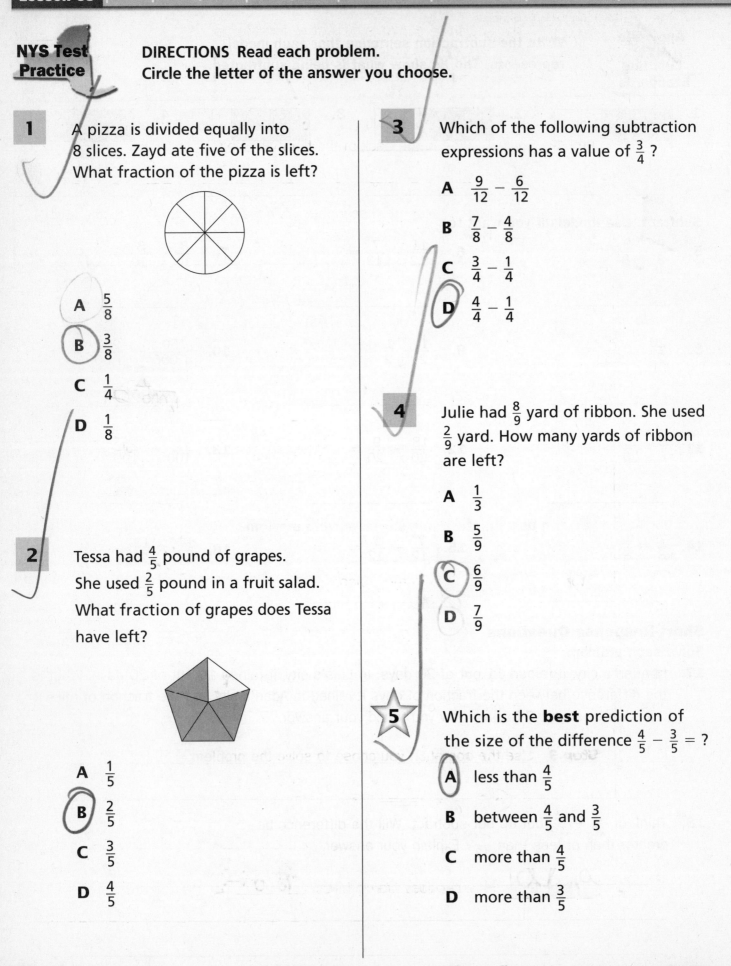

NYS Test Practice

DIRECTIONS Read each problem.
Circle the letter of the answer you choose.

1 A pizza is divided equally into 8 slices. Zayd ate five of the slices. What fraction of the pizza is left?

A $\frac{5}{8}$

B $\frac{3}{8}$

C $\frac{1}{4}$

D $\frac{1}{8}$

2 Tessa had $\frac{4}{5}$ pound of grapes. She used $\frac{2}{5}$ pound in a fruit salad. What fraction of grapes does Tessa have left?

A $\frac{1}{5}$

B $\frac{2}{5}$

C $\frac{3}{5}$

D $\frac{4}{5}$

3 Which of the following subtraction expressions has a value of $\frac{3}{4}$?

A $\frac{9}{12} - \frac{6}{12}$

B $\frac{7}{8} - \frac{4}{8}$

C $\frac{3}{4} - \frac{1}{4}$

D $\frac{4}{4} - \frac{1}{4}$

4 Julie had $\frac{8}{9}$ yard of ribbon. She used $\frac{2}{9}$ yard. How many yards of ribbon are left?

A $\frac{1}{3}$

B $\frac{5}{9}$

C $\frac{6}{9}$

D $\frac{7}{9}$

5 Which is the **best** prediction of the size of the difference $\frac{4}{5} - \frac{3}{5} = ?$

A less than $\frac{4}{5}$

B between $\frac{4}{5}$ and $\frac{3}{5}$

C more than $\frac{4}{5}$

D more than $\frac{3}{5}$

     Measuring Up® to the New York State Learning Standards

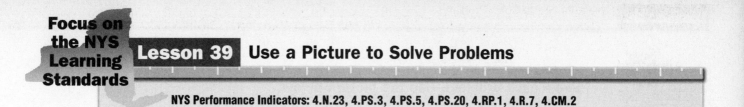

You can use a picture to help you solve word problems with fractions. Use the Problem-Solving Guide in the back of the book to help you.

Guided Instruction

Problem Marco bikes from school to his house. Then he bikes to the library. How far does Marco bike?

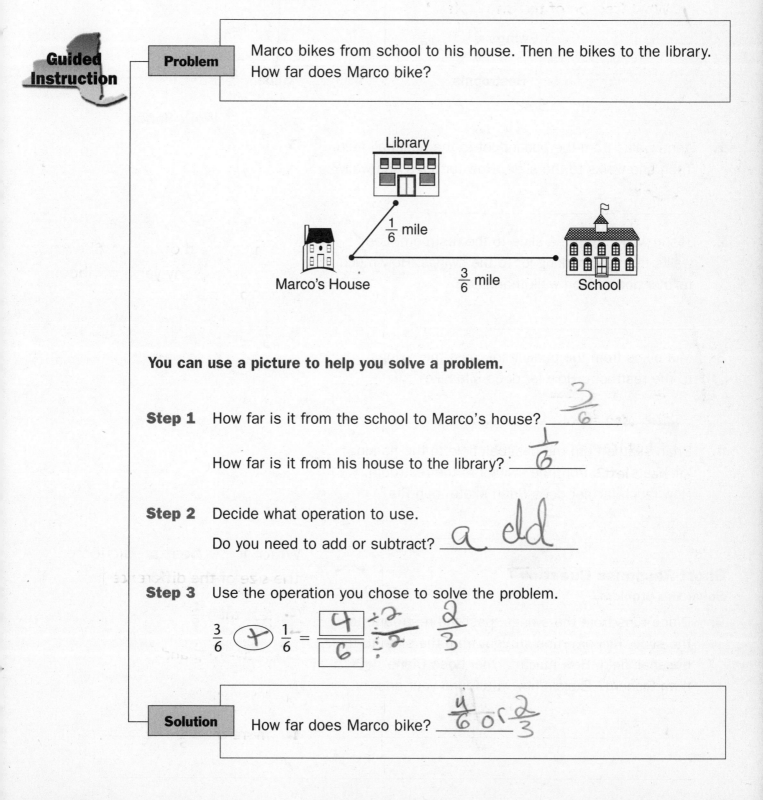

Library

$\frac{1}{6}$ mile

Marco's House $\frac{3}{6}$ mile   School

You can use a picture to help you solve a problem.

Step 1 How far is it from the school to Marco's house? ___$\frac{3}{6}$___

How far is it from his house to the library? ___$\frac{1}{6}$___

Step 2 Decide what operation to use.

Do you need to add or subtract? ___add___

Step 3 Use the operation you chose to solve the problem.

$\frac{3}{6}$ ⊕ $\frac{1}{6}$ = $\frac{4}{6}$ $\div 2 \atop \div 2$ $\frac{2}{3}$

Solution How far does Marco bike? ___$\frac{4}{6}$ or $\frac{2}{3}$___

Apply the NYS Learning Standards

Solve each problem. Use the picture below.

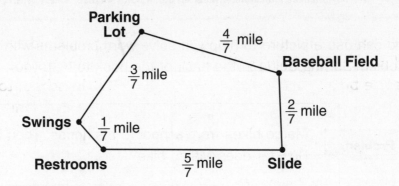

Parking Lot

$\frac{4}{7}$ mile

Baseball Field

$\frac{3}{7}$ mile

$\frac{2}{7}$ mile

Swings

$\frac{1}{7}$ mile

Restrooms

$\frac{5}{7}$ mile

Slide

Work Space

1. Anna walks from the parking lot to the baseball field. Then she walks to the slide. How far does she walk?

   $\frac{4}{7} + \frac{3}{7} = \frac{6}{7}$

2. Jason walks from the slide to the restroom. Lee walks from the parking lot to the swings. How much farther does Jason walk than Lee?

   $\frac{5}{7} - \frac{3}{7} = \frac{2}{7}$

3. Mia bikes from the parking lot, past the swings, to the restroom. How far does Mia bike?

   $\frac{3}{7} + \frac{1}{7} = \frac{4}{7}$

4. Brian skates from the baseball field to the parking lot. Ria skates from the swings to the restroom. How much farther does Brian skate than Ria?

   $\frac{4}{7} - \frac{1}{7} = \frac{3}{7}$

Short-Response Question
Solve the problem.

5. Diane runs from the swings, past the restroom, to the slide. Richard runs straight from the slide to the baseball field. How much farther does Diane run than Richard? Explain how you found your answer.

   First I added $\frac{1}{7} + \frac{5}{7}$ and got $\frac{6}{7}$ then I subtracted $\frac{6}{7} - \frac{2}{7}$ and got $\frac{4}{7}$

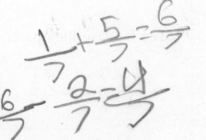

$\frac{1}{7} + \frac{5}{7} = \frac{6}{7}$

$\frac{6}{7} - \frac{2}{7} = \frac{4}{7}$

NYS Test Practice

DIRECTIONS Read each problem.
Circle the letter of the answer you choose.

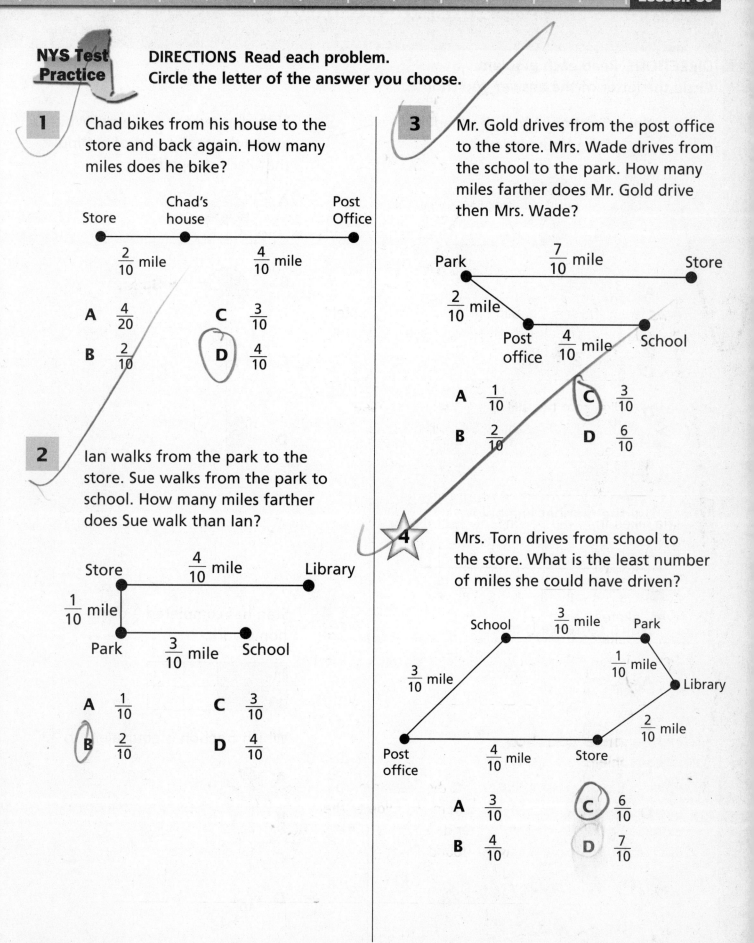

1 Chad bikes from his house to the store and back again. How many miles does he bike?

Store — Chad's house — Post Office

$\frac{2}{10}$ mile $\frac{4}{10}$ mile

A $\frac{4}{20}$ C $\frac{3}{10}$

B $\frac{2}{10}$ D $\frac{4}{10}$

2 Ian walks from the park to the store. Sue walks from the park to school. How many miles farther does Sue walk than Ian?

Store — $\frac{4}{10}$ mile — Library
$\frac{1}{10}$ mile
Park — $\frac{3}{10}$ mile — School

A $\frac{1}{10}$ C $\frac{3}{10}$

B $\frac{2}{10}$ D $\frac{4}{10}$

3 Mr. Gold drives from the post office to the store. Mrs. Wade drives from the school to the park. How many miles farther does Mr. Gold drive then Mrs. Wade?

Park — $\frac{7}{10}$ mile — Store
$\frac{2}{10}$ mile
Post office — $\frac{4}{10}$ mile — School

A $\frac{1}{10}$ C $\frac{3}{10}$

B $\frac{2}{10}$ D $\frac{6}{10}$

4 Mrs. Torn drives from school to the store. What is the least number of miles she could have driven?

School — $\frac{3}{10}$ mile — Park
$\frac{3}{10}$ mile $\frac{1}{10}$ mile — Library
Post office — $\frac{4}{10}$ mile — Store — $\frac{2}{10}$ mile

A $\frac{3}{10}$ C $\frac{6}{10}$

B $\frac{4}{10}$ D $\frac{7}{10}$

Building Stamina®

DIRECTIONS Read each problem.
Circle the letter of the answer you choose.

1 Which fraction names the shaded part of the figure below?

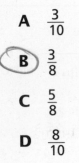

    A $\frac{3}{10}$

    B $\frac{3}{8}$

    C $\frac{5}{8}$

    D $\frac{8}{10}$

2 Use the number line below.

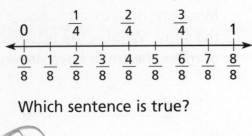

Which sentence is true?

    A $\frac{3}{4} < \frac{1}{4}$

    B $\frac{1}{8} > \frac{2}{8}$

    C $\frac{4}{8} > \frac{3}{8}$

    D $\frac{2}{4} < \frac{1}{4}$

3 Zach clapped for $\frac{1}{8}$ minute. Which model shows the part of a minute that Zach clapped?

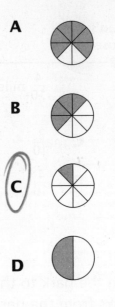

    A

    B

    C

    D

4 Stan has completed $\frac{4}{8}$ of his homework.

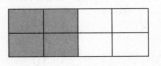

Which fraction is equivalent to $\frac{4}{8}$?

    A $\frac{3}{4}$

    B $\frac{1}{2}$

    C $\frac{1}{4}$

    D $\frac{1}{10}$

    Copying is illegal.   Measuring Up® to the New York State Learning Standards

5 The model below shows the fraction of fourth-grade students who take the bus to school.

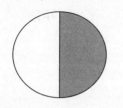

Fewer fourth graders walk to school than take the bus. Which fraction shows how many fourth graders might walk to school?

A $\frac{1}{6}$

B $\frac{1}{2}$

C $\frac{3}{4}$

D $\frac{7}{10}$

6 Which model shows equivalent fractions?

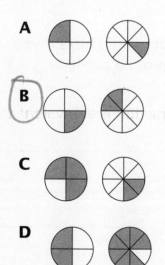

A

B

C

D

7 Find the sum.

$$\frac{6}{10} + \frac{3}{10} =$$

A $\frac{9}{10}$

B $\frac{9}{20}$

C $\frac{3}{10}$

D $\frac{3}{20}$

8 Chen's notebook weighs $\frac{3}{8}$ pound. His other school supplies weigh $\frac{2}{8}$ pound. How many pounds do the notebook and his other school supplies weigh altogether?

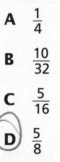

A $\frac{1}{4}$

B $\frac{10}{32}$

C $\frac{5}{16}$

D $\frac{5}{8}$

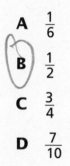

Extended-Response Questions
DIRECTIONS Read each question carefully before writing your response. Be sure to show your work when asked.

9 Label the cookies to show that
$\frac{1}{3}$ of them are chocolate chip cookies (CC);
$\frac{1}{2}$ of them are molasses cookies (M);
and the rest are sugar cookies (S).

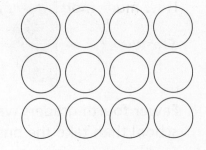

Part A

How many are sugar cookies?

Show your work.

Answer _____

What fraction are sugar cookies?

Answer _____

Part B

On the lines below explain how many oatmeal cookies you would have if you made the same number of cookies and wanted $\frac{1}{4}$ of them to be oatmeal.

_____

_____

_____

_____

_____

10 Jared is saving to buy a bicycle. In January he saved $\frac{2}{6}$ of the price of the bicycle, and in February he saved $\frac{1}{6}$ of the price.

Part A

How much more of the price does Jared have left to save?

Show your work.

Answer _____

Part B

Does Jared have more or less than half the price of the bicycle saved?

On the lines below, explain how you found your answer.

_____

_____

_____

_____

_____

164 Mathematics • Level D Copying is permitted.
Measuring Up® to the New York State Learning Standards

Decimals, like fractions, name part of a whole.

A **decimal** is a number that has one or more digits to the right of a decimal point.

Guided Instruction

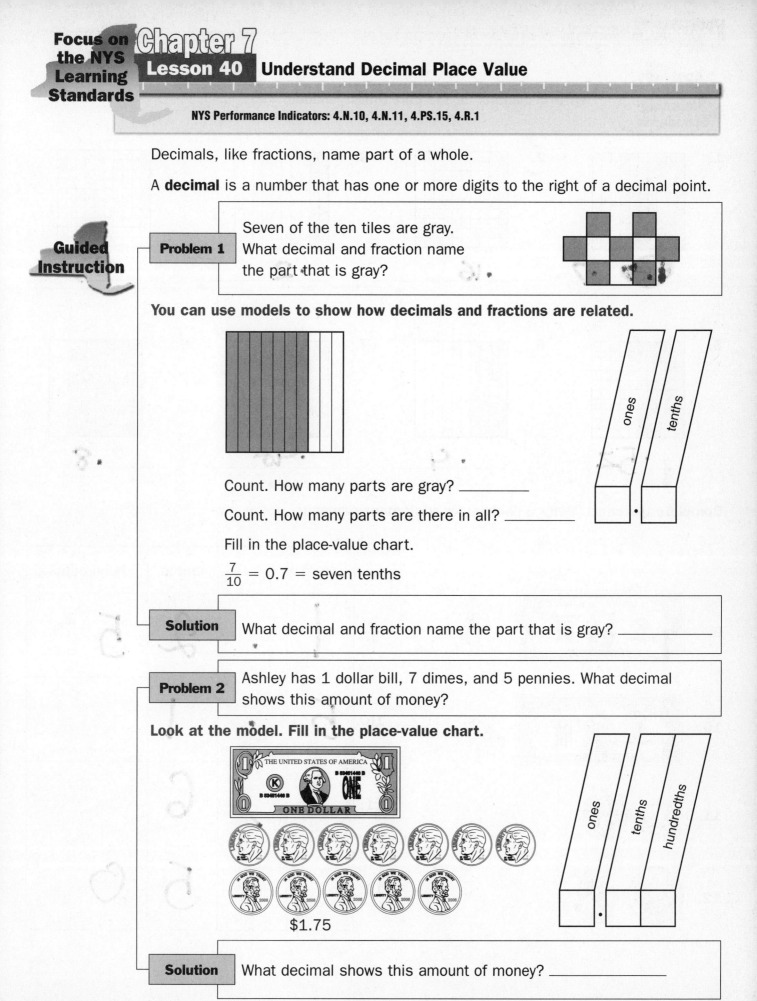

Problem 1 Seven of the ten tiles are gray. What decimal and fraction name the part that is gray?

You can use models to show how decimals and fractions are related.

Count. How many parts are gray? _____

Count. How many parts are there in all? _____

Fill in the place-value chart.

$\frac{7}{10}$ = 0.7 = seven tenths

ones   tenths

Solution What decimal and fraction name the part that is gray? _____

Problem 2 Ashley has 1 dollar bill, 7 dimes, and 5 pennies. What decimal shows this amount of money?

Look at the model. Fill in the place-value chart.

$1.75

ones   tenths   hundredths

Solution What decimal shows this amount of money? _____

Apply the NYS Learning Standards

Write a decimal for the part that is shaded.

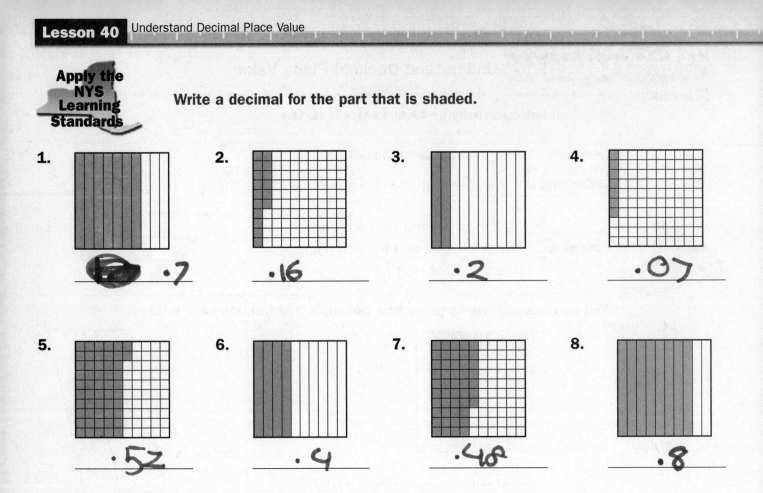

1. .7

2. .16

3. .2

4. .07

5. .52

6. .4

7. .48

8. .8

Complete the chart. Write a decimal for each money amount.

	ones	.	tenths	hundredths
9.	1	.	2	5
10.	5	.	1	
11.		.	6	
12.		.	5	6

DIRECTIONS Read each problem.
Circle the letter of the answer you choose.

1 What is the value of the underlined digit?

54.0<u>2</u>

A twenty

B 2

C two tenths

D two hundredths

2 Which number has a 7 in the hundredths place, a 0 in the tenths place, and an 8 in the ones place?

A $0.78   **C** $8.07

B $7.08   **D** $8.70

3 What part of the model is shaded?

A 0.2

B 0.27

C 0.72

D 2.7

4 Mike has 4 quarters, 3 dimes, 2 nickels, and 2 pennies. Which decimal shows Mike's amount of money?

A 0.42

B 1.42

C 14.2

D 142.1

5 A store sells pens. The model below shows how many cents a pen costs.

How much does a pen cost?

A $0.69

B $0.78

C $0.80

D $0.84

Lesson 41 Relate Fractions and Decimals

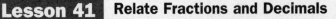

NYS Performance Indicators: 4.N.10, 4.N.24, 4.R.1

Both fractions and **decimals** are used to name part of a whole.

A **decimal point** is a period used to separate whole numbers from tenths.

A decimal can name the same number as a fraction. Example: six tenths

fraction = $\frac{6}{10}$ decimal = 0.6

$\frac{6}{10}$ = 0.6

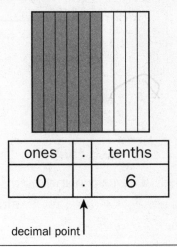

ones	.	tenths
0	.	6

↑
decimal point

Guided Instruction

Problem A box has 100 tiles. 75 tiles are used for a new floor. What decimal and fraction name the part that was used?

Look at the model. Fill in the place-value chart.

Step 1 How many parts are gray? _____

Step 2 How many parts are there in all? _____

Step 3 What fraction names the part that is gray? _____

Step 4 Write the decimal for the part that is gray in the chart below.

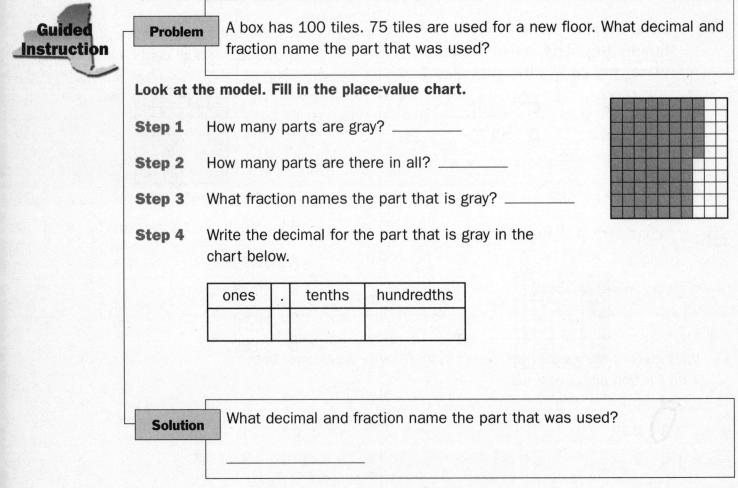

ones	.	tenths	hundredths

Solution What decimal and fraction name the part that was used?

_____

Write a decimal and a fraction for the part that is shaded.

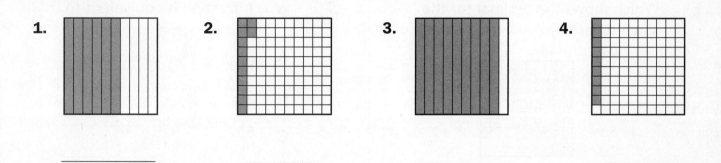

1. _____ 2. _____ 3. _____ 4. _____

Write the decimal equivalent next to each fraction.
Then shade the models to show each fraction.

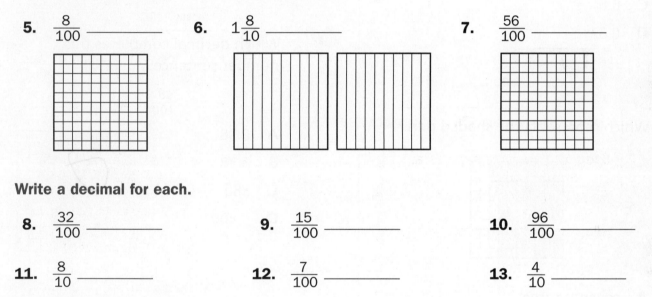

5. $\frac{8}{100}$ _____ 6. $1\frac{8}{10}$ _____ 7. $\frac{56}{100}$ _____

Write a decimal for each.

8. $\frac{32}{100}$ _____ 9. $\frac{15}{100}$ _____ 10. $\frac{96}{100}$ _____

11. $\frac{8}{10}$ _____ 12. $\frac{7}{100}$ _____ 13. $\frac{4}{10}$ _____

Short-Response Questions
Solve each problem.

14. Marta planted 89 out of 100 equal square plots in her garden. What part of the garden has been planted? Write the answer both as a fraction and a decimal.

_____

15. Jason has a page that holds 10 stickers. He puts 10 stickers on the page. In fraction and decimal form, write how much of the page is filled. Explain.

_____

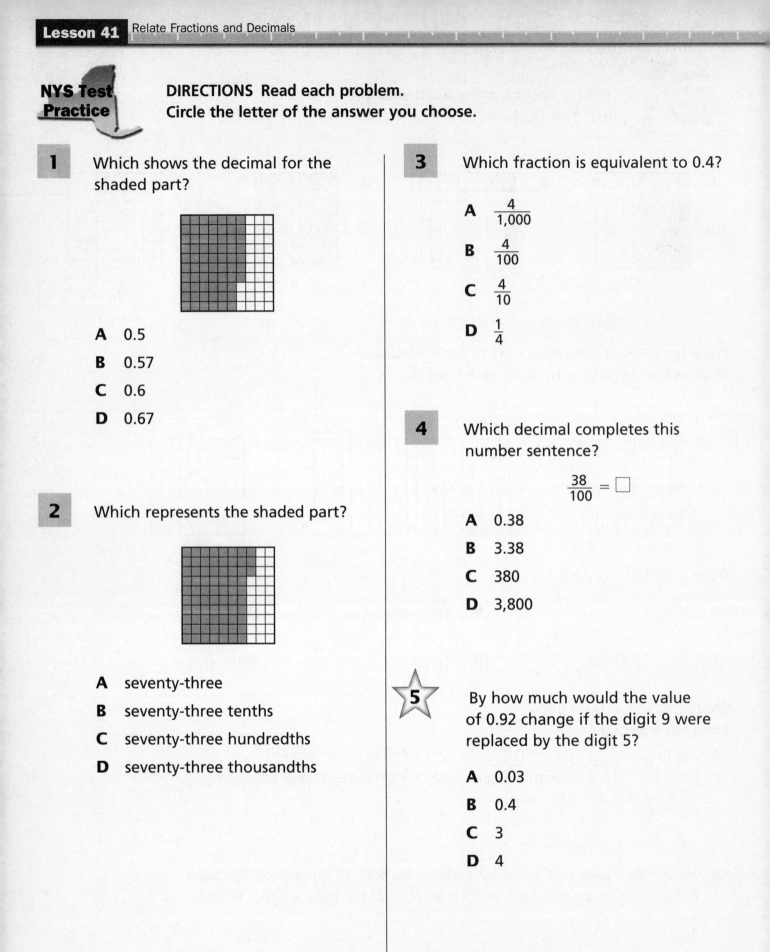

NYS Test Practice

DIRECTIONS Read each problem.
Circle the letter of the answer you choose.

1 Which shows the decimal for the shaded part?

A   0.5

B   0.57

C   0.6

D   0.67

2 Which represents the shaded part?

A   seventy-three

B   seventy-three tenths

C   seventy-three hundredths

D   seventy-three thousandths

3 Which fraction is equivalent to 0.4?

A $\frac{4}{1,000}$

B $\frac{4}{100}$

C $\frac{4}{10}$

D $\frac{1}{4}$

4 Which decimal completes this number sentence?

$$\frac{38}{100} = \square$$

A   0.38

B   3.38

C   380

D   3,800

5 By how much would the value of 0.92 change if the digit 9 were replaced by the digit 5?

A   0.03

B   0.4

C   3

D   4

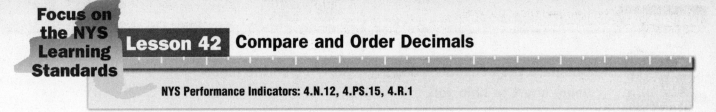

Lesson 42 Compare and Order Decimals

NYS Performance Indicators: 4.N.12, 4.PS.15, 4.R.1

You can use place value or a number line to compare and order decimals.
Use >, <, or = for is greater than, is less than, or is equal to.

Guided Instruction

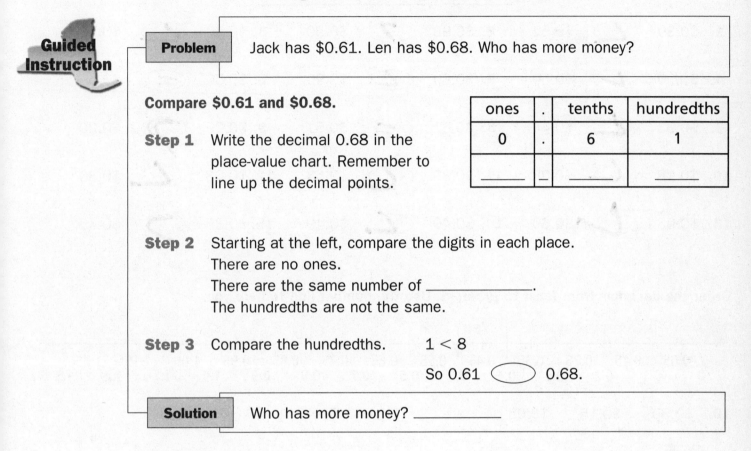

Problem	Jack has $0.61. Len has $0.68. Who has more money?

Compare $0.61 and $0.68.

ones	.	tenths	hundredths
0	.	6	1
___	_	___	___

Step 1 Write the decimal 0.68 in the place-value chart. Remember to line up the decimal points.

Step 2 Starting at the left, compare the digits in each place.
There are no ones.
There are the same number of _____.
The hundredths are not the same.

Step 3 Compare the hundredths.   1 < 8

So 0.61 ⬭ 0.68.

Solution	Who has more money? _____

Another Example

Compare and order $0.55, $0.90, and $0.35 from least to greatest.

Use a number line.

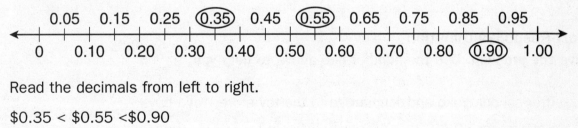

Read the decimals from left to right.

$0.35 < $0.55 <$0.90

Apply the NYS Learning Standards

Compare the decimals using <, >, or =. Use the place-value chart to help you.

ones	.	tenths	hundredths
	.		

1. $0.39 < $0.52   2. $0.98 > $0.90   3. $0.70 < $0.72

4. $0.20 < $0.50   5. $0.80 < $0.90   6. $0.50 = $0.50

7. $0.33 < $0.44   8. $0.51 = $0.51   9. $0.29 > $0.20

10. $0.18 < $0.28   11. $0.39 < $0.53   12. $0.03 < $0.30

13. $0.06 < $0.60   14. $0.40 < $0.49   15. $0.85 > $0.75

Order the decimals from *least* to *greatest*. Use the number line to help you.

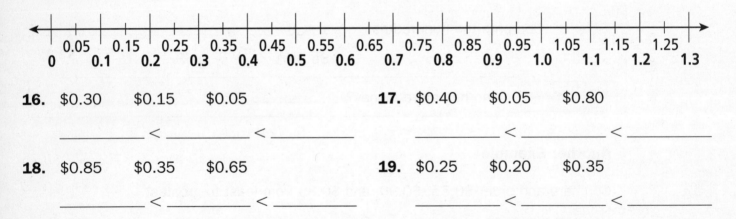

0   0.05   0.1   0.15   0.2   0.25   0.3   0.35   0.4   0.45   0.5   0.55   0.6   0.65   0.7   0.75   0.8   0.85   0.9   0.95   1.0   1.05   1.1   1.15   1.2   1.25   1.3

16. $0.30 $0.15 $0.05

_____ < _____ < _____

17. $0.40 $0.05 $0.80

_____ < _____ < _____

18. $0.85 $0.35 $0.65

_____ < _____ < _____

19. $0.25 $0.20 $0.35

_____ < _____ < _____

Short-Response Question

Solve the problem. Use the number line above to help you.

20. After school, Yoko and Jennifer go to the toy store. Yoko buys
a sticker for $0.49. Jennifer buys a whistle for $0.95.
Who spends the greater amount? _____

NYS Test Practice

DIRECTIONS Read each problem.
Circle the letter of the answer you choose.

1 Which statement is true? Use the place-value chart to help you.

ones	.	tenths	hundredths

A $0.81 = $0.18   C $0.81 > $0.18

B $0.81 < $0.18   D $0.81 < $0.81

2 Bob spent $0.73 yesterday. Dave spent less. Which shows the amount Dave might have spent?

A $0.83

B $0.91

C $0.75

D $0.70

3 Which of the following has the **greatest** value?

A $0.66

B $0.54

C $0.09

D $0.37

4 Which amount is represented by point *P* on this number line?

P
$0.30 $0.40 $0.50 $0.60 $0.70 $0.80

A $0.83

B $0.52

C $0.42

D $0.40

5 Use the number line below.

0   $0.25 $0.50 $0.75 $1.00

Which statement is not true?

A $0.25 < $0.50   C $0.50 > $0.75

B $0.50 = $0.50   D $0.75 = $0.75

6 Which could be the missing digit?

$3.51 > $3. □ 7 > $3.42

A 1

B 3

C 4

D 8

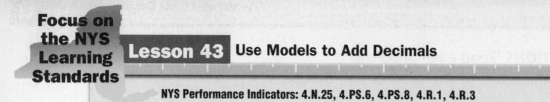
You can use models to add decimals with tenths and with hundredths.

Guided Instruction

Problem Jane ran 1.4 miles the first day and 0.8 mile the second day. How many miles did Jane run altogether?

Add to find the total number of miles.

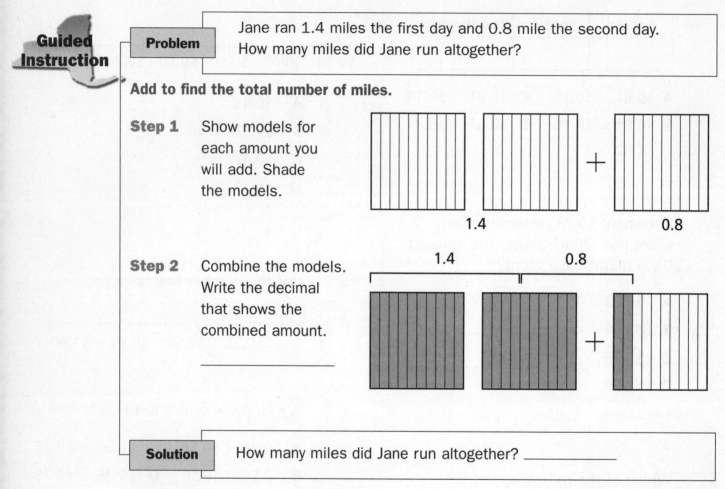

Step 1 Show models for each amount you will add. Shade the models.

1.4   0.8

Step 2 Combine the models. Write the decimal that shows the combined amount.

1.4   0.8

_____

Solution How many miles did Jane run altogether? _____

Another Example

Find the sum of 0.25 + 0.47.

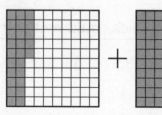

Combine the models. _____ + _____

How many squares will be shaded altogether? _____

Write the decimal that shows the combined amount. _____

Apply the NYS Learning Standards

Use models to find the sum.

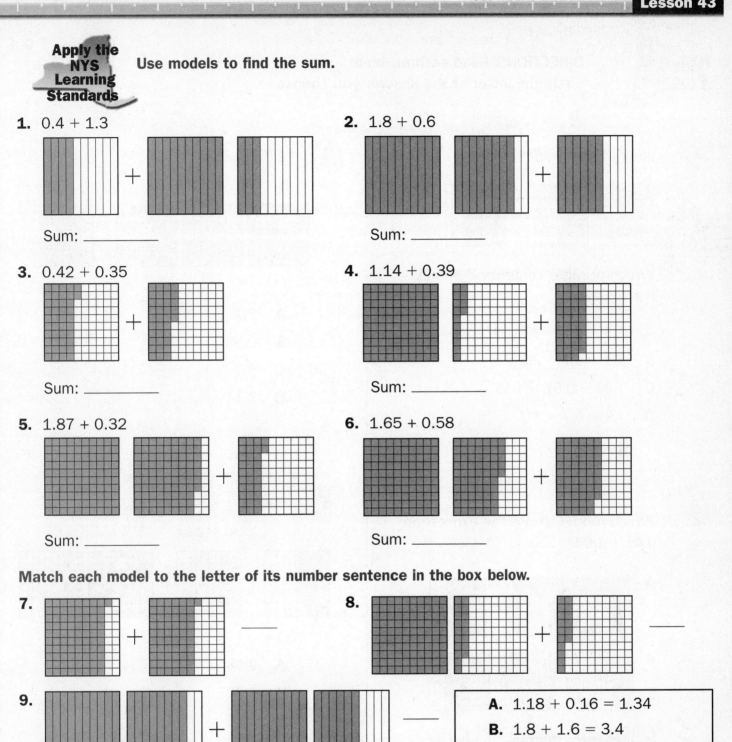

1. 0.4 + 1.3

Sum: _____

2. 1.8 + 0.6

Sum: _____

3. 0.42 + 0.35

Sum: _____

4. 1.14 + 0.39

Sum: _____

5. 1.87 + 0.32

Sum: _____

6. 1.65 + 0.58

Sum: _____

Match each model to the letter of its number sentence in the box below.

7. _____

8. _____

9. _____

A. 1.18 + 0.16 = 1.34

B. 1.8 + 1.6 = 3.4

C. 0.81 + 0.61 = 1.42

Short-Response Question

Solve. Use models if you need to.

10. Ted walks 0.76 mile to school and 0.76 mile from school. How far does he walk in all? Explain how you solved the problem.

_____

_____

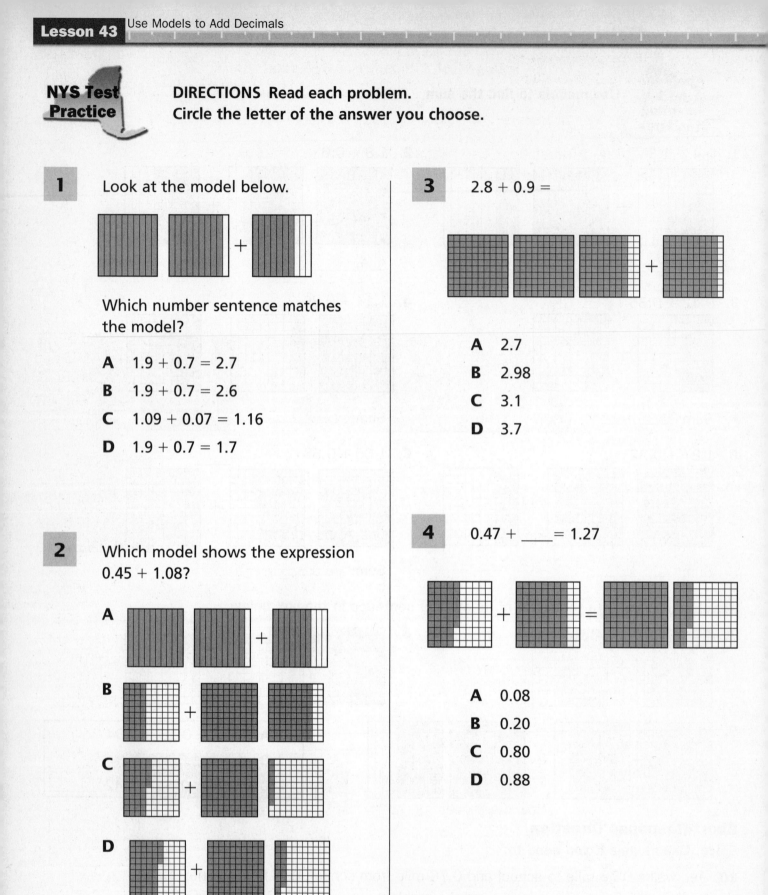

DIRECTIONS Read each problem.
Circle the letter of the answer you choose.

1 Look at the model below.

Which number sentence matches the model?

A 1.9 + 0.7 = 2.7

B 1.9 + 0.7 = 2.6

C 1.09 + 0.07 = 1.16

D 1.9 + 0.7 = 1.7

2 Which model shows the expression 0.45 + 1.08?

A

B

C

D

3 2.8 + 0.9 =

A 2.7

B 2.98

C 3.1

D 3.7

4 0.47 + _____ = 1.27

A 0.08

B 0.20

C 0.80

D 0.88

 Measuring Up® to the New York State Learning Standards

Lesson 44 Use Models to Subtract Decimals

NYS Performance Indicators: 4.N.25, 4.PS.6, 4.PS.8, 4.R.1, 4.R.3

Use decimal models to subtract decimals with tenths and with hundredths.

Guided Instruction

Problem

Gabe rode his bike 1.55 miles on Saturday and 2.80 miles on Sunday. How many more miles did Gabe ride on Sunday than on Saturday?

Use models to subtract 2.80 − 1.55.

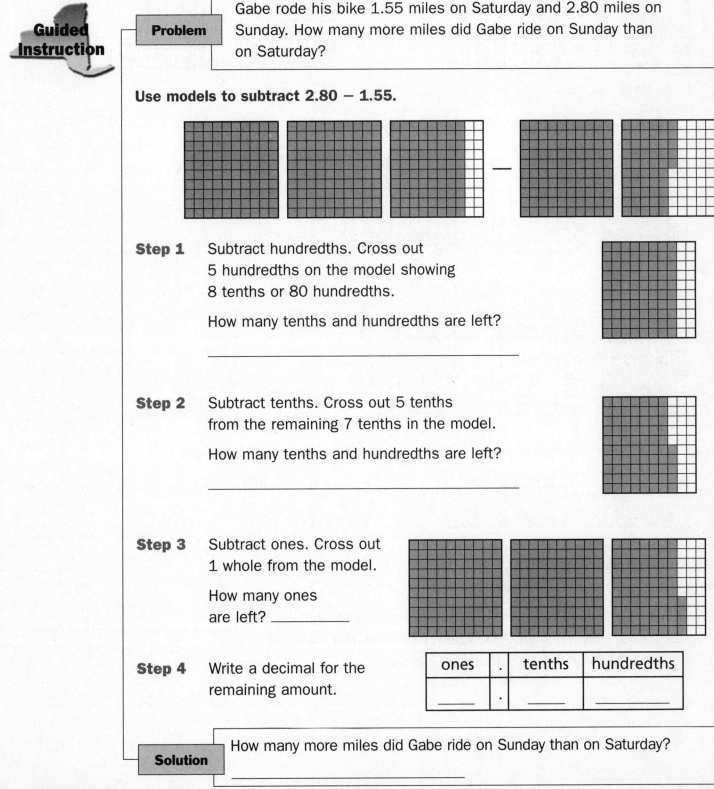

Step 1 Subtract hundredths. Cross out 5 hundredths on the model showing 8 tenths or 80 hundredths.

How many tenths and hundredths are left?

_____

Step 2 Subtract tenths. Cross out 5 tenths from the remaining 7 tenths in the model.

How many tenths and hundredths are left?

_____

Step 3 Subtract ones. Cross out 1 whole from the model.

How many ones are left? _____

Step 4 Write a decimal for the remaining amount.

ones	.	tenths	hundredths
_____	.	_____	_____

Solution

How many more miles did Gabe ride on Sunday than on Saturday?

_____

Apply the NYS Learning Standards

Use models to find each difference.

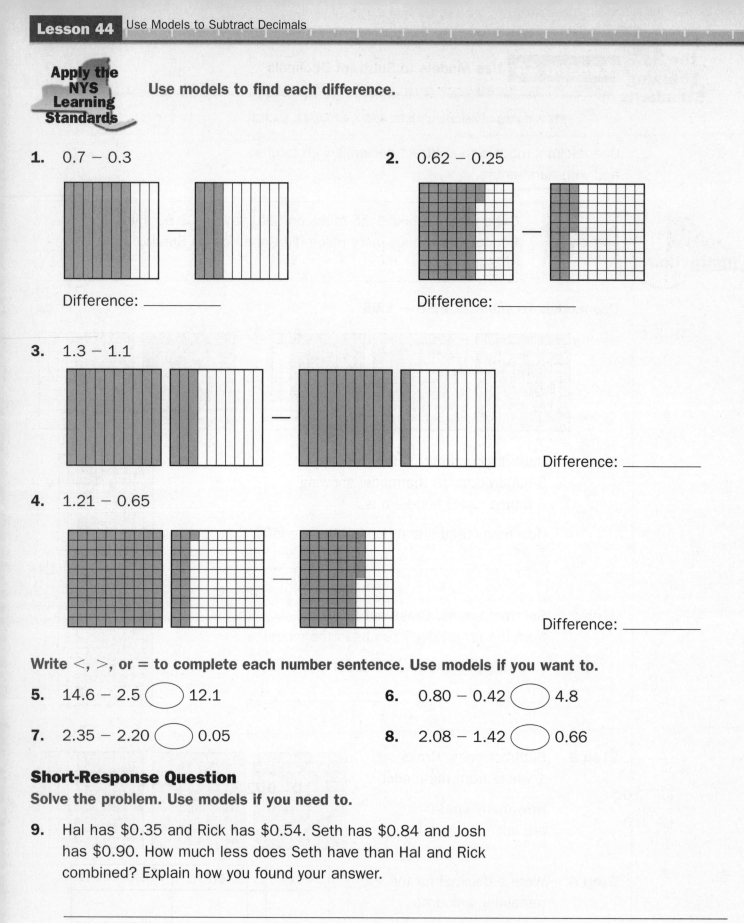

1. 0.7 − 0.3

Difference: _____

2. 0.62 − 0.25

Difference: _____

3. 1.3 − 1.1

Difference: _____

4. 1.21 − 0.65

Difference: _____

Write <, >, or = to complete each number sentence. Use models if you want to.

5. 14.6 − 2.5 ◯ 12.1

6. 0.80 − 0.42 ◯ 4.8

7. 2.35 − 2.20 ◯ 0.05

8. 2.08 − 1.42 ◯ 0.66

Short-Response Question

Solve the problem. Use models if you need to.

9. Hal has $0.35 and Rick has $0.54. Seth has $0.84 and Josh has $0.90. How much less does Seth have than Hal and Rick combined? Explain how you found your answer.

_____

_____

DIRECTIONS Read each problem.
Circle the letter of the answer you choose.

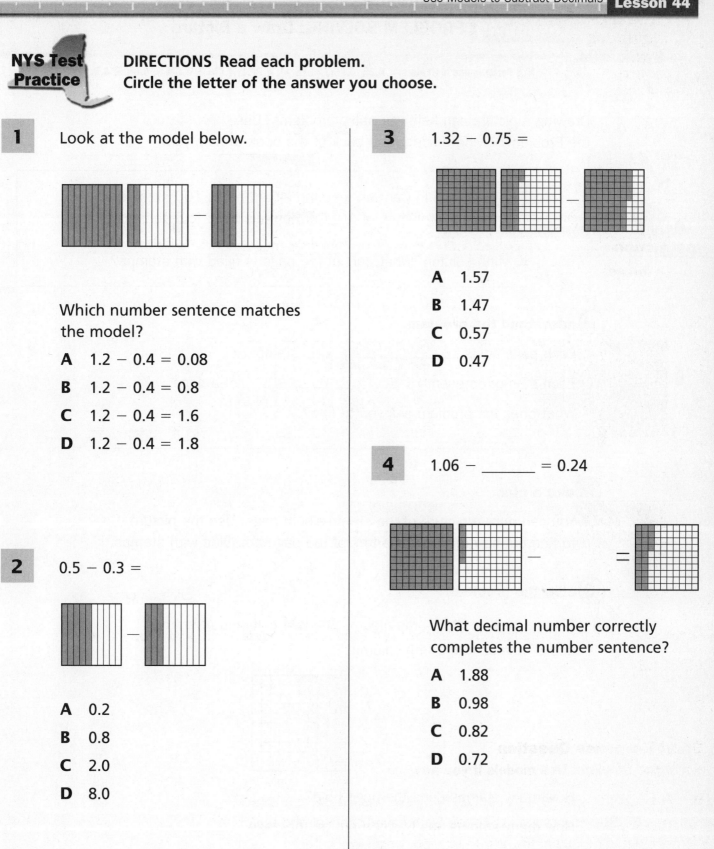

1 Look at the model below.

Which number sentence matches the model?

A $1.2 - 0.4 = 0.08$

B $1.2 - 0.4 = 0.8$

C $1.2 - 0.4 = 1.6$

D $1.2 - 0.4 = 1.8$

2 $0.5 - 0.3 =$

A 0.2

B 0.8

C 2.0

D 8.0

3 $1.32 - 0.75 =$

A 1.57

B 1.47

C 0.57

D 0.47

4 $1.06 - \underline{\hspace{1cm}} = 0.24$

What decimal number correctly completes the number sentence?

A 1.88

B 0.98

C 0.82

D 0.72

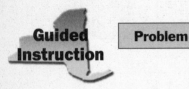
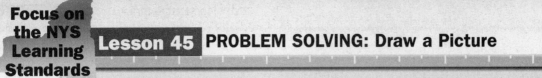

Lesson 45 PROBLEM SOLVING: Draw a Picture

NYS Performance Indicators: 4.N.25, 4.PS.7, 4.PS.11, 4.RP.1, 4.CM.2, 4.CM.5, 4.CN.5, 4.R.1

Drawing a picture can help you solve problems. Use
the Problem-Solving Guide in the back of the book to help you.

**Guided
Instruction**

| Problem |

Each page in Carmen's stamp album holds 100 stamps in
rows and columns of 10. Carmen has filled four columns
on the first page with stamps and has three stamps in the
fifth column. What part of the page is filled with stamps?

(U)nderstand the problem.

Each page holds _____ stamps.

Each stamp represents 1 _____ of a page.

What does the problem ask you to find?

_____

(M)ake a plan.

You can draw a picture of the stamp-album page. Use the picture
to find out how many hundredths of the page are filled with stamps.

(S)olve the problem.

Show a page in the stamp album. Shade 4 columns of stamps
and 3 stamps in the fifth column.

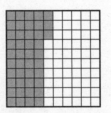

How many stamps does the page hold? _____

How many stamps has Carmen put on the page? _____

What part of the page is filled with stamps? _____

(C)heck your answer.

Does the picture show a model for 0.43? _____

Measuring Up® to the New York State Learning Standards

Apply the NYS Learning Standards

Draw a picture to help you solve each problem.

1. Brittany and Ruth collect stickers. Each page in their sticker albums holds 100 stickers, with 10 in each row and column. The first page in Brittany's sticker album has five rows filled plus six more stickers. Ruth's sticker album has one page filled and 75 stickers on the second page. How many more pages of stickers does Ruth have than Brittany?

_____

2. A carpenter cut a piece of wood measuring 2.75 meters from a 3-meter board. How much wood was left?

_____

3. Justin emptied the coins from his piggy bank. He wanted to exchange his coins for dollar bills. He had 48 dimes and 279 pennies. How much money did Justin have?

_____

4. Juanita and her sister Marla save pennies. They decided to put their pennies together to save for a birthday present for their dad. Juanita has $0.89. Marla has $0.25 more than Juanita. How much have they saved so far?

_____

Short-Response Question

Solve the problem.

5. A 10-kilometer race had four sections. The first section was 2.4 kilometers. The second section was 4.1 kilometers. The third section was 1.5 kilometers. How long was the fourth section? Explain how you found your answer.

_____

_____

_____

DIRECTIONS Read each problem.
Circle the letter of the answer you choose.

1 Craig jogs 1.8 miles on Mondays, Thursdays, and Saturdays. How many miles per week does Craig jog?

A 3.8

B 4.4

C 4.8

D 5.4

2 Anna filled 0.42 of a page in her sticker album with animal stickers. She filled another 0.15 of the page with rainbow stickers. The rest of the page is filled with butterfly stickers. The page holds 100 stickers. How many butterfly stickers are on the page?

A Page in Anna's Sticker Album

A 57

B 43

C 42

D 15

3 A bathroom floor needs ten rows of tile, with ten tiles in each row. A worker installs 28 hundredths of the tiles the first day. On the second day, the worker finishes the job. Which picture shows how many tiles were installed on day 2?

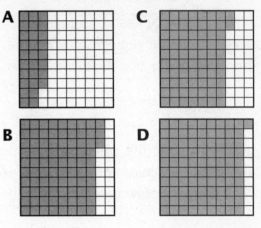

4 Lea has a pegboard that holds 100 pegs. She has 84 pegs on it now. Her sister pulls out 25 of the pegs. Which decimal shows what fraction of the pegboard is still filled?

A 1.9

B 0.69

C 0.61

D 0.59

Copying is illegal. Measuring Up® to the New York State Learning Standards

Building Stamina®

DIRECTIONS Read each problem.
Circle the letter of the answer you choose.

1 Kenya kept track of the weather for 100 days. She found that 0.27 of the days were cloudy. How many days were cloudy?

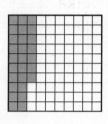

- **A** 0.27
- **B** 2.7
- **C** 27
- **D** 100

2 Marco has a sticker collection. Exactly $\frac{5}{10}$ of his collection are animal stickers. Which of the following has the same value as $\frac{5}{10}$?

- **A** 0.05
- **B** 0.5
- **C** 0.95
- **D** 5.0

3 A grid has 10 squares. Tina shaded in $\frac{9}{10}$ of the squares. Which statement is **not** true?

- **A** Tina shaded in 0.9 of the grid.
- **B** Tina shaded nine tenths of the grid.
- **C** Tina shaded 0.09 of the grid.
- **D** One tenth of the grid is not shaded.

4 A school store sells rulers, notebooks, and pencils. The models below show how many cents each costs.

A ruler costs less than a notebook, but more than a pencil. How much does a ruler cost?

- **A** $0.69
- **B** $0.78
- **C** $0.80
- **D** $0.84

5 Which model shows 1.16 + 0.59?

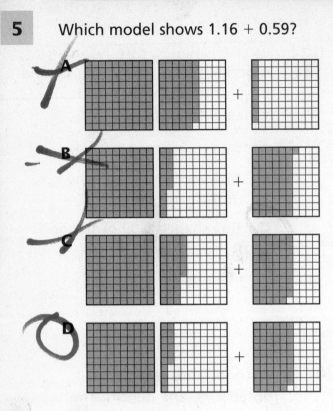

6 Which subtraction sentence does the model show?

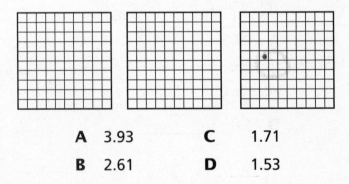

A $0.83 − $0.31 = $0.52

B $0.83 − $0.13 = $0.70

C $0.38 − $0.31 = $0.07

D $0.31 − $0.01 = $0.30

7 Yolanda bought 1.2 kilograms of apples and 1.3 kilograms of bananas. How many kilograms of fruit did Yolanda buy? Use the models below to help you.

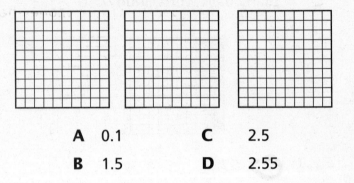

A 0.1   C 2.5

B 1.5   D 2.55

8 On Monday, Ms. Davis drove 2.73 miles to her sister's house. On Tuesday, she drove 1.2 miles to the mall. How many more miles did Ms. Davis drive on Monday than on Tuesday? Use the models below to help you.

A 3.93   C 1.71

B 2.61   D 1.53

Extended-Response Questions
DIRECTIONS Read each question carefully before writing your response.
Be sure to show your work when asked.

 Nicholas has 56 pennies. The model below represents $1.00.
Shade it to show how much money he has.

Part A

Write the fraction of the model that is shaded as a fraction and a decimal.

Show your work.

Answer _____

Write the fraction of the model that is not shaded as a fraction and a decimal.

Answer _____

Which decimal is **greater**?

Answer _____

Part B

On the lines below, explain how you found your answer.

_____

_____

_____

_____

★ **10** Tanya has 4 pieces of graph paper with 100 boxes on each piece of paper. On each piece of paper, there are 10 boxes in each row and column. She shades 1.56 of the 4 grids red. She shades 0.60 of the 4 grids blue.

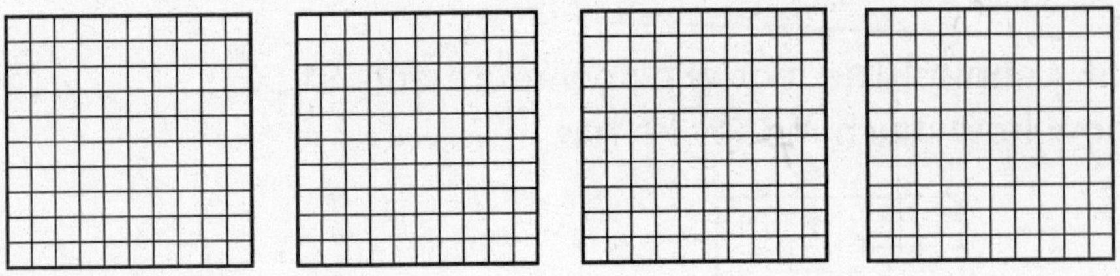

Part A

Shade in the models above to show what she shaded.

What decimal shows how many boxes were shaded in all?

Show your work.

Answer _____

Part B

On the lines below, explain how you found your answer.

_____

_____

_____

_____

NYS Performance Indicators: 4.G.2, 4.G.6, 4.CM.9, 4.CM.10

A **point** is a location in space. A **line** is a straight path of points that goes on forever in two directions. A **line segment** is part of a line and has two endpoints. A **plane** is a surface that extends in all directions.

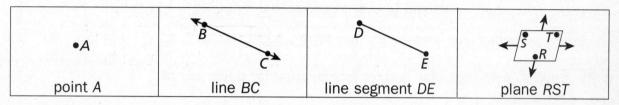

•A	line BC	line segment DE	plane RST
point A	line BC	line segment DE	plane RST

Intersecting lines go through the same point. **Parallel lines** are always the same distance apart. They never intersect. **Perpendicular lines** intersect to form 4 right angles.

intersecting lines	parallel lines	perpendicular lines

Guided Instruction

Problem Below is part of a map of a town. Find two streets that are parallel, two that are perpendicular, and two that intersect but not at right angles.

You can use what you know about geometric terms to identify lines.

Step 1 Which streets are the same distance apart along their entire lengths?
North St and Tremont St

Step 2 Which streets intersect at right angles? Look for square corners.
West Ave, North St or West Ave, Tremont St

Step 3 Which streets meet, but not at right angles? _____
Lake Ave, North St

Find two streets that are parallel, two that are perpendicular, and two that intersect but not at right angles.

Solution _____

_____

_____

Apply the NYS Learning Standards

Choose the correct word from the word box.

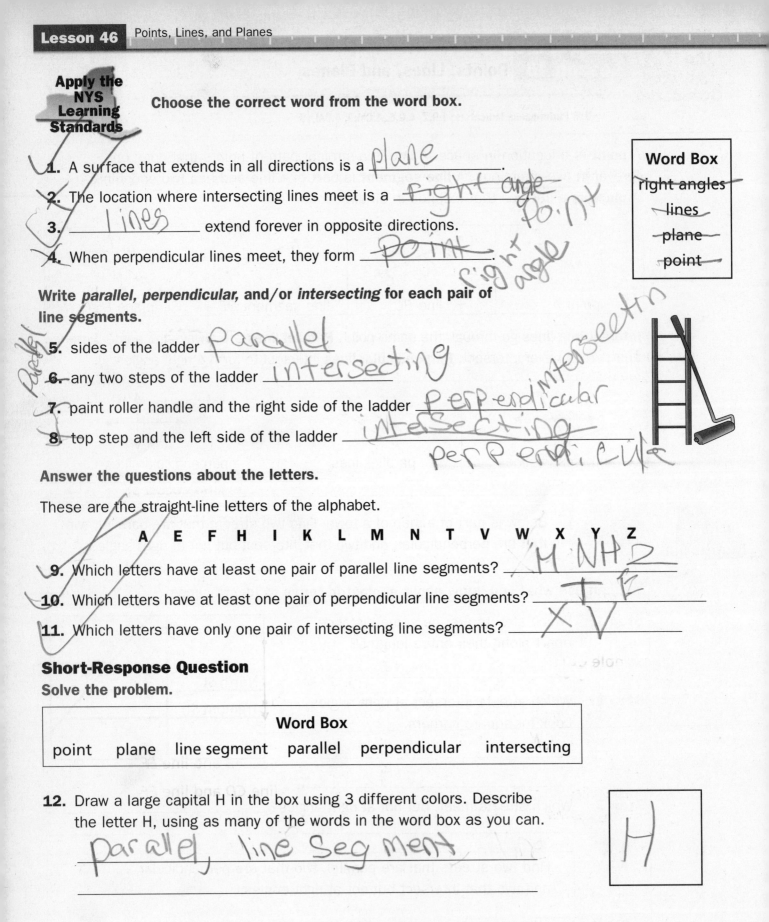

1. A surface that extends in all directions is a _plane_.

2. The location where intersecting lines meet is a ~~right angle~~ _point_.

3. _lines_ extend forever in opposite directions.

4. When perpendicular lines meet, they form ~~point~~ _right angle_.

Word Box
~~right angles~~
~~lines~~
~~plane~~
~~point~~

Write *parallel*, *perpendicular*, and/or *intersecting* for each pair of line segments.

5. sides of the ladder _parallel_

6. any two steps of the ladder _intersecting_

7. paint roller handle and the right side of the ladder _perpendicular_ ~~intersecting~~

8. top step and the left side of the ladder _intersecting_ _perpendicular_

Answer the questions about the letters.

These are the straight-line letters of the alphabet.

A   E   F   H   I   K   L   M   N   T   V   W   X   Y   Z

9. Which letters have at least one pair of parallel line segments? _M N H Z_

10. Which letters have at least one pair of perpendicular line segments? _T E_

11. Which letters have only one pair of intersecting line segments? _X V_

Short-Response Question

Solve the problem.

Word Box					
point	plane	line segment	parallel	perpendicular	intersecting

12. Draw a large capital H in the box using 3 different colors. Describe the letter H, using as many of the words in the word box as you can.

parallel, line segment

H

NYS Test Practice

**DIRECTIONS Read each problem.
Circle the letter of the answer you choose.**

1 How many line segments will you use to draw a square?

A 1   C 3

B 2   D 4

2 Which letter marks the point of intersection?

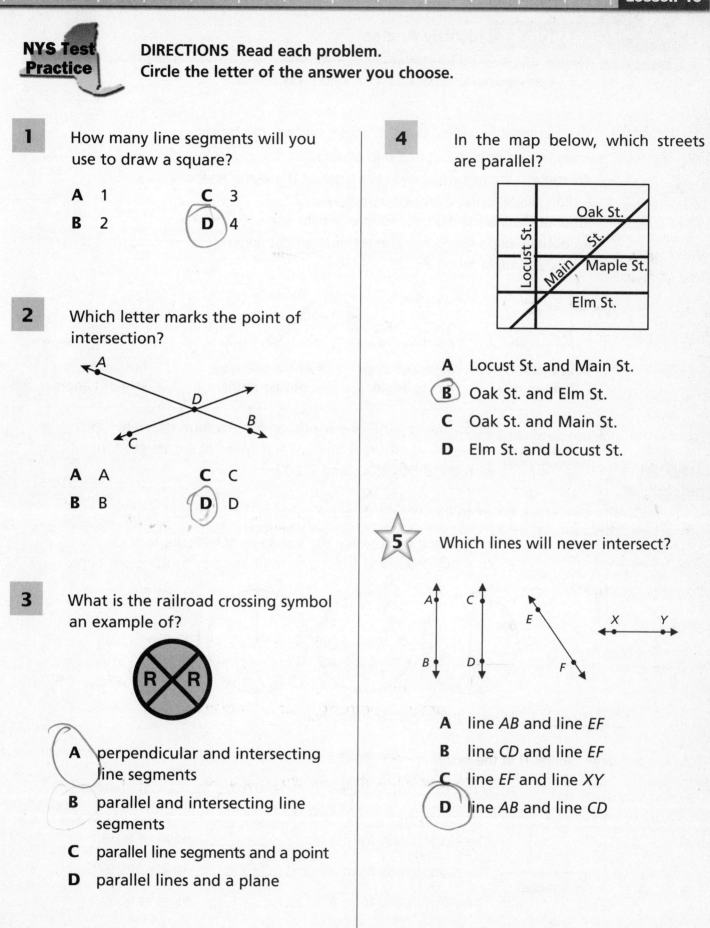

A A   C C

B B   D D

3 What is the railroad crossing symbol an example of?

A perpendicular and intersecting line segments

B parallel and intersecting line segments

C parallel line segments and a point

D parallel lines and a plane

4 In the map below, which streets are parallel?

A Locust St. and Main St.

B Oak St. and Elm St.

C Oak St. and Main St.

D Elm St. and Locust St.

5 Which lines will never intersect?

A line AB and line EF

B line CD and line EF

C line EF and line XY

D line AB and line CD

Lesson 47 Identify Angles

NYS Performance Indicators: 4.G.7, 4.G.8, 4.PS.11, 4.PS.12, 4.CM.6

You can identify angles as right, acute, obtuse, or straight.

A **ray** is part of a line. It has one endpoint.

An **angle** is formed when two rays meet at the same endpoint.

A **right angle** forms a square corner.

An **acute angle** measures less than a right angle.

An **obtuse angle** measures greater than a right angle.

A **straight angle** forms a line.

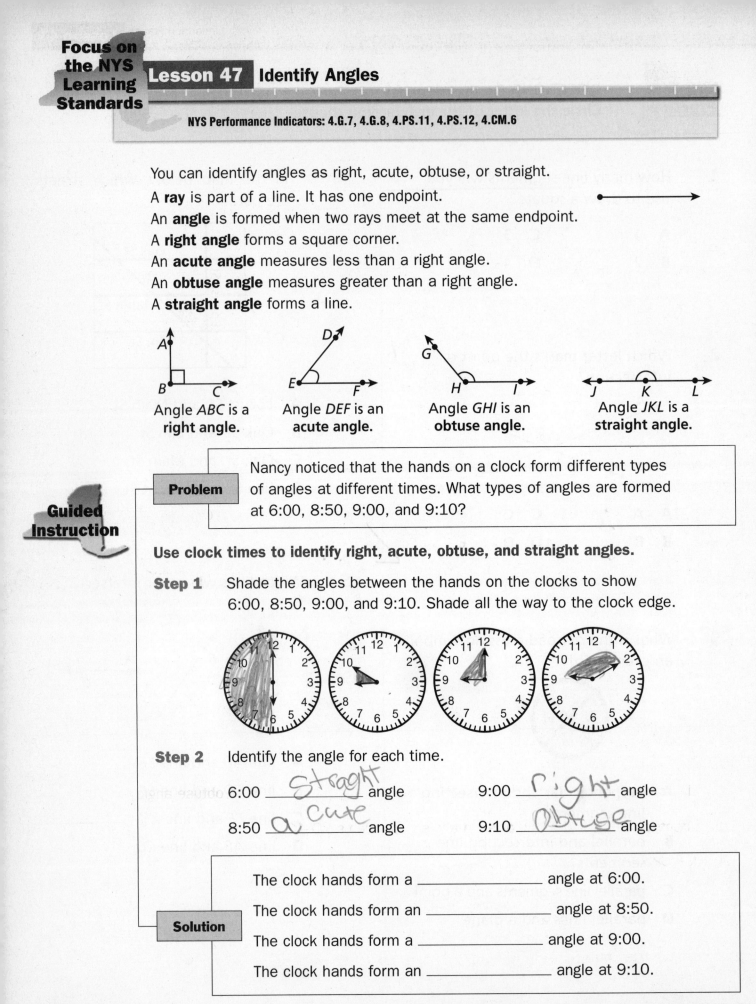

Angle *ABC* is a
right angle.

Angle *DEF* is an
acute angle.

Angle *GHI* is an
obtuse angle.

Angle *JKL* is a
straight angle.

Guided Instruction

Problem

Nancy noticed that the hands on a clock form different types of angles at different times. What types of angles are formed at 6:00, 8:50, 9:00, and 9:10?

Use clock times to identify right, acute, obtuse, and straight angles.

Step 1 Shade the angles between the hands on the clocks to show 6:00, 8:50, 9:00, and 9:10. Shade all the way to the clock edge.

Step 2 Identify the angle for each time.

6:00 _____Straght_____ angle   9:00 _____right_____ angle

8:50 _a__cute_____ angle   9:10 _____Obtuse_____ angle

Solution

The clock hands form a _____ angle at 6:00.

The clock hands form an _____ angle at 8:50.

The clock hands form a _____ angle at 9:00.

The clock hands form an _____ angle at 9:10.

Apply the NYS Learning Standards

Name each angle as *acute*, *right*, *straight*, or *obtuse*.

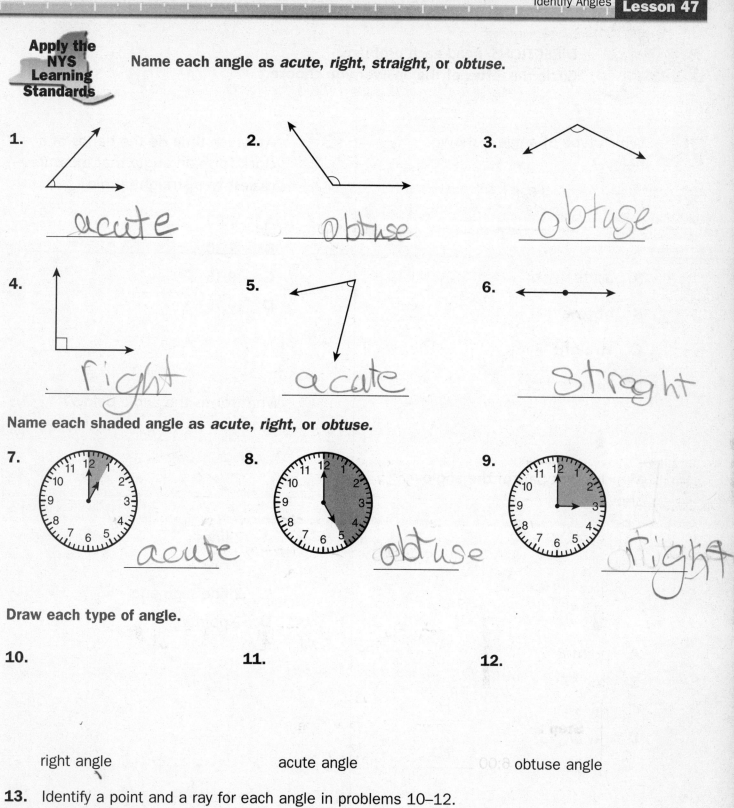

1. *acute*

2. *obtuse*

3. *obtuse*

4. *right*

5. *acute*

6. *straight*

Name each shaded angle as *acute*, *right*, or *obtuse*.

7. *acute*

8. *obtuse*

9. *right*

Draw each type of angle.

10.

11.

12.

right angle

acute angle

obtuse angle

13. Identify a point and a ray for each angle in problems 10–12.

Short-Response Question

Solve the problem.

14. Find objects in your classroom that have right, acute, and obtuse angles. Draw the objects with those angles. Share your drawings with classmates. Ask them to identify the angles.

DIRECTIONS Read each problem.
Circle the letter of the answer you choose.

1 Which type of angle is shown below?

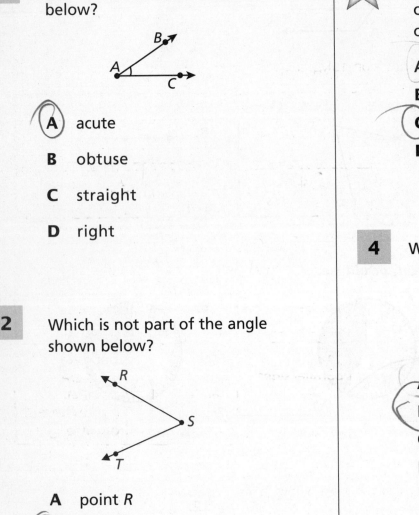

A acute

B obtuse

C straight

D right

2 Which is not part of the angle shown below?

A point *R*

B line *ST*

C ray *ST*

D ray *SR*

3 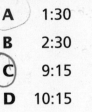 At which time do the hands of a clock form an angle that measures closest to a straight angle?

A 1:30

B 2:30

C 9:15

D 10:15

4 What forms the angle below?

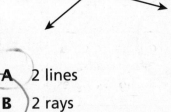

A 2 lines

B 2 rays

C 2 line segments

D 2 points

NYS Performance Indicators: 4.G.1, 4.G.2, 4.PS.16, 4.PS.21, 4.CM.11, 4.R.2

You can describe polygons by the number of angles and sides. A **polygon** is a flat, closed plane shape made up of three or more line segments called **sides**. A polygon with four sides and four angles is called a **quadrilateral**.

The table shows some common polygons. Complete the table.

Triangle	Quadrilateral	Pentagon	Hexagon	Octagon
△	▱	⬠	⬡	⯃
3 sides 3 angles	4 sides 4 angles	5 sides 5 angles	6 sides 6 angles	8 sides 8 angles

Quadrilaterals can be classified by their features.

Rectangle	Square	Trapezoid	Parallelogram	Rhombus
▭	◻	⏢	▱	◇
opposite sides are parallel; 4 right angles	4 equal sides and 4 right angles	1 pair of parallel sides	opposite sides are parallel and have equal lengths	opposite sides are parallel; 4 sides have equal lengths

Guided Instruction

Problem   Vanessa saw the sign below by her school. What is the shape of the sign?

Think about the features of the figure.

- How many sides does the sign have? ___5___

- How many angles does the sign have? ___5___

- Is the sign a quadrilateral? ___no___

- Are opposite sides parallel? ___yes___

- Which type of polygon does the sign look like? ___pentagon___

Solution   What is the shape of Vanessa's sign? ___pentagon___

Apply the NYS Learning Standards

Write the name of the polygon that matches the description.

Hexagon	Trapezoid	Triangle	Square
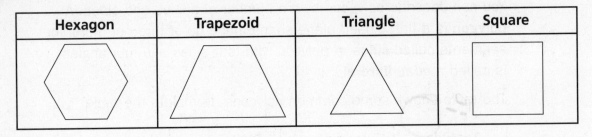			

1. 6 sides
6 angles
Hexagon

2. 4 equal sides
4 right angles
Square

3. 3 sides
3 angles
triangle

Draw an example of each shape. Write how many line segments you drew for each shape.

4. quadrilateral

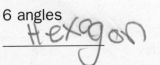

Square

5. triangle

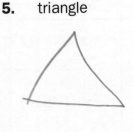

_____

6. octagon

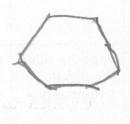

_____

Short-Response Questions

Solve each problem.

7. Suchi is thinking of a shape. It has 6 sides and 6 angles.
What shape is she thinking of?
Hetagon

8. Think of a polygon. Write down a description. Ask a partner to read
your description and name your polygon.

_____

_____

DIRECTIONS Read each problem.
Circle the letter of the answer you choose.

1 How many sides and angles does the stop sign have?

A   4 sides, 4 angles

B   6 sides, 6 angles

C   8 sides, 6 angles

D   8 sides, 8 angles

2 Suppose you wanted to draw a polygon with 6 line segments. Which polygon would you draw?

A   square

B   rectangle

C   hexagon

D   parallelogram

3 Which statement is not true?

A   A triangle has 3 angles.

B   A pentagon has 5 sides.

C   A square has 4 equal sides.

D   An octagon has 6 angles.

4 Which figure is not a polygon?

A

B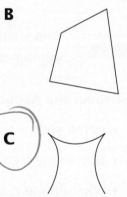

C

D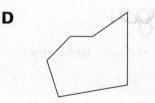

NYS Performance Indicators: 4.G.5, 4.PS.10, 4.PS.12, 4.CM.10, 4.CN.1, 4.R.2

A **solid shape** is a 3-dimensional shape that takes up space. A **face** is a flat surface of a solid shape. An **edge** is a line segment where two faces meet. A **vertex** is the point where three or more edges meet.

edge → ← face

vertex (plural: vertices)

These solid shapes have polygon faces. Complete the table.

Cube	Rectangular Prism	Triangular Prism	Square Pyramid	Triangular Pyramid
6 square faces ____edges 8 vertices	____faces ____edges ____vertices	2 triangular faces 3 rectangular faces ____edges ____vertices	1 square face 4 triangular faces ____edges ____vertices	____triangular faces ____edges ____vertices

Guided Instruction

Problem

Tina wants to build a cube out of cardboard. How many faces will her shape have? How many edges? How many vertices?

Think about the features of the shape.

- Is the shape a solid shape? _____
- How many faces does the shape have? _____
- What shape are the faces? _____
- How many edges does the shape have? _____
- How many vertices does the shape have? _____

Solution

Tina's shape will have _____ faces, _____ edges, and _____ vertices.

These solid shapes have curved surfaces and no edges.

Cylinder

2 circular faces

Cone

1 circular face

Sphere

Copying is illegal.

Measuring Up® to the New York State Learning Standards

Apply the NYS Learning Standards

Use the chart on the previous page to answer each question.

1. Name 2 three-dimensional shapes that have the same number of edges, faces, and vertices. _____

2. Name 2 three-dimensional shapes that have at least one square face.

_____

3. Name 2 three-dimensional shapes that have at least 2 rectangular faces.

_____

Circle the shape that looks like the face of the solid shape.

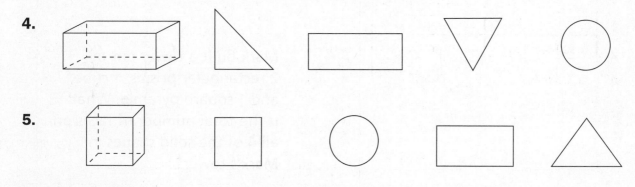

Solve each riddle.

6. I have two circular faces. What am I? _____

7. All six of my faces are the same shape and size. What am I? _____

8. I have 4 triangular faces and 2 more edges than vertices.
What am I? _____

Short-Response Questions

Solve each problem.

9. Diane was making lunch. She took out a box of crackers, a cube of cheese, and a can of soup. Which two items have the same number of vertices, faces, and edges?

_____

10. Larry made this pattern. If he folds it on the dotted lines, which solid shape will he form? Explain how you know.

_____

_____

NYS Test Practice

DIRECTIONS Read each problem.
Circle the letter of the answer you choose.

1 What is the total number of edges on the cone?

A 0

B 1

C 2

D 4

2 Which solid has the least number of vertices?

A triangular prism

B cube

C triangular pyramid

D rectangular prism

3 Which statement is not true?

A A cube has 6 square faces.

B A triangular prism has 6 vertices.

C A cone has 5 edges.

D A cylinder has 2 circular faces.

4 Mark built a tower out of 2 rectangular prisms, 1 cube, and 1 square pyramid. What is the total number of faces on all 4 of the solid shapes in Mark's tower?

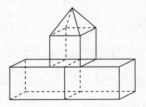

A 23

B 18

C 12

D 5

 Measuring Up® to the New York State Learning Standards

A pattern for a solid shape is called a **net**. You can use a model of a solid shape to make a net of the shape. You can use the problem-solving guide in the back of the book to help you.

Guided Instruction

| Problem | Lenny cut and folded a net to make this model of a cube. What does a net of Lenny's cube look like? | 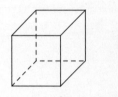 |

Understand the problem.

What do you need to do?

_____

Make a plan.

Use the cube.

Count the number of faces.

Look at the shape of the faces.

Solve the problem.

There are _____ faces on the cube.

Each face is in the shape of a _____.

Draw a net with 6 square faces that will fold up into the model of a cube.

Check your answer.

How many faces does the cube have? _____

How many faces does the net have? _____

What are the shapes of the faces on the cube? _____

What are the shapes of the faces on the net? _____

Use models of solids to help you.
Then name the solid.

Work Space

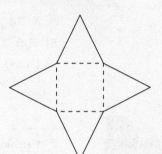

1. Madison drew the net to the right. When she folds it, what solid will it make?

   _____

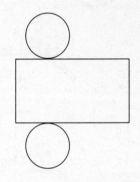

2. Nicholas drew the net to the right. What solid will the net become when it is folded?

   _____

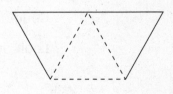

3. Emma has begun making a net for this solid shape. She is missing one face. Complete her net and name the solid shape it will make when it is folded.

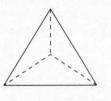

   _____

Short-Response Question

4. Jack wants to make a net for this rectangular prism. Draw what his net could look like. Explain how you drew your net.

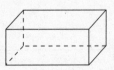

   _____

   _____

   _____

NYS Test Practice

DIRECTIONS Read each problem.
Circle the letter of the answer you choose.

1 Which net will fold up into this model?

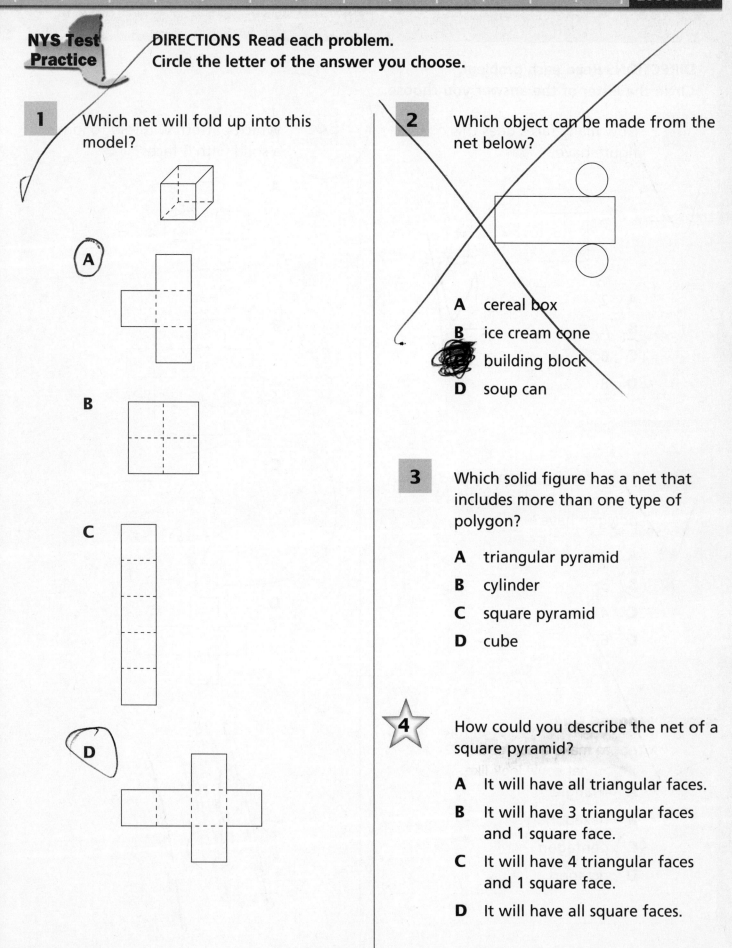

A

B

C

D

2 Which object can be made from the net below?

A cereal box

B ice cream cone

C building block

D soup can

3 Which solid figure has a net that includes more than one type of polygon?

A triangular pyramid

B cylinder

C square pyramid

D cube

4 How could you describe the net of a square pyramid?

A It will have all triangular faces.

B It will have 3 triangular faces and 1 square face.

C It will have 4 triangular faces and 1 square face.

D It will have all square faces.

DIRECTIONS Read each problem.
Circle the letter of the answer you choose.

1 How many faces does this figure have?

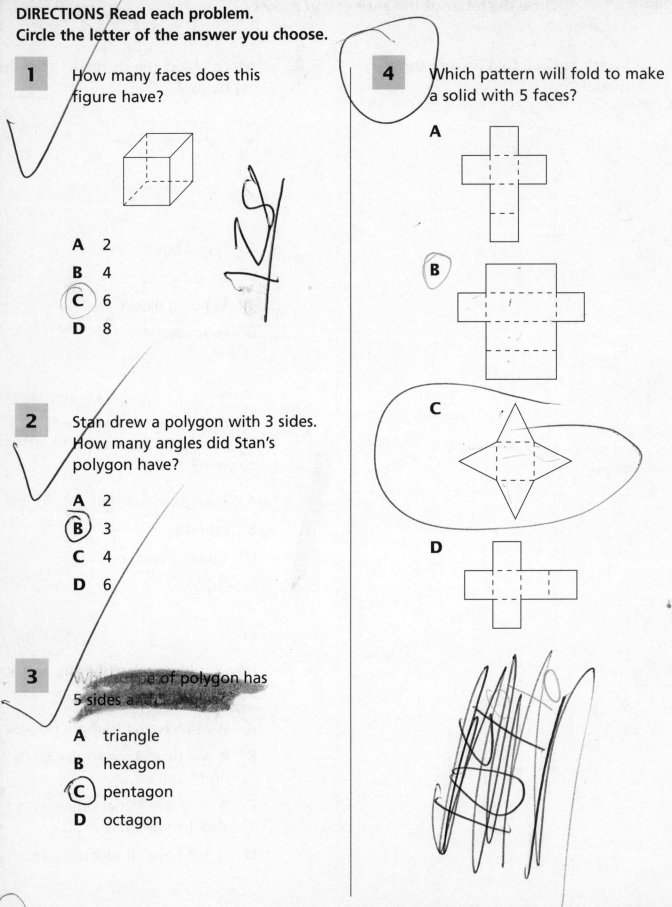

A 2

B 4

C 6

D 8

2 Stan drew a polygon with 3 sides. How many angles did Stan's polygon have?

A 2

B 3

C 4

D 6

3 Which type of polygon has 5 sides and 5 angles?

A triangle

B hexagon

C pentagon

D octagon

4 Which pattern will fold to make a solid with 5 faces?

A

B

C

D

5 Which letter marks the point of intersection?

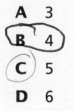

A   *A*

(B)   *B*

C   *C*

D   *D*

6 During which time do the hands of a clock form an acute angle?

A   3:00

B   6:00

C   9:00

(D)   11:00

7 How many line segments will you use to draw a quadrilateral?

A   3

(B)   4

(C)   5

D   6

8 What is the name of the figure below?

(A)   line

B   point

C   ray

D   line segment

9 Which figure or figures below show pairs of lines that appear to be perpendicular?

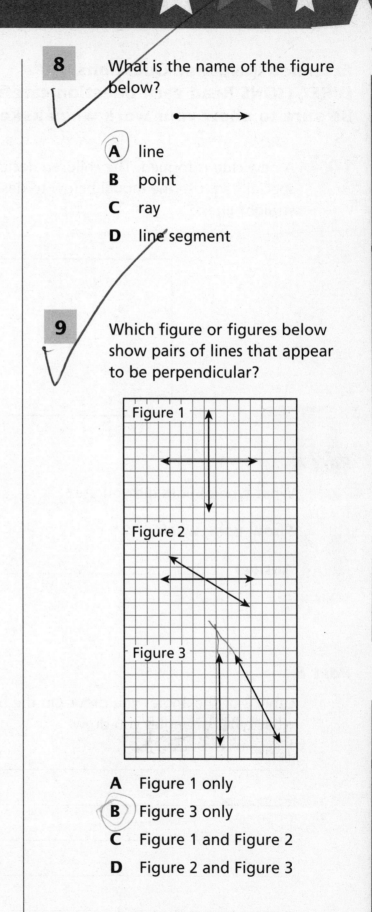

A   Figure 1 only

(B)   Figure 3 only

C   Figure 1 and Figure 2

D   Figure 2 and Figure 3

Extended-Response Questions
DIRECTIONS Read each question carefully before writing your response. Be sure to show your work when asked.

 10 A new club is formed. The children decide their new clubhouse should have a special flag. Use the model below to design a flag for the clubhouse using only straight lines.

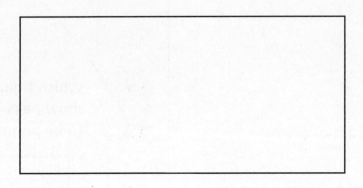

Part A

What type of lines did you use?

Show your work.

Answer _____

Part B

Label 2 of the angles you drew. On the lines below, explain how you knew what types of angles you drew.

_____

_____

_____

_____

11 Angie has a net. She is using the net to identify polygons and to make a solid shape.

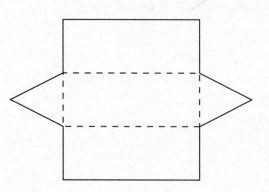

Part A

Name all the polygons that make up the net.

Answer _____

Part B

What three-dimensional shape will the net make? How many edges will the shape have?

Answer _____

On the lines below, explain how you found your answer.

_____

_____

_____

_____

_____

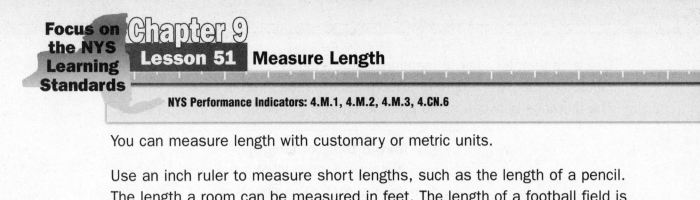

NYS Performance Indicators: 4.M.1, 4.M.2, 4.M.3, 4.CN.6

You can measure length with customary or metric units.

Use an inch ruler to measure short lengths, such as the length of a pencil. The length a room can be measured in feet. The length of a football field is measured in yards. Longer distances, such as the distance between cities, can be measured in miles.

> **Customary Units of Length**
> 12 inches (in.) = 1 foot (ft)
> 3 feet = 1 yard (yd)
> 5,280 feet = 1 mile (mi)

Guided Instruction

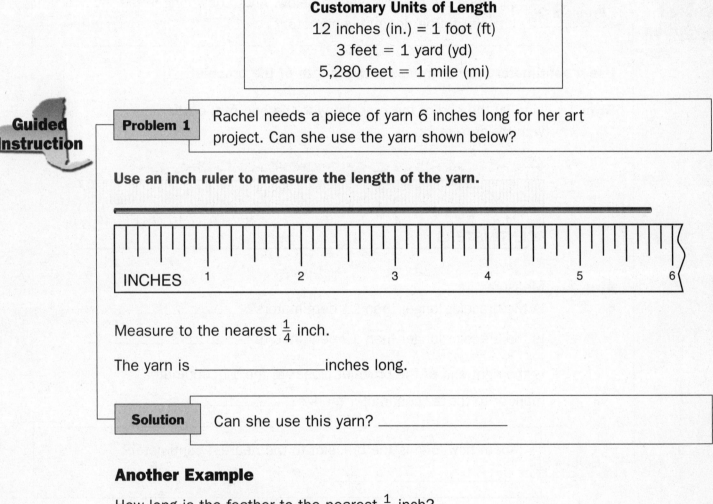

Problem 1 Rachel needs a piece of yarn 6 inches long for her art project. Can she use the yarn shown below?

Use an inch ruler to measure the length of the yarn.

Measure to the nearest $\frac{1}{4}$ inch.

The yarn is _____ inches long.

Solution Can she use this yarn? _____

Another Example

How long is the feather to the nearest $\frac{1}{2}$ inch?

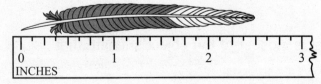

The feather is longer than 2 inches and shorter than 3 inches.

Measured to the nearest $\frac{1}{2}$ inch, the feather is $2\frac{1}{2}$ inches long.

Use a centimeter ruler to measure short lengths, such as the length of a piece of chalk. The length of a room can be measured in meters. The distance between home and the shopping mall can be in kilometers.

> **Metric Units of Length**
> 1 centimeter (cm) = 10 millimeters (mm)
> 1 meter (m) = 100 centimeters
> 1 kilometer (km) = 1,000 meters

Guided Instruction

Problem 2 Jill made the bracelet shown below. About how long is the bracelet to the nearest centimeter?

Use a centimeter ruler to measure the length of the bracelet.

Step 1 Line up the end of the bracelet with the end of the ruler or with the zero mark.

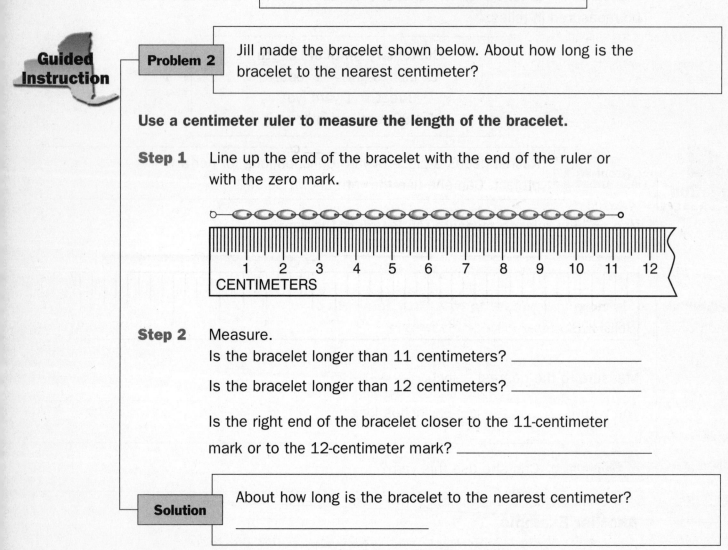

Step 2 Measure.
Is the bracelet longer than 11 centimeters? _____

Is the bracelet longer than 12 centimeters? _____

Is the right end of the bracelet closer to the 11-centimeter mark or to the 12-centimeter mark? _____

Solution About how long is the bracelet to the nearest centimeter?

_____

Another Example

Use the measuring tool that is closest to the object's length that you are measuring.

Use a centimeter ruler to measure the length of a pen.

Use a meterstick to measure the length of a truck.

Apply the NYS Learning Standards

Measure each object's length to the nearest $\frac{1}{4}$ inch.

1. Black

_____ inches

2.

_____ inches

Measure each length to the nearest centimeter.

3. ERASER

_____ centimeters

4.

_____ centimeters

Tell which unit is most appropriate to measure the length of each object. Write *inch*, *foot*, or *yard*.

5. kitchen table

_____

6. soccer field

_____

7. stapler

_____

Tell which tool is more appropriate to measure the length of each object. Write *centimeter ruler* or *meterstick*.

8. sticker

_____

9. bedroom

_____

10. airplane

_____

Short-Response Questions

Solve each problem.

11. Maggie drew a line 1 foot 9 inches long. How many inches is that? _____

12. Measure the length of the classroom. Which tool did you choose and why?

_____

_____

13. Diana wants to measure the length of her puppy's tail. Which metric unit of measure should she use? Explain how you decided which she should use.

_____

_____

NYS Test Practice

DIRECTIONS Read each problem.
Circle the letter of the answer you choose.

1 Use your ruler to help you solve this problem. Which is 3 centimeters long?

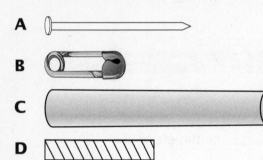

A

B

C

D

2 Corbett, Brett, Sean, and Evan each have a pet snake. Who has the longest snake?

Student	Length of Snake
Corbett	1 foot 8 inches
Brett	1 yard
Sean	13 inches
Evan	2 feet

A Corbett

B Brett

C Sean

D Evan

3 Use your ruler to help you solve this problem. How many inches long is the pencil to the nearest $\frac{1}{4}$ inch?

?

A 3

B $3\frac{1}{2}$

C $3\frac{1}{4}$

D 4

4 Which would most likely be measured in kilometers?

A fingernail

B classroom

C river

D door

You can use metric units to measure mass.

1 kilogram (kg) = 1,000 grams (g)

Guided Instruction

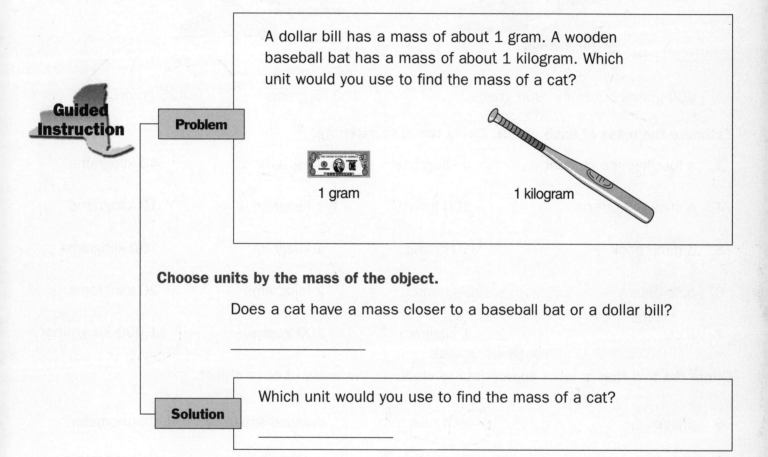

Problem

A dollar bill has a mass of about 1 gram. A wooden baseball bat has a mass of about 1 kilogram. Which unit would you use to find the mass of a cat?

1 gram

1 kilogram

Choose units by the mass of the object.

Does a cat have a mass closer to a baseball bat or a dollar bill?

_____

Solution

Which unit would you use to find the mass of a cat?

_____

Another Example

You can use a balance scale to find the mass of an object.
The mass of the can is 300 grams.

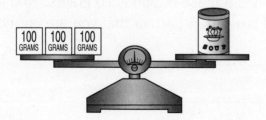

Apply the NYS Learning Standards

Circle the better estimate for the mass of each object.

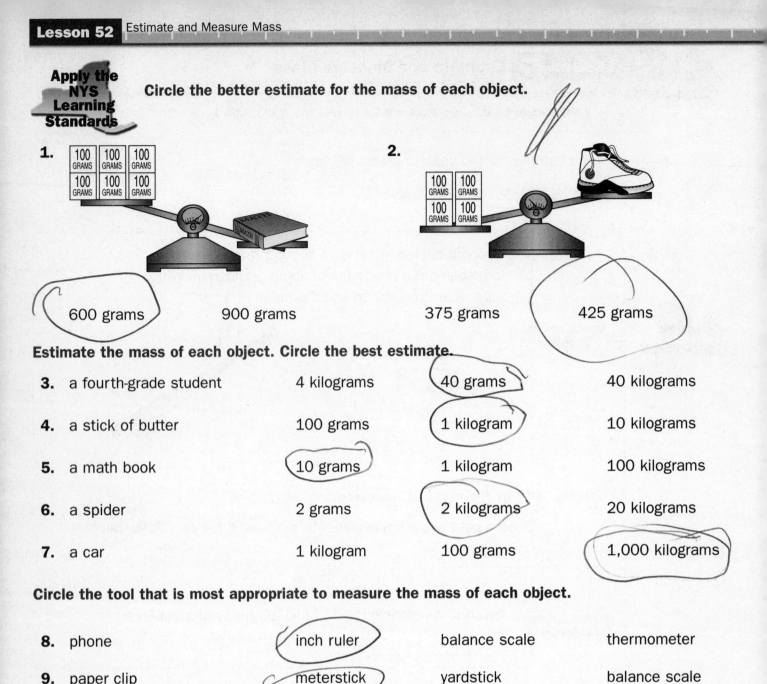

1.

100 GRAMS 100 GRAMS 100 GRAMS
100 GRAMS 100 GRAMS 100 GRAMS

(600 grams)   900 grams

2.

100 GRAMS 100 GRAMS
100 GRAMS 100 GRAMS

375 grams   (425 grams)

Estimate the mass of each object. Circle the best estimate.

3.	a fourth-grade student	4 kilograms	(40 grams)	40 kilograms
4.	a stick of butter	100 grams	(1 kilogram)	10 kilograms
5.	a math book	(10 grams)	1 kilogram	100 kilograms
6.	a spider	2 grams	(2 kilograms)	20 kilograms
7.	a car	1 kilogram	100 grams	(1,000 kilograms)

Circle the tool that is most appropriate to measure the mass of each object.

8.	phone	(inch ruler)	balance scale	thermometer
9.	paper clip	(meterstick)	yardstick	balance scale

Short-Response Question

Solve the problem.

10. Look around the room. Find an object that has a mass of about 10 grams. Find a partner and share your answers. Explain how you could prove to a partner that you are correct.

_____

_____

_____

_____

 Measuring Up® to the New York State Learning Standards

NYS Test Practice

DIRECTIONS Read each problem.
Circle the letter of the answer you choose.

1 Anita uses a balance scale to compare the mass of a loaf of bread and the mass of a container of milk.

Anita knows the bread has a mass of 500 grams. Which of the following statements could be true?

A The bread has more mass than the milk.

B The milk has a mass of 500 grams.

C The milk has more mass than 500 grams.

D The milk has a mass that is less than 500 grams.

2 Which unit of measure is **best** for measuring the mass of an envelope?

A gram

B kilogram

C centimeter

D meter

3 Samantha wants to find the mass of her hairbrush. Which tool should she use?

A balance scale

B yardstick

C inch ruler

D centimeter ruler

4 Look at the picture below.

Which of the following is the **best estimate** of the weight of 2 books?

A 5 grams

B 50 grams

C 500 grams

D 1 kilogram

How much a container can hold is called **capacity**.

You can measure capacity in metric units.

1 liter (L) = 1,000 milliliters (mL)

1 milliliter   1 liter

Guided Instruction

| Problem 1 | Which metric unit would you use to measure the capacity of a mug? |

Choose units by the size of the object.

A mug holds a small amount of water. Use a small metric unit.

Use _____.

| Solution | Which metric unit would you use to measure the capacity of a mug? _____ |

| Problem 2 | Which metric unit would you use to measure the capacity of a fish tank? |

Use liters to measure capacity of larger objects.

A fish tank holds a large amount of water.

Use a large metric unit. Use _____.

| Solution | Which metric unit would you use to measure the capacity of a fish tank? _____ |

Apply the NYS Learning Standards

Tell which unit is more appropriate to measure the capacity of each object. Write *liter* or *milliliter*.

1. juice glass

_____

2. sink

_____

3. pool

_____

4. soup can (empty)

_____

5. medicine cup

_____

6. lake

_____

Estimate the capacity of each object. Circle the better estimate.

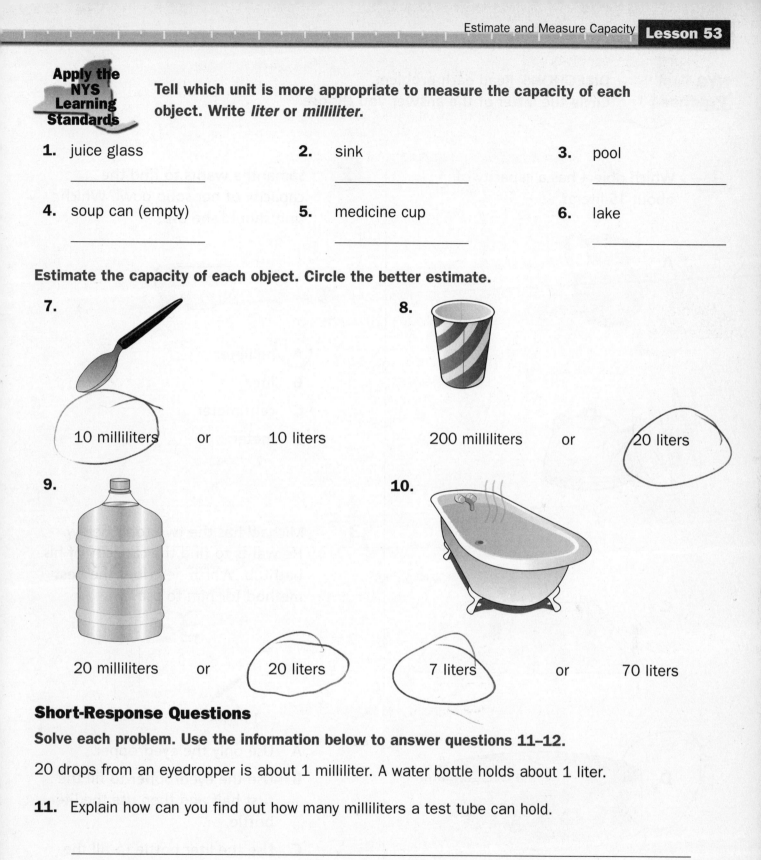

7.

10 milliliters   or   10 liters

8.

200 milliliters   or   20 liters

9.

20 milliliters   or   20 liters

10.

7 liters   or   70 liters

Short-Response Questions

Solve each problem. Use the information below to answer questions 11–12.

20 drops from an eyedropper is about 1 milliliter. A water bottle holds about 1 liter.

11. Explain how can you find out how many milliliters a test tube can hold.

_____

_____

12. Explain how can you find out how many liters a pitcher can hold.

_____

_____

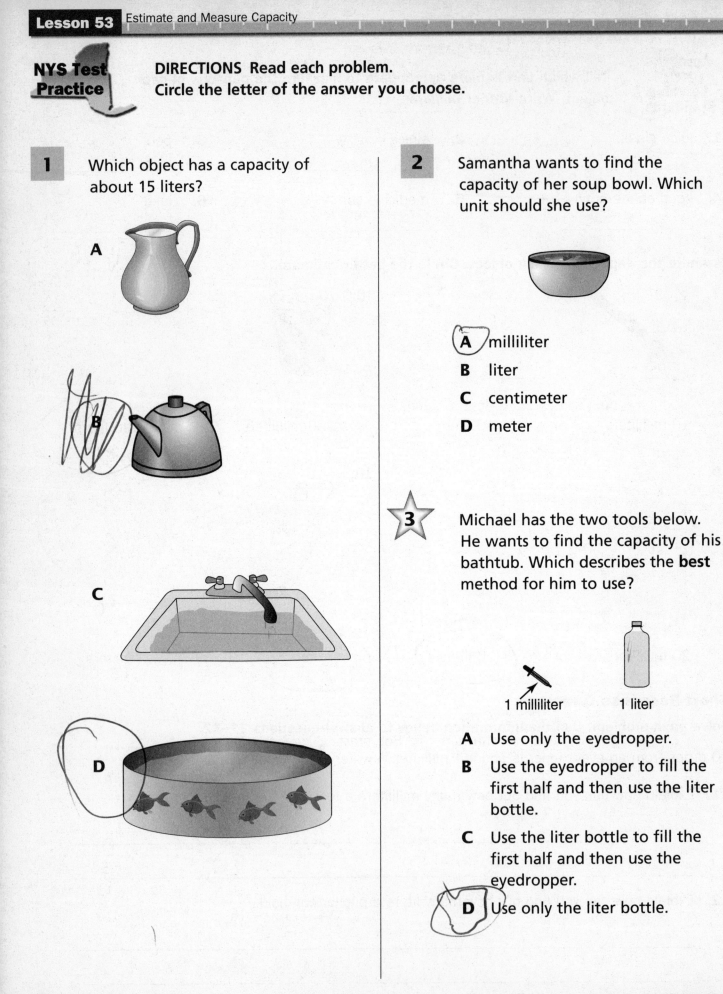

NYS Test Practice

DIRECTIONS Read each problem.
Circle the letter of the answer you choose.

1 Which object has a capacity of about 15 liters?

A

B

C

D

2 Samantha wants to find the capacity of her soup bowl. Which unit should she use?

A milliliter

B liter

C centimeter

D meter

3 Michael has the two tools below. He wants to find the capacity of his bathtub. Which describes the **best** method for him to use?

1 milliliter   1 liter

A Use only the eyedropper.

B Use the eyedropper to fill the first half and then use the liter bottle.

C Use the liter bottle to fill the first half and then use the eyedropper.

D Use only the liter bottle.

Measuring Up® to the New York State Learning Standards

Lesson 54 Find Elapsed Time

NYS Performance Indicators: 4.M.9, 4.M.10, 4.PS.5, 4.CN.1, 4.CN.6

Use the information below to help you work with units of time.

1 minute = 60 seconds   1 day = 24 hours

1 hour = 60 minutes   1 week = 7 days

Elapsed time is the amount of time that has passed.

Guided Instruction

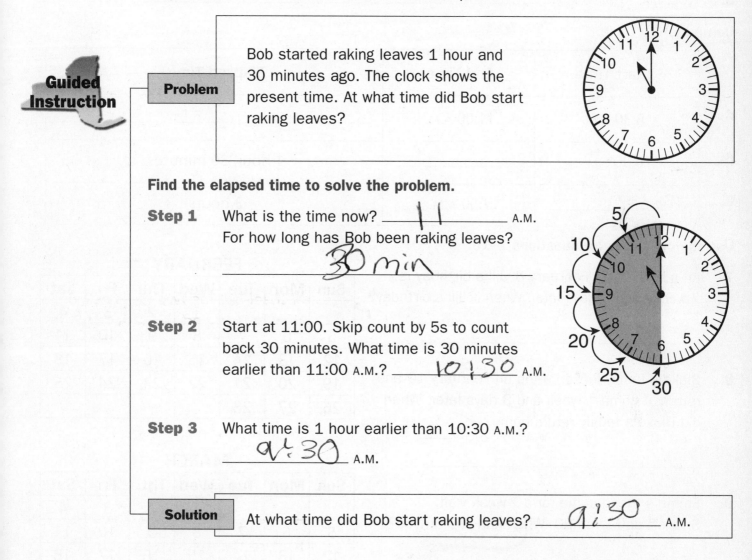

Problem

Bob started raking leaves 1 hour and 30 minutes ago. The clock shows the present time. At what time did Bob start raking leaves?

Find the elapsed time to solve the problem.

Step 1   What is the time now? _____11_____ A.M.
For how long has Bob been raking leaves?
_____30 min_____

Step 2   Start at 11:00. Skip count by 5s to count back 30 minutes. What time is 30 minutes earlier than 11:00 A.M.? ___10:30___ A.M.

Step 3   What time is 1 hour earlier than 10:30 A.M.?
_____9:30_____ A.M.

Solution   At what time did Bob start raking leaves? ___9:30___ A.M.

Another Example

Joan's next flight is one week and two days after April 10.

On which day and date is Joan's next flight?

_____Fri 19_____

APRIL

Sun	Mon	Tue	Wed	Thu	Fri	Sat
	1	2	3	4	5	6
7	8	9	10	11	12	13
14	15	16	17	18	19	20
21	22	23	24	25	26	27
28	29	30				

Apply the NYS Learning Standards

Find each elapsed time. Use hours and minutes.

1. 3:00 P.M. to 3:30 P.M. _____

2. 3:30 A.M. to 5:00 A.M. _____

3. 7:00 P.M. to 9:00 P.M. _____

Complete the table.

	Start Time	End Time	Elapsed Time
4.	8:30 A.M.	11:00 A.M.	
5.	6:30 P.M.		1 hour, 30 minutes
6.		7:00 A.M.	3 hours

Use the calendars for questions 7–10.

7. Ari's birthday is February 8. Jill's birthday is 2 weeks and 3 days later. When is Jill's birthday?

_____

8. Blake's family left on a trip on February 19 and returned home 1 week and 3 days later. When did Blake's family return home?

_____

9. Emma's friend came for a 2-week visit. She left on March 20. When had she arrived?

_____

FEBRUARY

Sun	Mon	Tue	Wed	Thu	Fri	Sat
			1	2	3	4
5	6	7	8	9	10	11
12	13	14	15	16	17	18
19	20	21	22	23	24	25
26	27	28				

MARCH

Sun	Mon	Tue	Wed	Thu	Fri	Sat
			1	2	3	4
5	6	7	8	9	10	11
12	13	14	15	16	17	18
19	20	21	22	23	24	25
26	27	28	29	30	31	

Short-Response Question
Solve the problem.

10. The Science Exhibit started on February 23 and ended on March 5. The History Exhibit started on March 6 and ended on March 18. Which exhibit was longer? Explain.

_____

NYS Test Practice

DIRECTIONS Read each problem.
Circle the letter of the answer you choose.

1 The clock shows when Christina started to read a book.

If Christina read for 1 hour 30 minutes, at what time did she stop reading?

A   4:40 P.M.

B   4:30 P.M.

C   5:00 P.M.

D   5:30 P.M.

2 Annie left her house at 8:30 A.M. She arrived at school at 9:00 A.M. How long did it take Annie to get to school?

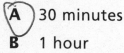

A   30 minutes

B   1 hour

C   1 hour, 30 minutes

D   2 hours

3 Kayla is leaving on a trip to Miami on August 25. She is returning home on September 6. How long will Kayla be away from home?

AUGUST

Sun	Mon	Tue	Wed	Thu	Fri	Sat
	1	2	3	4	5	6
7	8	9	10	11	12	13
14	15	16	17	18	19	20
21	22	23	24	25	26	27
28	29	30	31			

SEPTEMBER

Sun	Mon	Tue	Wed	Thu	Fri	Sat
				1	2	3
4	5	6	7	8	9	10
11	12	13	14	15	16	17
18	19	20	21	22	23	24
25	26	27	28	29	30	

A   2 weeks

B   1 week and 5 days

C   1 week and 1 day

D   1 week

4 Barry is spending two weeks away at summer camp. How many days will he be away from home?

A   7

B   10

C   12

D   14

You can use what you have learned about measurement to estimate and find perimeter. **Perimeter** is the distance around a figure.

Guided Instruction

Problem

Paul wants to build a fence around his garden. The garden is a rectangle 10 feet long and 8 feet wide. How many feet of fencing will Paul need?

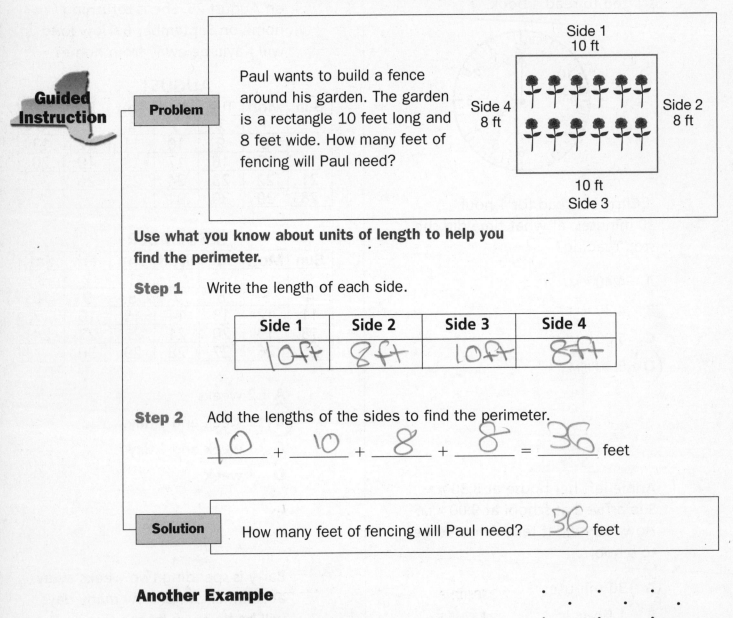

Use what you know about units of length to help you find the perimeter.

Step 1 Write the length of each side.

Side 1	Side 2	Side 3	Side 4
10 ft	8 ft	10 ft	8 ft

Step 2 Add the lengths of the sides to find the perimeter.

10 + 10 + 8 + 8 = 36 feet

Solution How many feet of fencing will Paul need? 36 feet

Another Example

Find the perimeter of the polygon.
Start at the top and go to the right. Write how many units long each side is. Add to find the perimeter.

1 + 2 + 1 + 1 + 2 + 1 = 8

The perimeter of the polygon is _____ units.

Find the perimeter of each figure.

1.

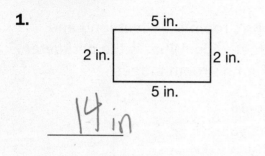

5 in.

2 in.   2 in.

5 in.

14 in

2.

3 m

3 m   3 m

3 m

12m

3.

10 cm   15 cm

18 cm

43 cm

4.

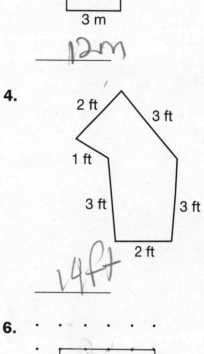

2 ft

3 ft

1 ft

3 ft   3 ft

2 ft

14ft

5.

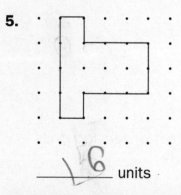

_____ 16 units

6.

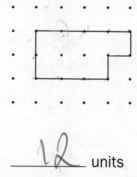

_____ 12 units

Short-Response Question

Solve the problem.

7. Katrina's room was rectangular in shape. The perimeter measured 48 feet. The width of her room was 11 feet. What was the length of her room? Explain how you found your answer.

13 feet

_____

_____

_____

_____

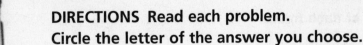

DIRECTIONS Read each problem.
Circle the letter of the answer you choose.

1 A drawing of Adam's garden is shown below.

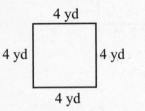

4 yd

4 yd   4 yd

4 yd

What is the perimeter, in yards, of the garden?

A 4

B 8

C 12

D 16

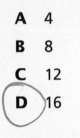

2 Julia's patio was 3 yards by 3 yards. Then she doubled the size of the patio. Which describes how the perimeter of the patio changed?

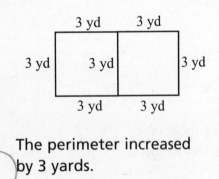

3 yd   3 yd

3 yd   3 yd   3 yd

3 yd   3 yd

A The perimeter increased by 3 yards.

B The perimeter increased by 6 yards.

C The perimeter doubled.

D The perimeter tripled.

3 John's room is 11 feet long and 8 feet wide. What is the perimeter of John's room in feet?

A 18

B 29

C 30

D 38

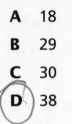

4 Melody wants to build a fence around her yard shown below.

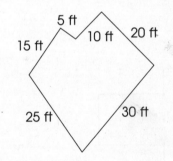

5 ft

15 ft   10 ft   20 ft

25 ft   30 ft

How many feet of fencing does Melody need?

A 50

B 100

C 105

D 110

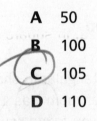

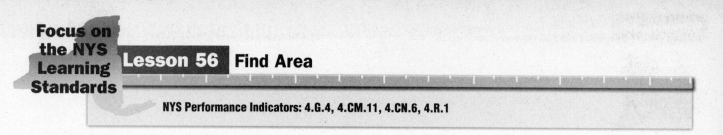
Area is a measure of how many square units it takes to cover a two-dimensional shape exactly.

Guided Instruction

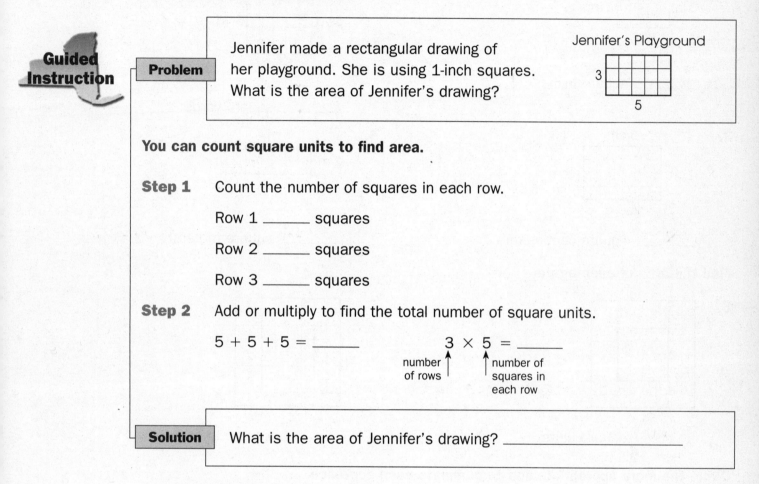

Problem Jennifer made a rectangular drawing of her playground. She is using 1-inch squares. What is the area of Jennifer's drawing?

Jennifer's Playground

3
5

You can count square units to find area.

Step 1 Count the number of squares in each row.

Row 1 _____ squares

Row 2 _____ squares

Row 3 _____ squares

Step 2 Add or multiply to find the total number of square units.

$5 + 5 + 5 =$ _____ $3 \times 5 =$ _____

number of rows   number of squares in each row

Solution What is the area of Jennifer's drawing? _____

Another Example

This is a diagram of Mr. Simon's kitchen. What is the area, in square meters, of the kitchen?

Count the number of squares in each row.
$6 + 6 + 6 + 6 = 24$ $4 \times 6 = 24$

The key says that each square equals 1 square meter.

The area of the kitchen is 24 square meters.

Kitchen

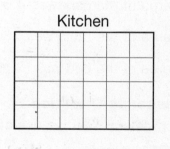

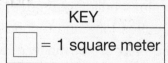

KEY
☐ = 1 square meter

Count the squares to find the area of each figure.

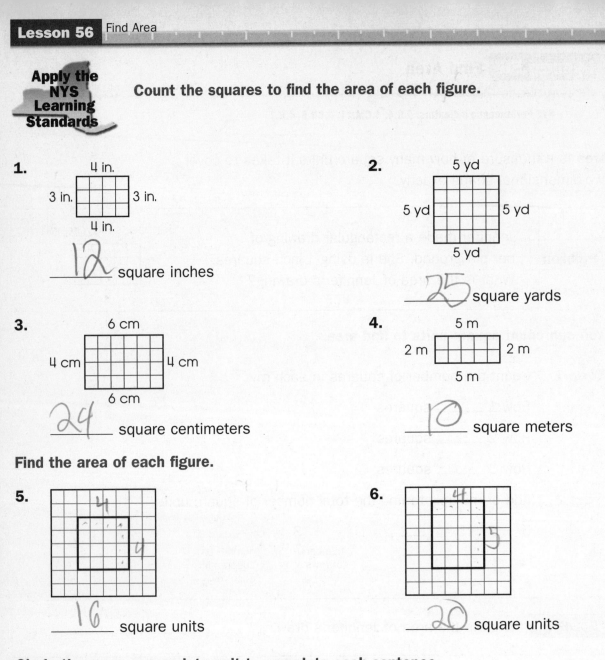

1.

4 in.

3 in. 3 in.

4 in.

_12_ square inches

2.

5 yd

5 yd 5 yd

5 yd

_25_ square yards

3.

6 cm

4 cm 4 cm

6 cm

_24_ square centimeters

4.

5 m

2 m 2 m

5 m

_10_ square meters

Find the area of each figure.

5.

4

4

_16_ square units

6.

4

5

_20_ square units

Circle the more appropriate unit to complete each sentence.

7. The area of the park was 4,000 (square feet or square inches).

8. The area of the table was 160 (square centimeters or square meters).

9. The area of the bed was (3 square meters or 3 square centimeters).

Short-Response Question

Solve the problem. You can use cubes to help.

10. Georgia is building a model of a garden she is planning. Her model
is 6 cubes long and 6 cubes wide. She is using 1-inch cubes. What
is the area of her model? Explain.

36 square inches

         Measuring Up® to the New York State Learning Standards

 **NYS Test Practice**

DIRECTIONS Read each problem.
Circle the letter of the answer you choose.

1 What is the area of this figure?

A 11 square units
B 22 square units
C 28 square units
D 30 square units

 2 The area of the rectangle below is 12 square meters.

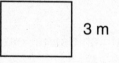 3 m

What is the length of the rectangle in meters?

A 3
B 4
C 6
D 8

3 Which is the most appropriate unit to measure the area of a playground?

A square inches
B square feet
C square yards
D square miles

4 Dean was making a design using white and gray tiles. What is the area of the gray part of the design?

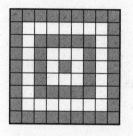

□ = one square inch

A 49 inches
B 49 square inches
C 36 inches
D 36 square inches

5 The shaded part of the figure shows the part of Cora's garden that is planted with corn. What is the area of the garden that is not planted with corn?

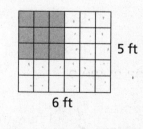 5 ft

6 ft

A 9 square feet
B 21 square feet
C 22 square feet
D 30 square feet

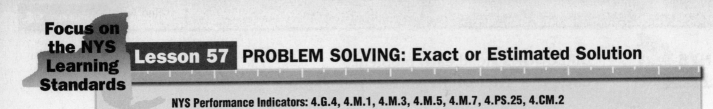
Decide whether to estimate or to find an exact solution in order
to solve a problem. You can use the problem-solving guide in the back of the book
to help you.

Guided Instruction

Problem	Jack measured the length of his desk and the length of his bed. His desk is 3 feet 2 inches long. His bed is 5 feet 11 inches long. About how much longer is Jack's bed than his desk?

nderstand the problem.

What do you need to find?

_____

_____

ake a plan.

Decide if you need an exact solution or if you can use an estimate.

The word *about* in the question is a clue that an estimate can be used.

Solve the problem.

Estimate. Round each length to the nearest foot. Then subtract.

Bed: 5 feet 11 inches ⟶ ☐

Desk: 3 feet 2 inches ⟶ − ☐
_____
☐

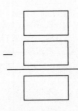

About how much longer is Jack's bed than his desk?

about _____ feet

Check your answer.

If you add the estimated length of the desk and the difference you found,
the result should be the estimated length of the bed.

3 feet + 3 feet = 6 feet

Apply the NYS Learning Standards

Decide if an exact answer or an estimate should be used. Then solve each problem.

Work Space

1. Amanda is making banners. The red banner is 26 inches long. The blue banner is 1 yard long, and the green banner is 2 feet long. About how many feet long are the 3 banners put end to end?

_____

2. Dylan has a basket of apples that has a mass of 720 grams. He adds another 206 grams of apples. What is the total mass of his apples?

_____

3. It is 52 kilometers to the hotel from Amanda's house. It is 39 kilometers to the ocean from the hotel. It is 58 kilometers to the amusement park from the ocean. Amanda drove from her house to the hotel, from the hotel to the ocean, and then from the ocean to the amusement park. About how many kilometers did she drive?

_____

Short-Response Question

4. John has a square copper sheet. The sheet has an area of 64 square centimeters. Does he have enough copper to make the bookmark at the right? Explain how you solved the problem.

_____

_____

_____

John's Bookmark

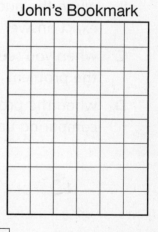

☐ = 1 square centimeter

NYS Test Practice

DIRECTIONS Read each problem.
Circle the letter of the answer you choose.

1 Which statement is not true?

A You could use a ruler to find out how much longer one pencil is than another.

B You could use a measuring cup to find out about how much more juice was in one bottle than another.

C You could use a balance scale to find out how much longer one piece of string is than another.

D You could use a tape measure to find out about how much taller one fourth grader is than another.

2 How do you know when an **estimated** solution is needed for a problem?

A when you see the word *about* in the problem

B when the question asks for an exact answer

C when you see the word *solve* in the problem

D when the problem involves comparing units

3 Which expression would be **best** to use to find about how much heavier Fido is than Fifi?

Fifi
5 kilograms 25 grams

Fido
8 kilograms 7 grams

A 10 kilograms − 8 kilograms

B 8 kilograms − 5 kilograms

C 9 kilograms − 7 kilograms

D 9 kilograms − 6 kilograms

4 A fish tank holds 40 liters of water. How many liters of water are in the fish tank if it is exactly half full?

A about 60

B about 40

C about 30

D exactly 20

 Measuring Up® to the New York State Learning Standards

Building Stamina

DIRECTIONS Read each problem.
Circle the letter of the answer you choose.

1 SuLin is 48 inches tall. How many feet is that?

A 2

B 4

C 8

D 12

2 Use your ruler to help you solve this problem. How many inches long is the nail below to the nearest $\frac{1}{2}$ inch?

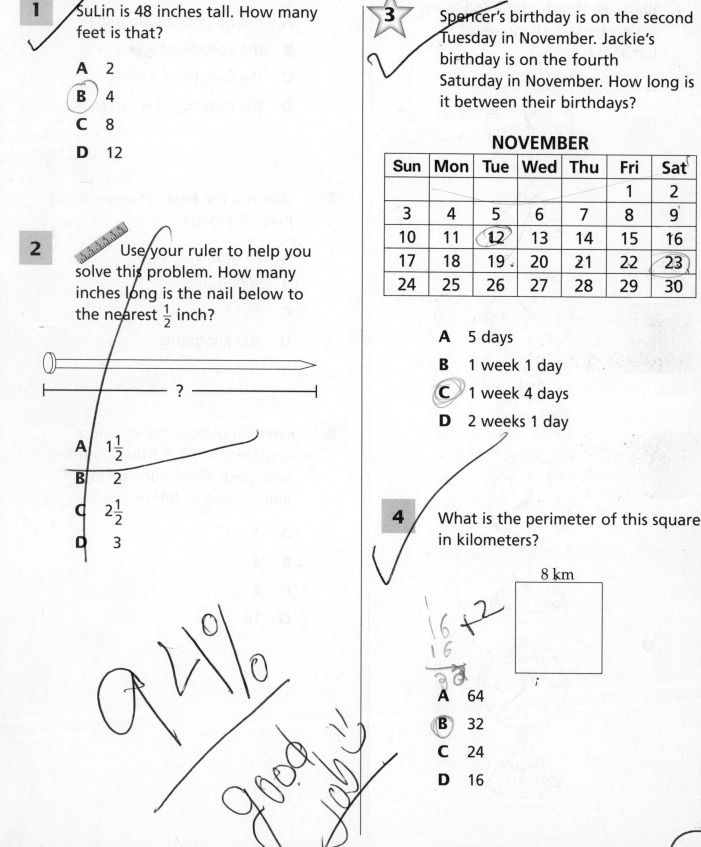

?

A $1\frac{1}{2}$

B 2

C $2\frac{1}{2}$

D 3

3 Spencer's birthday is on the second Tuesday in November. Jackie's birthday is on the fourth Saturday in November. How long is it between their birthdays?

NOVEMBER

Sun	Mon	Tue	Wed	Thu	Fri	Sat
					1	2
3	4	5	6	7	8	9
10	11	12	13	14	15	16
17	18	19	20	21	22	23
24	25	26	27	28	29	30

A 5 days

B 1 week 1 day

C 1 week 4 days

D 2 weeks 1 day

4 What is the perimeter of this square in kilometers?

8 km

A 64

B 32

C 24

D 16

5 Sally's mother sent her to the grocery store to buy 3 kilograms of bananas. Which of the following scales shows 3 kilograms of bananas?

A

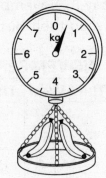

B

C

D

6 Which of the following would you measure using a yardstick?

A the height of a flagpole

B the volume of a bathtub

C the weight of a book

D the capacity of a fish tank

7 Which is the **best estimate** of the mass of a dog?

A 25 grams

B 200 grams

C 25 kilograms

D 200 kilograms

8 Emma is using a 100-milliliter container to fill a 1-liter thermos with juice. How many times will Emma need to fill the cup?

A 2

B 4

C 8

D 10

Extended-Response Questions
DIRECTIONS Read each question carefully before writing your response. Be sure to show your work when asked.

 9 Kevin drew the diagram below of his dog's exercise yard.

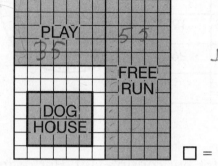

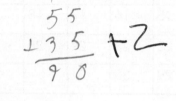

☐ = 1 square foot

Part A

What is the total area of the "play" and "free run" part of the dog pen?

Show your work.

Answer ___90___

Part B

On the lines below, explain how you found your answer.

_____

_____

_____

_____

_____

_____

10 Ms. Ellery's birthday is on May 16. Her cousin will be visiting soon.

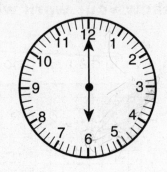

MAY						
Sunday	Monday	Tuesday	Wednesday	Thursday	Friday	Saturday
		1	2	3	4	5
6	7	8	9	10	11	12
13	14	15	16	17	18	19
20	21	22	23	24	25	26
27	28	29	30	31		

Part A

Ms. Ellery will practice making a recipe for her cousin's visit. Her recipe will take a total of 1 hour 30 minutes to make. If she wants to serve it at 6:00, what time should she begin cooking?

Show your work.

Answer _____

4:30

Part B

Ms. Ellery's cousin is coming to visit 1 week and 4 days after her birthday. What day is her cousin coming to visit?

Answer _Sunday_

On the lines below, explain how you found your answer.

_____

_____

_____

_____

_____

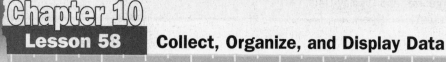
A pictograph can make information easier to see. A **pictograph** is a graph that uses pictures or symbols and a key to show **data**. The **key** tells what each symbol stands for.

Guided Instruction

Problem The table shows the results of a survey of some fourth-grade students for their favorite type of music. How does the pictograph show the students' favorite type of music?

FAVORITE TYPE OF MUSIC

Type of Music	Number of Votes
Rock	20
Country	8
Rap	12
Jazz	2

TITLE: _____

Type of Music	Number of Votes
Rock	

KEY	
◯ = _____ votes	

Step 1 Write a title and the name of each type of music.

Step 2 Choose a number to use for the key. Since most of the data are multiples of 4, let each ◯ mean 4 votes. Complete the key.

Step 3 Draw the correct number of ◯ for each type of music to complete the graph. Use a half picture ◖ to show half the number given in the key.

Solution How does the pictograph show the students' favorite type of music?

_____

_____

Apply the NYS Learning Standards

Use the data in the table to make a pictograph.

1. Write a title for the pictograph.

2. Write the types of books in the left column of the pictograph.

3. Use the key. In the pictograph, draw the symbols for each type of book.

4. How can you check if the number of symbols in your graph is correct?

_____

_____

_____

5. Suppose each symbol means 5 votes. How many symbols would you draw for space books?

_____

FAVORITE TYPE OF BOOK

Type of Book	Number of Votes
Nature	10
History	15
Story	30
Space	40

TITLE: _____

Type of Book	Number of Votes

KEY
☐ = 10 votes

Short-Response Questions
Solve the problems.

6. Joe is making a pictograph showing the number of residents in each of 3 towns. Each town has over 1,000 residents. Which key would be best for him to use on his graph? ☐ = 5, ☐ = 10, or ☐ = 100. Explain your choice.

_____

_____

7. Susie created a pictograph showing how many cans each student recycled. She used the symbol ◯ to stand for 50 cans. Explain how Susie can show 125 cans on the pictograph.

_____

_____

 Measuring Up® to the New York State Learning Standards

NYS Test Practice

**DIRECTIONS Read each problem.
Circle the letter of the answer you choose.**

1 Anna surveyed some students about their favorite type of pizza. The table shows the survey results.

FAVORITE TYPE OF PIZZA

Type of Pizza	Number of Votes
Plain	25
Pepperoni	30
Vegetable	10
Sausage	15

What question might Anna have asked?

A How many slices of pizza do you eat?

B How often do you eat pizza?

C What type of pizza do you like the best?

D What type of pizza do you like the least?

2 Mark is making a pictograph to show how many books students read. He uses the symbol ☐ to stand for 10 books. Which can he use to show 35 books on the graph?

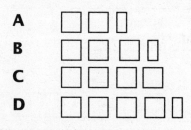

3 The pictograph below shows the number of hours Robin spends reading over four weeks.

ROBIN'S READING

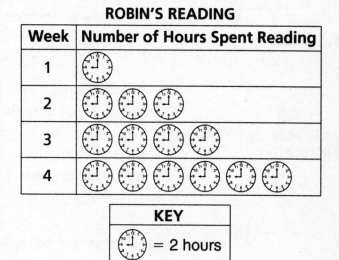

KEY
🕐 = 2 hours

If Robin reads for 10 hours in Week 5, how many clocks will she need to draw for that week on the pictograph?

A 20

B 10

C 5

D 4

4 Each symbol on a pictograph stands for 5 hours. How many hours are shown by three and one half symbols?

A $10\frac{1}{2}$

B 15

C $17\frac{1}{2}$

D 20

You can show data by using **bar graphs.** A bar graph has bars of different lengths to show the data. On the side or bottom of the graph there is a **scale** that tells you what numbers the bars stand for. The difference between two numbers on a scale is an interval.

Guided Instruction

Problem

The table shows how students get to school. Use the table to complete the bar graph. Which way do most students use to get to school?

Ways to Get to School	Number of Students
Van	150
Carpool	225
Bike	100
Bus	325
Walk	50

The bars on the graph can be vertical or horizontal.

Step 1 Write a title. Label the side and bottom of the graph.

The side label for this graph is about the number of

_____.

The bottom label for this graph is about

_____.

Step 2 The interval on the scale is

_____.

Complete the scale.
What number will come after 100?

_____.

The bar for carpool ends halfway between _____ and _____.

Step 3 Use the table to complete the bar graph.

The bar for Bus should go between _____ and _____.

The bar for Walk goes up to _____.

Solution Which way do most students use to get to school? _____

Apply the NYS Learning Standards

Use the table to complete the bar graph.

Doug collected information from the students in his school about their favorite type of music. The results for the school are recorded in the table below.

FAVORITE MUSIC

Type of Music	Number of Students
Rock	180
Rap	160
Country	100
Classical	40
Jazz	70

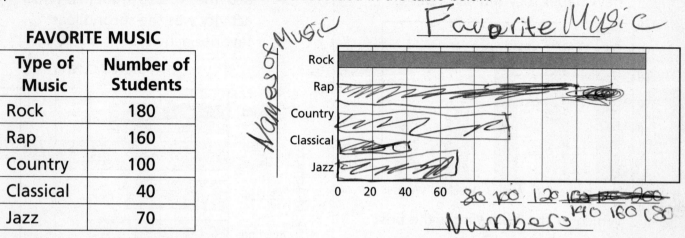

1. Write a title for the graph.
2. Label the side and bottom of the graph.
3. What is the interval on the scale? _____
4. Complete the scale of the graph.
5. Use the information from the table to complete the horizontal bar graph.

Use the graph you made to answer questions 6–11.

6. Where does the bar for jazz end? _beetween the 60 and 80_
7. Which type of music is least popular? _Classical 645_
8. How many students are represented in the graph? _645_
9. How many more students like rock than like classical music? _60_

Short-Response Questions

Solve each problem.

10. If another 500 students were surveyed about their favorite music, do you think classical would become the favorite? Explain.

_____

_____

11. What prediction can you make based on the data shown above for another class of students being surveyed about their favorite music? Explain.

_____

_____

_____

_____

NYS Test Practice

DIRECTIONS Read each problem.
Circle the letter of the answer you choose.

1 The graph shows the amount of newspaper recycled each week.

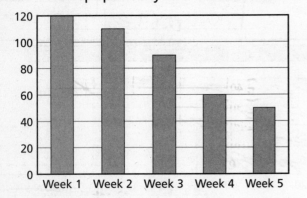

Which of the following is the **best** title for the graph?

A Newspapers Read

B Number of Newspapers Sold

C Pounds of Newspaper Recycled

D Newspaper Advertising

2 Look at the graph below. In all, how many miles were run by all of the members?

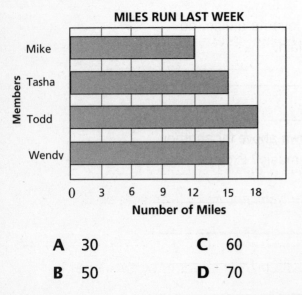

MILES RUN LAST WEEK

A 30   **C** 60

B 50   **D** 70

3 The graph below shows the favorite activities of 225 students. Which activity was the second least favorite activity?

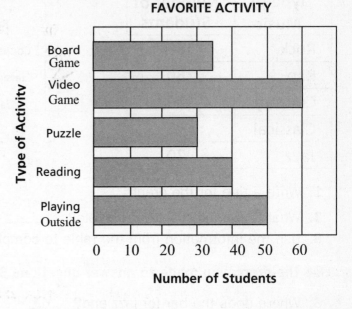

FAVORITE ACTIVITY

A Movie

B Board Game

C Puzzle

D Reading

Measuring Up® to the New York State Learning Standards

Lesson 60 Interpret Line Graphs

NYS Performance Indicators: 4.S.4, 4.S.5, 4.S.6

A **line graph** is a graph that uses a line to show how data change over a period of time. You can use the data on a line graph to answer questions.

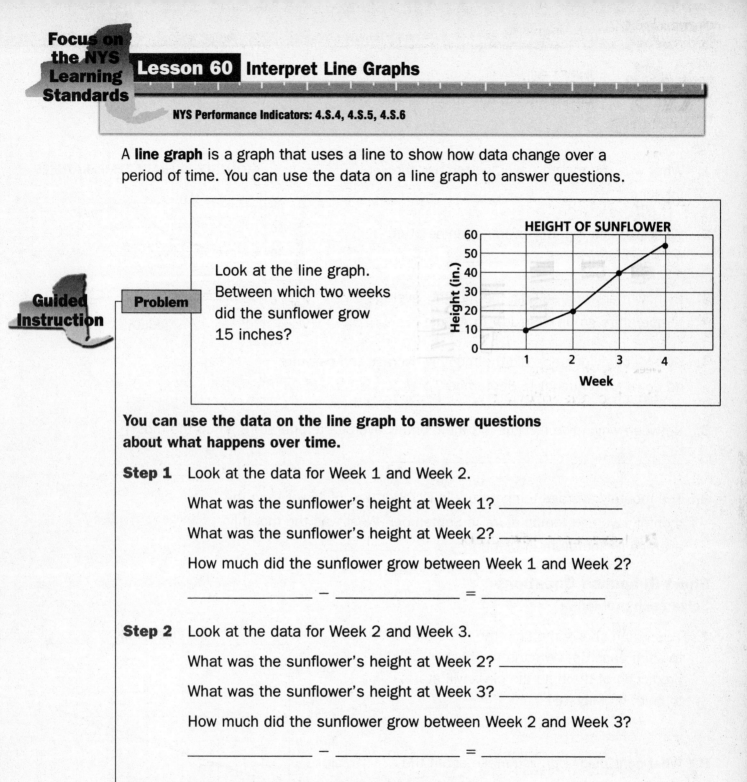

Guided Instruction

Problem

Look at the line graph. Between which two weeks did the sunflower grow 15 inches?

You can use the data on the line graph to answer questions about what happens over time.

Step 1 Look at the data for Week 1 and Week 2.

What was the sunflower's height at Week 1? _____

What was the sunflower's height at Week 2? _____

How much did the sunflower grow between Week 1 and Week 2?

_____ – _____ = _____

Step 2 Look at the data for Week 2 and Week 3.

What was the sunflower's height at Week 2? _____

What was the sunflower's height at Week 3? _____

How much did the sunflower grow between Week 2 and Week 3?

_____ – _____ = _____

Step 3 Look at the data for Week 3 and Week 4.

What was the sunflower's height at Week 3? _____

What was the sunflower's height at Week 4? _____

How much did the sunflower grow between Week 3 and Week 4?

_____ – _____ = _____

Solution

Between which two weeks did the sunflower grow 15 inches?

_____

Apply the NYS Learning Standards

Use the line graph for problems 1–6.

1. What was the monthly average temperature for June? _____

2. What was the monthly average temperature for September? _____

3. By how many degrees did the monthly average temperature go up from July to August? _____

4. By how many degrees did the monthly average temperature go down from August to September? _____

5. Between which two months did the monthly average temperature go up the most?

_____

6. The monthly average temperature in October was 5° lower than the monthly average temperature in September. What was the monthly average temperature in October? _____

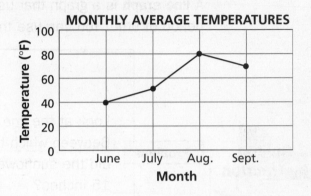

MONTHLY AVERAGE TEMPERATURES

Short-Response Questions

Solve each problem.

7. This graph shows the time the birds start to chirp each day. What is the best prediction of the time the birds will start to chirp on May 16?

_____

8. What conclusion can you make about the time the birds start to chirp in May?

_____

_____

_____

TIME BIRDS CHIRP

 Measuring Up® to the New York State Learning Standards

NYS Test Practice

**DIRECTIONS Read each problem.
Circle the letter of the answer you choose.**

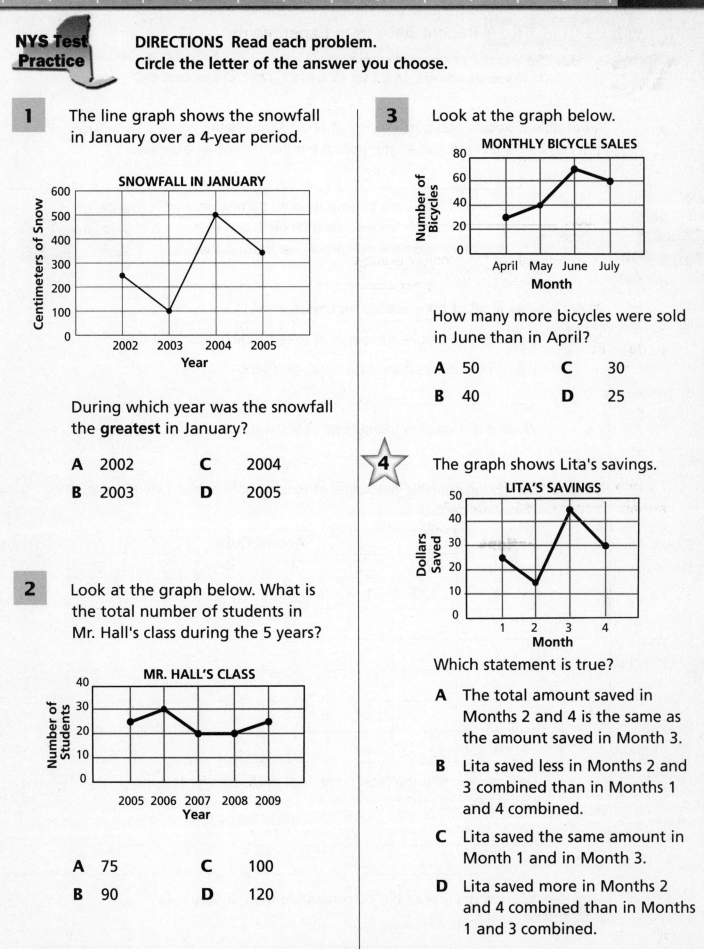

1 The line graph shows the snowfall in January over a 4-year period.

SNOWFALL IN JANUARY

During which year was the snowfall the **greatest** in January?

A 2002   C 2004

B 2003   D 2005

2 Look at the graph below. What is the total number of students in Mr. Hall's class during the 5 years?

MR. HALL'S CLASS

A 75   C 100

B 90   D 120

3 Look at the graph below.

MONTHLY BICYCLE SALES

How many more bicycles were sold in June than in April?

A 50   C 30

B 40   D 25

4 The graph shows Lita's savings.

LITA'S SAVINGS

Which statement is true?

A The total amount saved in Months 2 and 4 is the same as the amount saved in Month 3.

B Lita saved less in Months 2 and 3 combined than in Months 1 and 4 combined.

C Lita saved the same amount in Month 1 and in Month 3.

D Lita saved more in Months 2 and 4 combined than in Months 1 and 3 combined.

A **possible outcome** is a possible result of an experiment.

You can use a table to find all the possible outcomes of an experiment.

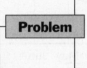
Guided Instruction

Problem

Brad and Marti are playing a board game. They use two number cubes, each labeled 1 to 6. How many possible outcomes are there if they toss both cubes?

Make a table of all of the possible outcomes.

Step 1 List all the possible outcomes of tossing each cube one time.

Which numbers can the first cube land on?

_____

Which numbers can the second cube land on?

_____

Step 2 List all the possible outcomes of tossing both cubes together one time. Complete the table.

First Cube	Second Cube					
	1	2	3	4	5	6
1	1, 1	1, 2	1, 3	1, 4		
2						
3						
4						
5						
6						

How can you find the total number of outcomes for tossing two cubes one time?

_____

Solution

How many possible outcomes are there if they toss both cubes? _____

List all possible outcomes for each experiment. You may use a diagram or chart to help you.

1. Two spinners are spun.

red ⟨ 1 _____
     2 _____

blue ⟨ 1 _____
      2 _____

2. Two quarters are tossed at once.

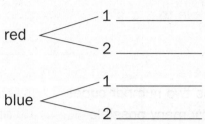

Quarter 1	Quarter 2
_____	_____
_____	_____
_____	_____
_____	_____

3. The spinner is spun once.

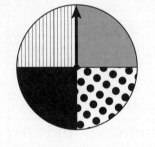

_____

_____

4. A letter card is picked.

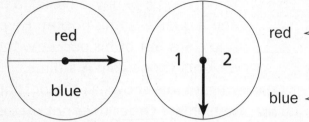

_____

_____

5. The spinner is spun once.

_____

_____

Short-Response Question

Solve the problem.

6. Suppose you want to take two crayons from the crayon box without looking. The order of the colors does not matter. What are the possible outcomes?

_____

_____

NYS Test Practice

DIRECTIONS Read each problem.
Circle the letter of the answer you choose.

1 Look at the spinners below.

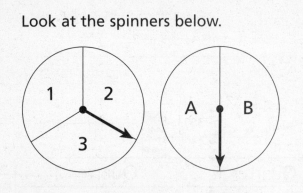

Which list shows all the possible outcomes if you spin a number and then a letter?

A 1A, 2A, 3A

B 1A, 2A, 3B

C 1A, 2A, 3A, 1B, 2B, 3B

D 1, 2, 3, A, B

2 If you toss a pair of number cubes each labeled 1 to 6 and find the sum of the numbers you toss, which outcome is not possible?

A 2

B 8

C 12

D 20

3 Tommy has a penny, a nickel, a dime, and a quarter in his pocket. He pulls two coins out of his pocket without looking. If one coin is a dime, which table shows all the possible outcomes? Order does not matter.

A

penny	dime
nickel	quarter
dime	quarter

B

penny	nickel
nickel	dime
dime	quarter

C

penny	dime
nickel	dime
quarter	dime

D

penny	penny
nickel	nickel
dime	dime

You can use a graph to identify a trend. A trend is a pattern of change in an upward or downward direction. You can use the problem-solving guide in the back of the book to help you.

Guided Instruction

| Problem |

Ronnie made a bar graph to show the number of museum visitors from November to February. What trend can you identify on Ronnie's graph?

MUSEUM VISITORS

Number of Visitors (y-axis: 0, 50, 100, 150, 200, 250, 300)

Nov. ≈ 230, Dec. ≈ 200, Jan. = 100, Feb. ≈ 75

Month (x-axis: Nov., Dec., Jan., Feb.)

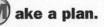**nderstand the problem.**

What do you need to do?

_____

M ake a plan.

Use the graph. See where the data increases, decreases, or stays the same.

S olve the problem.

List the data.

November: _____ visitors   December: _____ visitors

January: _____ visitors   February: _____ visitors

Identify the trend.

Does the data show the number of visitors staying the same from month to month? _____

Does the data show an increase in the number of visitors from month to month? _____

Does the data show a decrease in the number of visitors from month to month? _____

The trend is that the number of museum visitors _____ from month to month.

C heck your answer.

Look at the graph. Does it start at a larger number of visitors and go down to a smaller number of visitors? _____

Use the data on each graph to determine the trend.

1. LaToya made a graph of the DVDs sold by the Town and Country store. What trend do you see?

_____

_____

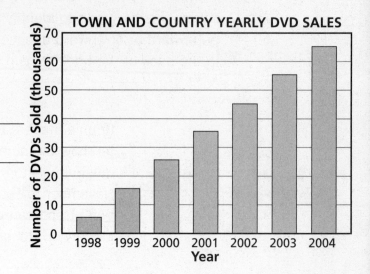

TOWN AND COUNTRY YEARLY DVD SALES

2. Every day Emma records how many minutes it takes her to complete Level 6 of her video game. She puts the data on a line graph. What trend do you see in her line graph?

_____

_____

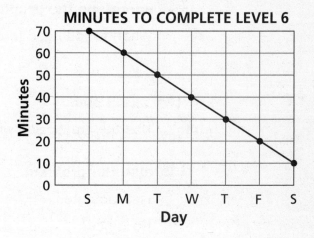

MINUTES TO COMPLETE LEVEL 6

Short-Response Question

Solve the problem.

3. Ryan made a line graph of the average monthly temperature for the months February through July. What trend do you see in his graph? Explain your answer.

_____

_____

_____

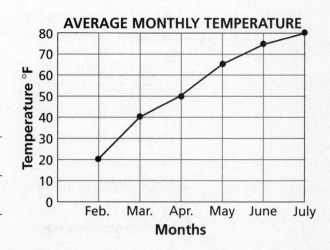

AVERAGE MONTHLY TEMPERATURE

NYS Test Practice

DIRECTIONS Read each problem.
Circle the letter of the answer you choose.

1 Jack made the line graph below to show the temperature each hour starting at 7:00 A.M. for his science class.

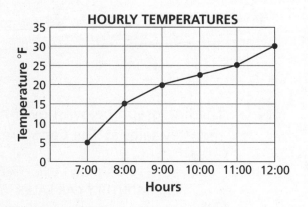

HOURLY TEMPERATURES

What trend can you see?

A The temperature decreased between 7:00 and 12:00.

B The temperature decreased between 7:00 and 10:00 and then increased.

C The temperature increased between 7:00 and 12:00.

D The temperature increased between 7:00 and 10:00 and then decreased.

2 If the trend shown in the line graph below continues, what will the membership be in 2010?

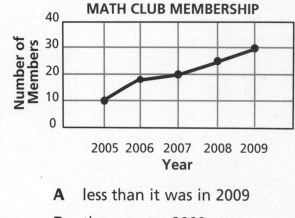

MATH CLUB MEMBERSHIP

A less than it was in 2009

B the same as 2009

C more than it was in 2009

D less than it was in 2005

3 Based on the trend shown in the bar graph below, predict how many videos will be rented in August.

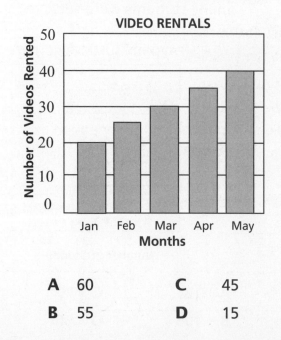

VIDEO RENTALS

A	60	C	45
B	55	D	15

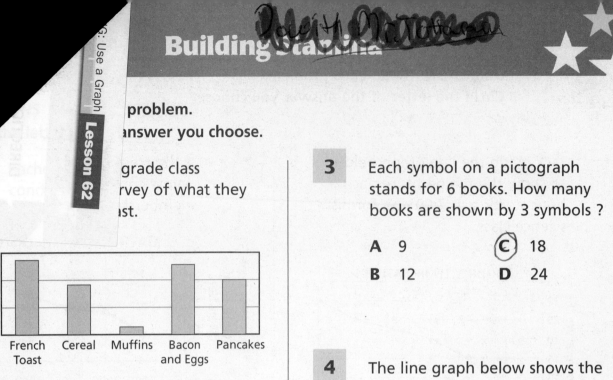

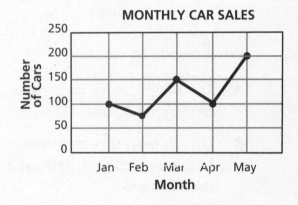

G: Use a Graph

Lesson 62

...problem.

...answer you choose.

...grade class ...rvey of what they ...ast.

Which of the following is the **best** title for the graph?

A   Favorite Breakfast Place

B   Favorite Pizza Place

C   Favorite Breakfast Food

D   Favorite Lunch Food

2   Look at the bar graph below. How many students were surveyed?

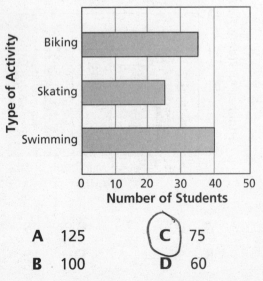

FAVORITE SUMMER ACTIVITY

A   125   **C**   75

B   100   **D**   60

3   Each symbol on a pictograph stands for 6 books. How many books are shown by 3 symbols ?

A   9   **C**   18

B   12   D   24

4   The line graph below shows the monthly sales at The Car Store.

MONTHLY CAR SALES

During which two months did the car sales increase the most?

A   January to February

B   February to March

C   March to April

D   April to May

5 Mr. Marino owns a pizza shop. What is the **best** thing he can do to help him order the toppings he will need?

A order his favorite topping

B count how many tables are in his shop

C take a survey of favorite toppings

D make a list of how many types of plates he has

6 Carlos has a yellow counter, a red counter, a green counter, and a white counter in a bag. He pulls two counters out of the bag without looking. If one counter is white, which table shows the possible outcomes?

A

white counter	red counter
white counter	green counter
white counter	white counter

B

white counter	red counter
white counter	yellow counter
white counter	blue counter

C

red counter	white counter
white counter	yellow counter
white counter	white counter

D

white counter	yellow counter
white counter	red counter
white counter	green counter

7 The line graph shows the number of centimeters of rain over a 5-day period.

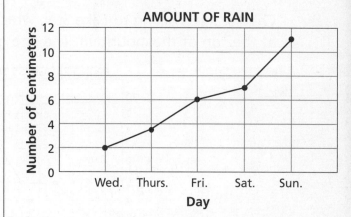

If the trend shown in the line graph continues, how much rain will there be on Monday?

A less than on Thursday

B less than on Friday

C the same as on Sunday

D more than on Sunday

Extended-Response Questions
DIRECTIONS Read each question carefully before writing your response. Be sure to show your work when asked.

8 Chad started biking to Lake Star, which is 10 miles from the campsite at the top of the mountain. The line graph shows Chad's progress so far.

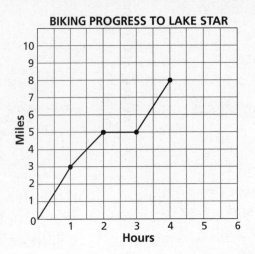

BIKING PROGRESS TO LAKE STAR

Part A

How many miles did Chad bike between hours 1-2 and hours 3-4 combined?

Show your work.

Answer _____ miles

Part B

On the lines below, tell how many miles Chad biked between hours 2 and 3 and explain why the line graph is flat.

_____

_____

_____

_____

_____

 Measuring Up® to the New York State Learning Standards

9 Honnia has the two spinners shown below.

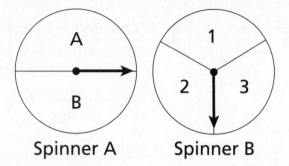

Spinner A   Spinner B

Part A

What are all of the possible outcomes if Spinners A and B are spun at the same time?

Answer _____

Part B

How many possible outcomes would there be if the letter "C" were added to spinner A?

Show your work.

Answer _____

On the lines below, explain how you found your answer.

_____

_____

_____

_____

_____

DIRECTIONS Read each problem.
Circle the letter of the answer you choose.

1 Which is the **best estimate** for the capacity of a pen cap?

   A 1 liter

   B 1 milliliter

   C 10 liters

   D 100 milliliters

2 1.24 + 0.86 =

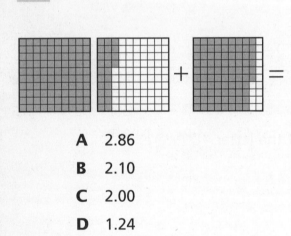

   A 2.86

   B 2.10

   C 2.00

   D 1.24

3 Tom is making a rectangular design with links that are 5 inches long. His design is 6 links long by 3 links wide. What is the perimeter of Tom's design in inches?

   A 18

   B 90

   C 120

   D 150

4 The models below are shaded to show 3 fractions.

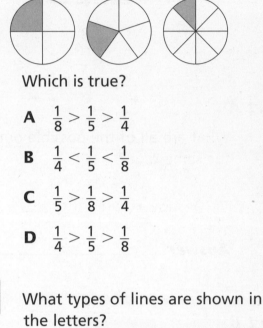

Which is true?

   A $\frac{1}{8} > \frac{1}{5} > \frac{1}{4}$

   B $\frac{1}{4} < \frac{1}{5} < \frac{1}{8}$

   C $\frac{1}{5} > \frac{1}{8} > \frac{1}{4}$

   D $\frac{1}{4} > \frac{1}{5} > \frac{1}{8}$

5 What types of lines are shown in the letters?

MATH

   A perpendicular

   B parallel

   C both perpendicular and parallel

   D neither perpendicular or parallel

6 Lena has $\frac{7}{8}$ of the markers on her desk. $\frac{2}{8}$ of them fall on the floor. What fraction of the markers is still on Lena's desk?

   A $\frac{7}{10}$ **C** $\frac{5}{8}$

   B $\frac{8}{8}$ **D** $\frac{4}{8}$

7 What fraction is **best** represented by the point *B* on this number line?

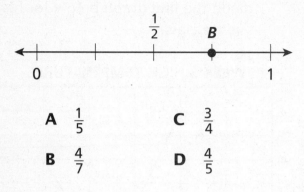

A $\frac{1}{5}$ **C** $\frac{3}{4}$

B $\frac{4}{7}$ **D** $\frac{4}{5}$

8 Which shows the correct order of the fractions from least to greatest?

A $\frac{3}{4}, \frac{2}{4}, \frac{1}{4}$

B $\frac{3}{4}, \frac{2}{4}, \frac{1}{4}$

C $\frac{1}{4}, \frac{2}{4}, \frac{3}{4}$

D $\frac{1}{4}, \frac{3}{4}, \frac{2}{4}$

9 A grid has 100 squares. Rosa shaded in $\frac{50}{100}$ of the squares. Which statement is not true?

A Rosa shaded 0.5 of the grid.

B Rosa shaded 0.05 of the grid.

C Rosa shaded $\frac{1}{2}$ of the grid.

D Rosa shaded 50 of the squares on the grid.

10 Which decimal and fraction is shown by the shaded part of this model?

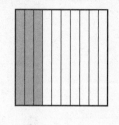

A 0.7, $\frac{7}{10}$

B 0.5, $\frac{1}{2}$

C 0.3, $\frac{3}{10}$

D 0.03, $\frac{3}{10}$

11 How many line segments would you need to draw a quadrilateral?

A 8   **C** 5

B 6   **D** 4

12 A new three-person couch was delivered to the Cohen family yesterday. Which of the following is the **best estimate** of the mass of the couch?

A 60 grams

B 600 grams

C 6 kilograms

D 60 kilograms

13 How many edges does the figure have?

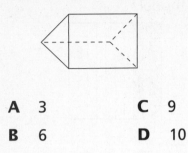

A 3   C 9

B 6   D 10

14 What 2 polygons are the faces of the shape?

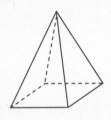

A   square and triangles

B   pentagons and rectangles

C   rectangles and squares

D   rectangles and triangles

15 Ricky shaded $\frac{1}{5}$ of a grid blue and $\frac{1}{5}$ red. How much of the grid did Ricky shade?

A $\frac{0}{5}$ C $\frac{1}{4}$

B $\frac{2}{10}$ D $\frac{2}{5}$

16 Max recorded the high temperature of the day for 5 days. Then he made the line graph below for his science class.

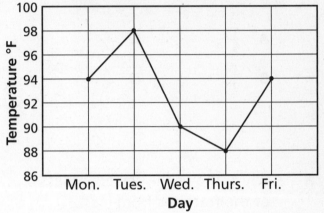

Which day had the highest temperature?

A   Monday

B   Tuesday

C   Thursday

D   Friday

17 Each symbol on a pictograph stands for 8 people. How many people are shown by 5 symbols?

A   40

B   30

C   15

D   13

18 Look at the angle below. Which of the following statements is true?

A The angle is an acute angle.

B The angle is a right angle.

C The angle is a straight angle.

D The angle is an obtuse angle.

19 A shape has 6 sides. What type of polygon is it?

A quadrilateral

B pentagon

C hexagon

D octagon

20 Jake found the capacity of his bathtub. Which unit did Jake most likely use?

A liters

B milliliters

C pounds

D grams

21 What is the area of Derek's garden?

Derek's Garden

☐ = 1 square yard

A 10 yards

B 10 square yards

C 24 yards

D 24 square yards

22 Which unit of measure is **best** for measuring the amount of water in a fish tank?

A meter

B gram

C liter

D milliliter

 23 If a ladybug took 2 minutes to walk 6 inches, how long would it take the same ladybug to walk 2 feet?

A 8 minutes

B 12 minutes

C 24 minutes

D 1 hour

Short-Response Questions
DIRECTIONS Read each question carefully before writing your response. Be sure to show your work when asked.

24 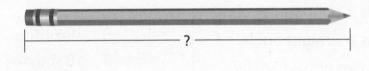 Use your inch ruler to help you solve this problem.

How many inches long is the pencil to the nearest $\frac{1}{2}$ inch?

?

_____ inches

25 Meaghan is leaving for vacation on May 4. She will be coming home 1 week and 3 days later. What day will she be returning home?

_____

MAY						
Sunday	Monday	Tuesday	Wednesday	Thursday	Friday	Saturday
		1	2	3	4	5
6	7	8	9	10	11	12
13	14	15	16	17	18	19
20	21	22	23	24	25	26
27	28	29	30	31		

26 Ashley drew the shape to the right by connecting points.

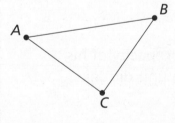

Part A

Name the shape she drew. _____

Part B

How many points did Ashley connect to draw her shape?

_____ points

27 Josh wants to put an outline of
string around the outside of his
house. How long a piece of string
will he need?

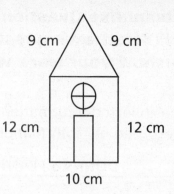

9 cm   9 cm

12 cm   12 cm

10 cm

_____ centimeters

28 Look at the data below.

Color	Votes
red	16
blue	18
yellow	12

FAVORITE COLOR

Color	Votes
red	
blue	
yellow	

KEY
Each ◯ = 4

Part A

Complete the pictograph using the data from the table.

Part B

Which color received 4 **fewer** votes than red?

Show your work.

_____

29 How many edges does the shape below have?

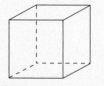

_____ edges

Extended-Response Questions
DIRECTIONS Read each question carefully before writing your response. Be sure to show your work when asked.

30 Donna collected information on the growth of her plant over 13 weeks. She recorded her information on the two graphs shown below.

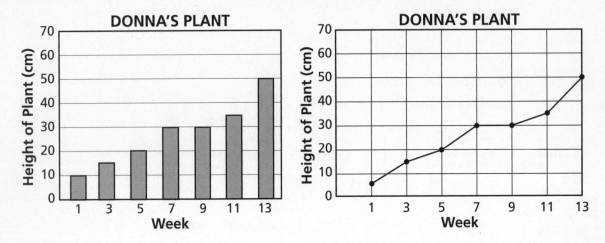

Part A

About how tall do you think Donna's plant will be in Week 14?

Answer _____

Part B

On the lines below, explain which graph would be **best** to use to find the height of the plant at Week 2 and why.

_____

_____

_____

_____

_____

31 Dylan and Anna each had identical large candy bars. Dylan broke his into 8 equal pieces and Anna broke hers into 12 equal pieces. They each ate one fourth of a candy bar.

Dylan

Anna

Part A

How many pieces did each child eat?

Dylan _____ pieces

Anna _____ pieces

Part B

Dylan and Anna each ate more pieces without finishing their candy bars. Both children have eaten the same amount.

On the lines below, write how many pieces in all each child could have eaten and what fraction of the candy bar they ate. Explain how you found your answer.

_____

_____

_____

_____

End-of-Book
Building Stamina®

The End-of-Book **Building Stamina**® is a

comprehensive review of the

New York State Learning Standards

covered in the lessons.

By practicing with these challenging,

broad-based, higher-order thinking questions,

you will be building up your stamina

to succeed on the New York State Test

and in other academic endeavors

that require higher-order thinking.

Building Stamina®

DIRECTIONS Read each problem.
Circle the letter of the answer you choose.

1 What does the model below show?

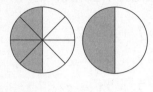

A $\frac{8}{8} = \frac{1}{2}$

B $\frac{4}{8} = \frac{1}{2}$

C $\frac{4}{6} = \frac{1}{2}$

D $\frac{3}{5} = \frac{1}{2}$

2 The fourth grade is planning an end-of-year party. There are 79 students and 4 teachers. If each table seats 6 people, how many tables will be needed?

A   12

B   13

C   14

D   15

3 A snack bar has 15 cases of juice. Each case contains 24 bottles. How many bottles of juice are there?

A   350

B   360

C   370

D   460

4 How does changing *a* affect *b*?

a	40	30	20	10
b	20	15	10	5

A   When *a* decreases, *b* increases.

B   When *a* increases, *b* decreases.

C   When *a* decreases, *b* decreases.

D   Both *a* and *b* decrease, by the same amount.

5 Which is the missing number below?

$(98 \times 47) \times 102 = 98 \times (47 \times \square)$

A   98

B   102

C   147

D   198

6 Josh sold 6 plates of cookies at a bake sale. There were 18 cookies on each plate. Which shows how many cookies he sold?

A   3

B   68

C   75

D   108

7 Which array models 3 × 7?

A 🌐🌐🌐🌐🌐🌐🌐
🌐🌐🌐🌐🌐🌐🌐
🌐🌐🌐🌐🌐🌐🌐

B 🌐🌐🌐🌐🌐🌐🌐
🌐🌐🌐🌐🌐🌐🌐
🌐🌐🌐🌐🌐🌐🌐

C 🌐🌐🌐🌐🌐🌐
🌐🌐🌐🌐🌐🌐
🌐🌐🌐🌐🌐🌐
🌐🌐🌐🌐🌐🌐
🌐🌐🌐🌐🌐🌐
🌐🌐🌐🌐🌐🌐

D 🌐🌐🌐🌐🌐🌐🌐
🌐🌐🌐🌐🌐🌐🌐
🌐🌐🌐🌐🌐🌐🌐
🌐🌐🌐🌐🌐🌐🌐
🌐🌐🌐🌐🌐🌐🌐

8 Cory is making kites. It takes 6 feet of string for each kite. He has 80 feet of string. How many kites can he make?

A 13

B 14

C 24

D 74

9 26
×8

A 34 C 148

B 68 D 208

10 Jackie has 7 CDs. Kris and Jackie together have 21 CDs. Which number sentence shows how to find the number of Kris's CDs?

A $7 + c = 21$

B $7 \times 21 = c$

C $7 + 21 = c$

D $21 \div c = 7$

11 Which of the following groups contains **only** letters that have perpendicular lines?

A H, K, Z

B N, E, F

C Z, L, M

D L, F, H

12 Which of these triangles contains an obtuse angle?

A

B

C

D

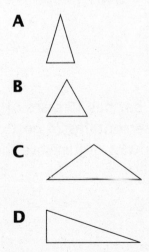

Measuring Up® to the New York State Learning Standards

13 Bobby practiced for his track meet by running every day. The table shows how far he ran each day in the week before the race.

Day	Miles
Monday	$\frac{7}{8}$
Tuesday	$\frac{4}{8}$
Wednesday	$\frac{1}{8}$
Thursday	$\frac{3}{8}$
Friday	$\frac{2}{8}$

On which day did Bobby have the shortest run?

A Monday

B Tuesday

C Wednesday

D Friday

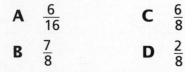

14 Jason ran $\frac{4}{8}$ mile on Monday and $\frac{2}{8}$ mile on Tuesday. What is the total number of miles he ran for Monday and Tuesday?

A $\frac{6}{16}$ **C** $\frac{6}{8}$

B $\frac{7}{8}$ **D** $\frac{2}{8}$

15 Dora has $\frac{8}{10}$ pound of grapes. She eats 0.5 pound. How many pounds of grapes are left?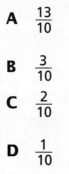

A $\frac{13}{10}$

B $\frac{3}{10}$

C $\frac{2}{10}$

D $\frac{1}{10}$

16 Which correctly lists the fractions in order from least to greatest?

A $\frac{1}{5}, \frac{1}{4}, \frac{1}{2}$

B $\frac{1}{4}, \frac{1}{2}, \frac{1}{5}$

C $\frac{1}{4}, \frac{1}{5}, \frac{1}{2}$

D $\frac{1}{2}, \frac{1}{5}, \frac{1}{4}$

17 LeeAnn's class recycled 121 cans in January and 209 cans in February. About how many cans did her class recycle in those two months?

A between 100 and 200

B between 200 and 300

C between 300 and 400

D between 400 and 500

18 Jason owns two dogs that have a combined weight of 120 pounds. Use the graph to find the names of Jason's dogs.

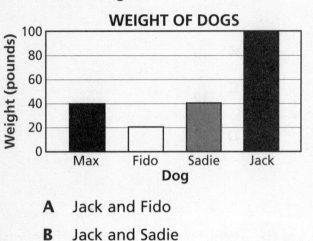

WEIGHT OF DOGS

A Jack and Fido

B Jack and Sadie

C Sadie and Max

D Max and Fido

19 Look at the graph below. Which statement is true?

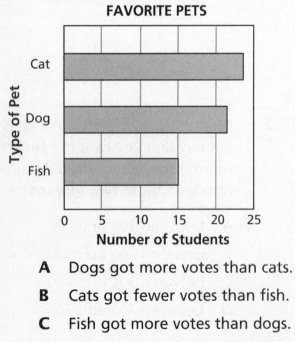

FAVORITE PETS

A Dogs got more votes than cats.

B Cats got fewer votes than fish.

C Fish got more votes than dogs.

D Dogs got more votes than fish.

20 Which of the tables below represents the same data as in the bar graph?

SAVINGS

A

Week	Money Saved
1	$9
2	$3
3	$6

B

Week	Money Saved
1	$3
2	$6
3	$9

C

Week	Money Saved
1	$3
2	$9
3	$6

D

Week	Money Saved
1	$6
2	$9
3	$3

21 The town wants to enclose the town swimming pool, which is a rectangle that is 50 yards by 40 yards. How many feet of fencing does the town need?

A 540

B 200

C 180

D 90

22 Marrisa used the rule below to describe her pattern.

subtract 3, add 2, subtract 3, add 2

Which pattern was made using her rule, starting with the number 40?

A 40, 42, 39, 41, 38

B 40, 37, 35, 32, 30

C 40, 37, 39, 36, 38

D 40, 43, 45, 48, 50

23 Which of the following decimals is equivalent to $\frac{23}{100}$?

A 0.023

B 0.23

C 2.3

D 230

24 The line graph shows the number of e-mails Farrah received over a 5-day period.

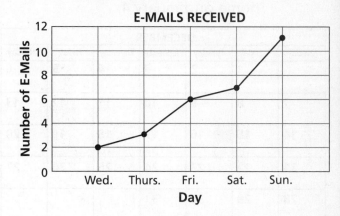

If the pattern continues, how many e-mails will Farrah receive on Monday?

A fewer than on Thursday

B fewer than on Friday

C more than on Sunday

D the same as on Sunday

25 A grid has 100 squares. Chen shaded in $\frac{45}{100}$ of the grid. Which statement is not true?

A Chen shaded forty-five hundredths of the grid.

B Chen shaded less than half of the grid.

C Chen shaded 0.45 of the grid.

D Fifty-five hundredths of the grid is shaded.

26 Liza is spending one week at her grandmother's house and 5 days at her aunt's house. She will return home on January 4.

DECEMBER						
Sunday	Monday	Tuesday	Wednesday	Thursday	Friday	Saturday
	1	2	3	4	5	6
7	8	9	10	11	12	13
14	15	16	17	18	19	20
21	22	23	24	25	26	27
28	29	30	31			

JANUARY						
Sunday	Monday	Tuesday	Wednesday	Thursday	Friday	Saturday
				1	2	3
4	5	6	7	8	9	10
11	12	13	14	15	16	17
18	19	20	21	22	23	24
25	26	27	28	29	30	31

When will Liza leave home?

A December 28

B December 23

C December 21

D December 7

27 Which polygon has more sides than a triangle but **fewer** sides than a pentagon?

A hexagon   C rectangle

B octagon   D circle

28 Which is the most reasonable number of gumballs in the full machine?

25 gumballs   ? gumballs

A 25

B 100

C 250

D 500

29 Ms. Young's landscaping business has 24 clients. Ms. Young wants to mow the same number of lawns each day and work **only** Monday through Saturday. Which related division and multiplication facts can you use to find how many lawns she must mow each day?

A $24 \div 2 = 12$ and $2 \times 12 = 24$

B $36 \div 6 = 6$ and $6 \times 6 = 36$

C $24 \div 6 = 4$ and $6 \times 4 = 24$

D $24 \div 24 = 1$ and $24 \times 1 = 24$

30 How many edges does this tent have?

- **A** 10
- **B** 9
- **C** 8
- **D** 6

31 Which measuring tool would be **best** to use when finding the mass of a watermelon?

- **A** meterstick
- **B** balance scale
- **C** thermometer
- **D** measuring cup

32 Which two are not equivalent?

- **A** 12 + 3 and 1 ten 5 ones
- **B** 108 − 3 and
  1 hundred 0 tens 5 ones
- **C** 441 + 100 and
  4 hundreds 4 tens 1 one
- **D** 735 − 500 and
  2 hundreds 3 tens 5 ones

33 If the digit 6 in the number 6,881 is changed to a 9, how will the value of the number change?

- **A** increase by 3
- **B** increase by 30
- **C** increase by 300
- **D** increase by 3,000

34 Laura's family bought a new television. Which of the following could be the mass of the television?

- **A** 16 grams
- **B** 400 grams
- **C** 16 kilograms
- **D** 400 kilograms

35 Look at this pattern.

$$83 \times 1 = 83$$
$$83 \times 10 = 830$$
$$83 \times 100 = 8,300$$

Which comes next?

- **A** $83 \times 1,000 = 83,000$
- **B** $83 + 1,000 = 1,083$
- **C** $8,300 - 1,000 = 7,300$
- **D** $8,300 \times 1,000 = 8,300,000$

36 Jasper found the capacity of his bathtub. Which unit did Jasper most likely use?

A   milliliters

B   liters

C   pounds

D   square feet

37 Which figure has an area of 4 square units and a perimeter of 8 units?

A

B

C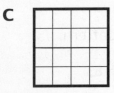

D

38 Which number is one thousand four hundred three?

A   1,430

B   1,403

C   1,304

D   143

39 If $x > 3$, which whole numbers from 0 to 5 could x be?

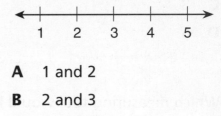

A   1 and 2

B   2 and 3

C   3 and 4

D   4 and 5

40 Which equals 10,000?

A   1,000 ones

B   100 thousands

C   1,000 tens

D   1,000 thousands

41 Which is true?

A $1,050 \neq 1,050$

B $8,467 > 8,476$

C $9,017 < 9,107$

D $6,931 = 6,913$

42 On Monday, 6,802 people visited the zoo. On Tuesday, 7,528 people visited the zoo. How many more people visited the zoo on Tuesday than on Monday?

    A   14,330

    B   1,726

    C   730

    D   726

43 Mrs. Gold is drawing a rectangle.

How many more line segments does she need to draw?

    A   2   **C**   4

    B   3   **D**   8

44 Look at the number sentence below.

$$\frac{1}{4} < \square$$

Which could be the missing fraction?

    A $\frac{1}{3}$

    B $\frac{1}{5}$

    C $\frac{1}{6}$

    D $\frac{1}{8}$

45 Which tool would be **best** for measuring the length of a football field?

    A   yardstick

    B   inch ruler

    C   balance scale

    D   centimeter ruler

46 Mr. Moore finished his basketball game at 6:30. His game lasted for $1\frac{1}{2}$ hours. What time did his game start?

    A   8:00

    B   5:30

    C   5:00

    D   4:30

47 What shape comes next in the pattern below?

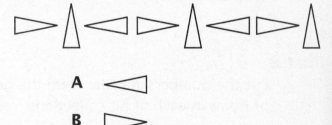

    A

    B

    C

    D

Short-Response Questions
DIRECTIONS Read each question carefully before writing your response. Be sure to show your work when asked.

48   Draw a set of parallel lines below.

49   Usher has 3 collections. He has 2,459 baseball cards. The number of stamps he has is 2 more hundreds, 1 less thousand, 5 less ones, and 1 more ten than his baseball cards. The number of stickers he has is 3 more tens, 2 less hundreds, 1 more thousand, and 4 less ones than his baseball cards.

	thousands	hundreds	tens	ones
stamps				
baseball cards				
stickers				

Part A
Fill in the chart to show the numbers in each collection.

Part B
Put the numbers in order from the greatest number to the least number of items in each of his collections.

Answer _____

50 Write the decimal and fraction for the shaded part.

_____

 51 Pat says when you multiply an odd number by an odd number the product will always be even. Is her statement true? _____ Prove your answer showing examples.

Show your work.

52 John's container holds 20 liters of water. He fills the container to the top and empties it into the kiddy pool 7 times. How much water is in the kiddy pool?

Show your work.

_____ liters

53 A banner is 24 inches long. How many feet long is the banner?

_____ feet

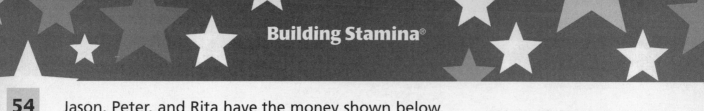

54 Jason, Peter, and Rita have the money shown below.

| Jason | Peter | Rita |

Write a decimal for each money amount in order from least to greatest.

_____

55 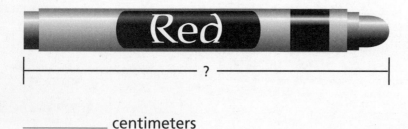 Use your centimeter ruler to solve this problem. Measure the crayon to the nearest centimeter.

Red

?

_____ centimeters

56 Mrs. Cho bought a magazine for $1.50 and a package of gum for $0.75. She gave the clerk $5.00. How much did she receive in change?

Show your work.

_____

Extended-Response Questions

DIRECTIONS Read each question carefully before writing your response. Show your work when asked.

57 Ryan wrote the number pattern shown below.

1, 6, 11, 9, 14, 19, 17, 22, 27, 25

Part A

What is the rule for Ryan's pattern?

Answer _____

On the lines below, describe how you found your answer.

_____

_____

_____

_____

_____

Part B

On the lines below write a pattern that uses the same rule as Ryan's pattern. Do not use any of the same numbers that Ryan used.

Pattern _____, _____, _____, _____, _____, _____, _____

58 Jose is making a pictograph showing the number of books in each box.

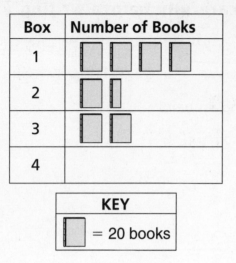

Box	Number of Books
1	
2	
3	
4	

KEY
= 20 books

Part A

How many more books are in box 1 than in box 2?

Show your work.

Answer _____

Part B

There are 50 books in box 4. Complete the pictograph to show this information.

On the lines below explain how you knew what to draw in the pictograph.

_____

_____

_____

_____

_____

59 A circus was in town for three nights.

- On Friday night, the attendance was 769.

- On Saturday night, the attendance was 315 more than Friday night.

- On Sunday night, the attendance was 176 less than Friday night.

Part A

What was the total attendance for the 3 nights?

Show your work.

Answer _____

Part B

On the lines below, explain how you found your answer.

_____

_____

_____

_____

Problem-Solving Guide

To solve some mathematics problems, you need to think about the question in a different way. You need to use special problem-solving skills like the ones below. You can use these four steps to solve any problem. Just follow the steps one at a time. Now you're on your way to becoming a good problem solver.

Step 1	**Understand the problem.** Think about what you need to do to solve the problem. • Read the problem carefully. • What does the problem ask you to find? • What information do you need to solve the problem?
Step 2	**Make a plan.** Choose a strategy that works best for the problem. • Draw a picture • Make a table • Look for a pattern • Use logical reasoning • Guess and check • Make a list • Make a model
Step 3	**Solve the problem.** Follow your plan to solve the problem. • How can you use the strategy to help solve the problem? • Think about the steps you need to follow. • Show all your work. • Record your answer.
Step 4	**Check your answer.** • Look back at the problem. • Did you answer the question that the problem asks? • Does your answer make sense? • How else could you solve the problem? Do you get the same answer?

Use the chart on the next page to organize your thinking while solving problems.

Use this problem-solving organizer to help you solve problems.

Step 1 Understand the problem.
Write what the problem asks you to find.

Step 2 Make a plan.
Write the steps you'll take to solve the problem.

Step 3 Solve the problem.
Show your work and record your answer.

Step 4 Check your answer.
Explain why your answer makes sense.

2-Point Holistic Rubric

Score Points:

2 Points	A two-point response is complete and correct. This response • demonstrates a thorough understanding of the mathematical concepts and/or procedures embodied in the task • indicates that the student has completed the task correctly, using mathematically sound procedures • contains clear, complete explanations and/or adequate work when required
1 Point	A one-point response is only partially correct. This response • indicates that the student has demonstrated only a partial understanding of the mathematical concepts and/or procedures embodied in the task • addresses some elements of the task correctly but may be incomplete or contain some procedural or conceptual flaws • may contain an incorrect solution but applies a mathematically appropriate process • may contain a correct numerical answer but required work is not provided
0 Points	A zero-point response is incorrect, irrelevant, incoherent, or contains a correct response arrived at using an obviously incorrect procedure. Although some parts may contain correct mathematical procedures, holistically they are not sufficient to demonstrate even a limited understanding of the mathematical concepts embodied in the task.

Condition Code A

Condition Code A is applied whenever a student who is present for a test session leaves an <u>entire</u> open-ended item in that session blank (no response).

3-Point Holistic Rubric

Score Points:

3 Points	A three-point response is complete and correct. This response • demonstrates a thorough understanding of the mathematical concepts and/or procedures embodied in the task • indicates that the student has completed the task correctly, using mathematically sound procedures • contains clear, complete explanations and/or adequate work when required
2 Points	A two-point response is partially correct. This response • demonstrates partial understanding of the mathematical concepts and/or procedures embodied in the task • addresses most aspects of the task, using mathematically sound procedures • may contain an incorrect solution but provides complete procedures, reasoning, and/or explanations • may reflect some misunderstanding of the underlying mathematical concepts and/or procedures
1 Point	A one-point response is incomplete and exhibits many flaws but is not completely incorrect. This response • demonstrates only a limited understanding of the mathematical concepts and/or procedures embodied in the task • may address some elements of the task correctly but reaches an inadequate solution and/or provides reasoning that is faulty or incomplete • exhibits multiple flaws related to a misunderstanding of important aspects of the task, misuse of mathematical procedures, or faulty mathematical reasoning • reflects a lack of essential understanding of the underlying mathematical concepts • may contain a correct numerical answer but required work is not provided
0 Points	A zero-point response is incorrect, irrelevant, incoherent, or contains a correct response arrived at using an obviously incorrect procedure. Although some parts may contain correct mathematical procedures, holistically they are not sufficient to demonstrate even a limited understanding of the mathematical concepts embodied in the task.

Tools

Ruler

Counters

Pattern Blocks

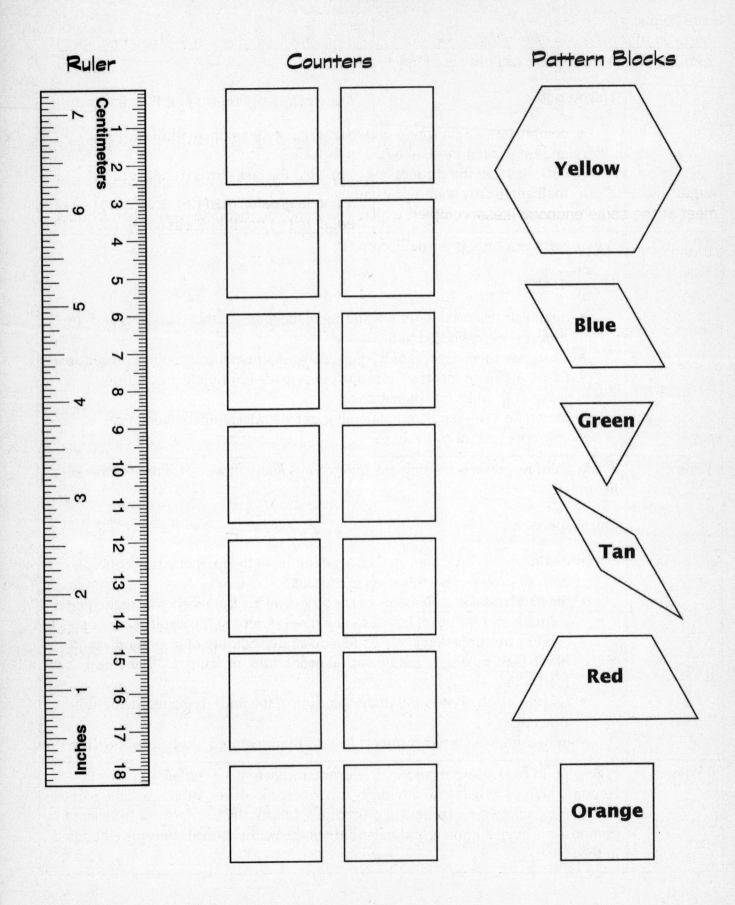

Measuring Up® to the New York State Learning Standards

Glossary

A

acute angle an angle with a measure less than a right angle (Lesson 47)

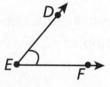

angle the shape formed when two rays meet at the same endpoint (Lesson 47)

area a measure of how many square units it takes to cover a two-dimensional shape exactly (Lesson 56)

array arrangement of objects in rows and columns (Lesson 13)

Associative Property of Multiplication the grouping of the factors does not change the product (Lesson 15)

B

bar graph graph that uses bars of different lengths to show data (Lesson 59)

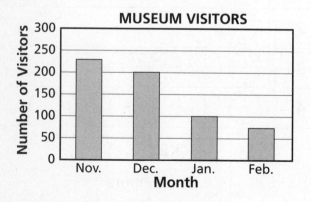

benchmark a measurement that you know, which you can use to estimate other measurements (Lesson 7)

C

capacity how much a container can hold (Lesson 53)

Commutative Property of Multiplication factors can be multiplied in any order and the product will be the same (Lesson 15)

compare examination of numbers to see if one is *greater than* (>), *less than* (<) or *equal to* (=) another (Lesson 3)

D

data information (Lessons R3, 58)

decimal a number that has one or more digits to the right of a decimal point; it names parts of a whole (Lessons 40, 41)

decimal point a period used to separate whole numbers from tenths (Lesson 41)

denominator the bottom number in a fraction; it tells the total number of equal parts (Lesson 34)

Distributive Property the multiplication property that states that to multiply a sum by a number, you can multiply each addend by the number and then add the products example:
$5 \times 14 = 5 \times (10 + 4) = (5 \times 10) + (5 \times 4) = 50 + 20$ (Lesson 16)

dividend the number being divided in a division problem (Lesson 22)

divisor the number you are dividing by in a division problem (Lesson 22)

E

edge a line segment where two faces meet (Lesson 49)

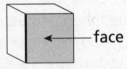

elapsed time the amount of time that has passed (Lesson 54)

equation a number sentence with an equal sign (Lessons 19, 30)

equivalent numbers that describe the same amount (Lesson 2)

equivalent fractions fractions that name the same amount (Lessons R1, 35)

estimate rounding numbers when an exact answer is not necessary (Lesson 11)

expression a part of a number sentence using numbers, operations, and sometimes variables (Lesson 30)

F

face a flat surface of a solid shape (Lesson 49)

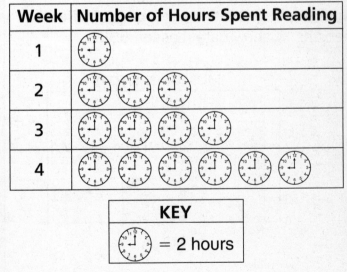

face

fact family a group of related facts that use the same numbers (Lesson 23)

factors the numbers you multiply (Lesson 13)

fraction a number that names part of a whole or part of a group (Lesson 34)

I

Identity Property of Multiplication the product of any number and 1 is that number (Lesson 15)

inequality a number sentence that uses one of these symbols: $<$, $>$, $\neq$ (Lesson 31)

intersecting lines lines that go through the same point (Lesson 46)

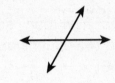

K

key the part of a pictograph that tells what each picture or drawing stands for (Lesson 58)

ROBIN'S READING

Week	Number of Hours Spent Reading
1	(1 clock)
2	(3 clocks)
3	(4 clocks)
4	(6 clocks)

KEY
(clock) = 2 hours

L

line a straight path of points that goes on forever in two directions (Lesson 46)

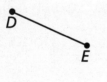

line graph graph that uses a line to show how data change over a period of time (Lesson 60)

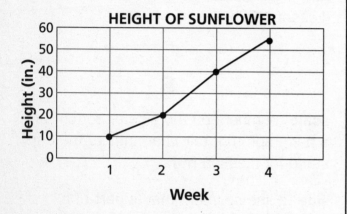

line segment a part of a line with two endpoints (Lesson 46)

N

net a pattern for a solid shape (Lesson 50)

numerator the top number in a fraction; it tells the number of parts of the whole being described (Lesson 34)

O

obtuse angle an angle with a measure greater than a right angle (Lesson 47)

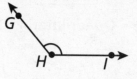

order listing numbers in a series, such as least to greatest or greatest to least (Lesson 4)

P

parallel lines lines that are always the same distance apart (Lesson 46)

perimeter the distance around a figure (Lesson 55)

perpendicular lines lines that intersect to form 4 right angles (Lesson 46)

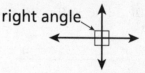

pictograph a graph that uses pictures or symbols and a key to show data (Lesson 58)

plane a surface that extends in all directions (Lesson 46)

point a location in space (Lesson 46)

polygon a flat, closed-plane shape made up of three or more line segments (Lesson 48)

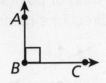

Triangle   Quadrilateral   Pentagon

Hexagon   Octagon

possible outcome a possible result of an experiment (Lesson 61)

product the answer in a multiplication problem (Lesson 13)

Q

quadrilateral a polygon with four sides and four angles (Lesson 48)

quotient the answer in a division problem (Lesson 22)

R

ray a part of a line with one endpoint (Lesson 47)

reasonable a possible answer that makes sense (Lesson 12)

regroup rename a number, such as changing 10 ones to 1 ten, 10 tens to 1 hundred, and so on (Lessons 9, 17)

related facts facts in the same fact family (Lesson 23)

remainder the amount left over when a whole number cannot be divided evenly (Lesson 25)

right angle two rays meeting to form a square corner (Lesson 47)

rounding using an estimate, such as the nearest ten or nearest hundred, to make a problem easier (Lesson 20)

rule how the numbers in a pattern change (Lesson 29)

S

scale numbers on the side or bottom of a bar graph that tell what number the bars stand for (Lesson 59)

side a line segment that is part of a polygon (Lesson 48)

solid shape a 3-dimensional shape that takes up space (Lesson 49)

Cube   Rectangular Prism   Triangular Prism   Square Pyramid

Triangular Pyramid   Cylinder   Cone   Sphere

straight angle an angle that forms a line (Lesson 47)

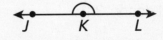

Measuring Up® to the New York State Learning Standards

survey data collected by asking a question and recording answers (Lesson R3)

U

unit fraction a fraction with a numerator of 1 (R2)

V

variable a letter or symbol that stands for an unknown number (Lesson 30)

vertex a point where three or more edges meet (Lesson 49)

vertex (plural: vertices)

Z

Zero Property of Multiplication the product of any number and zero is 0 (Lesson 15)

Copy Master 1
Fraction Bars

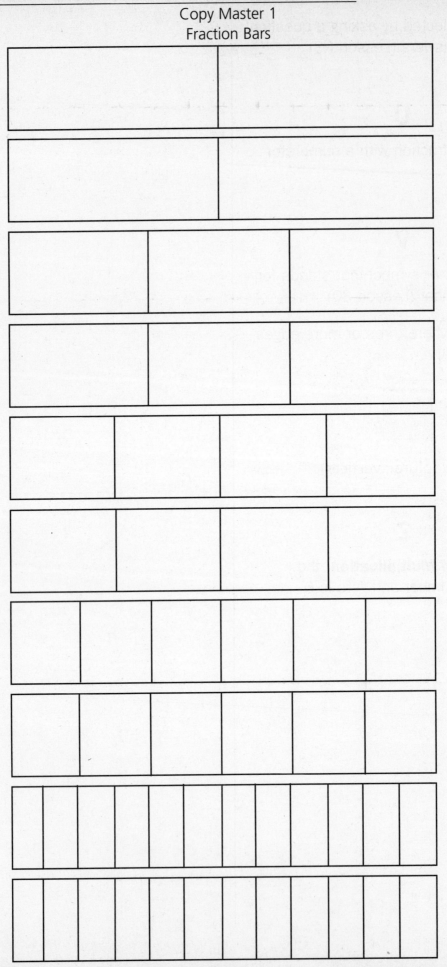

Copying is permitted. Measuring Up® to the New York State Learning Standards

Name _____

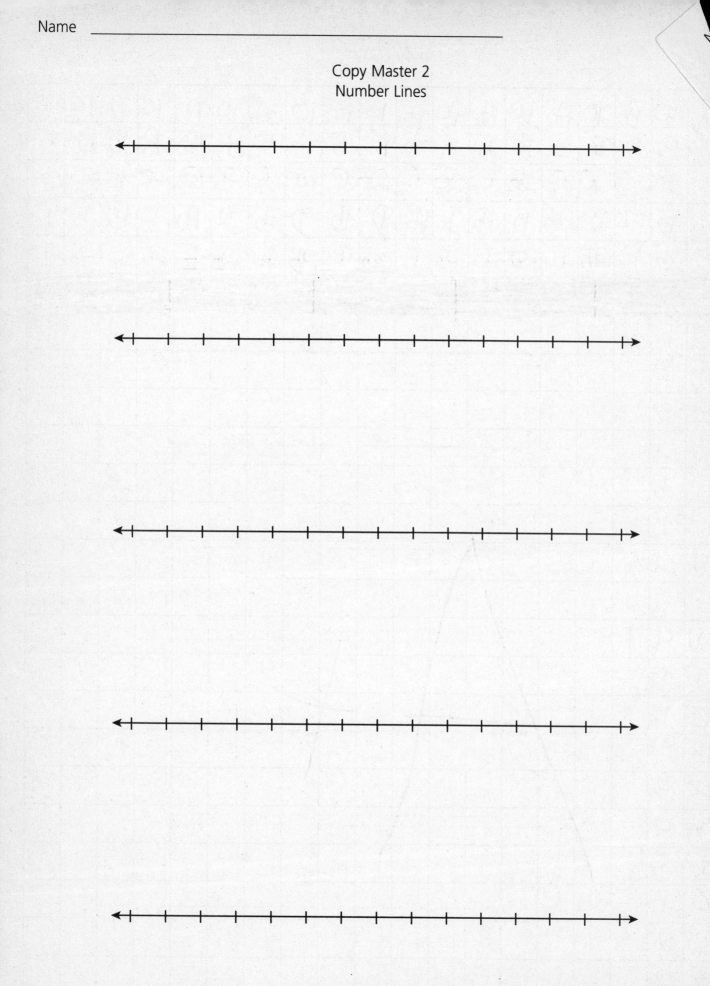

Copying is permitted.

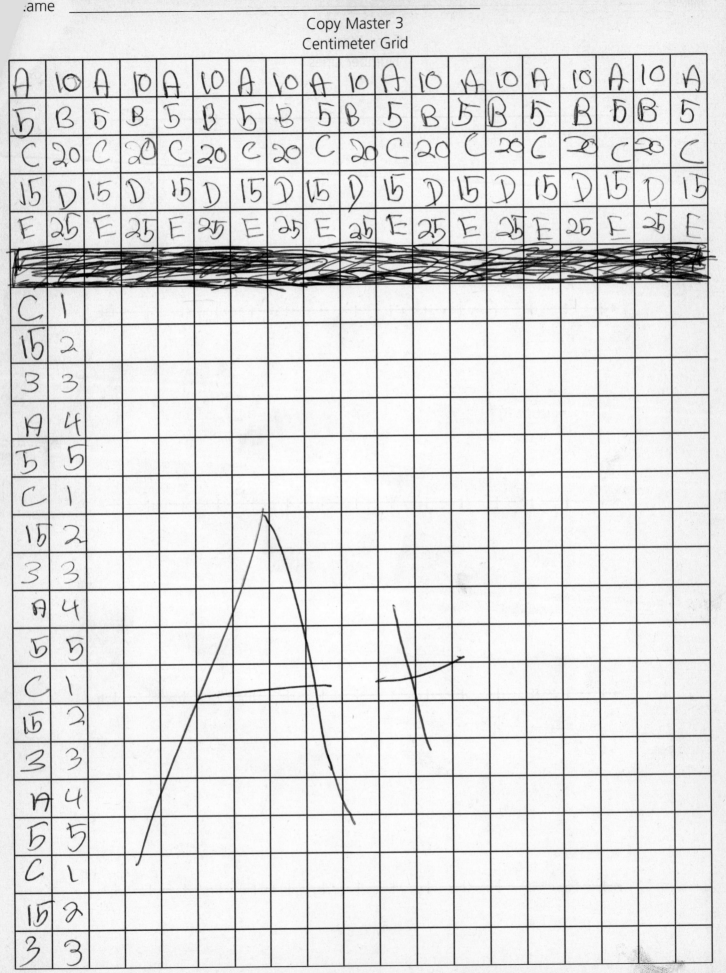

A	10	A	10	A	10	A	10	A	10	A	10	A	10	A	10	A	10	A
B	B	B	B	B	B	B	B	B	B	B	B	B	B	B	B	B	B	B	B
C	20	C	20	C	20	C	20	C	20	C	20	C	20	C	20	C	20	C
15	D	15	D	15	D	15	D	15	D	15	D	15	D	15	D	15	D	15
E	25	E	25	E	25	E	25	E	25	E	25	E	25	E	25	E	25	E

C	1
15	2
3	3
A	4
5	5
C	1
15	2
3	3
A	4
5	5
C	1
15	2
3	3
A	4
5	5
C	1
15	2
3	3

Copying is permitted.
Measuring Up® to the New York State Learning Standards

Percent Models

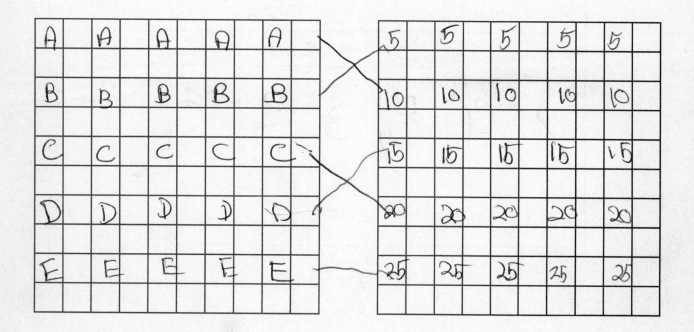

A	A	A	A	A		5	5	5	5	5	
B	B	B	B	B		10	10	10	10	10	
C	C	C	C	C		15	15	15	15	15	
D	D	D	D	D		20	20	20	20	20	
E	E	E	E	E		25	25	25	25	25	

C	C	C	C	C		1	1	1	1	1	
15	15	15	15	15		2	2	2	2	2	
3	3	3	3	3		3	3	3	3	3	
A	A	A	A	A		4	4	4	4	4	
5	5	5	5	5		5	5	5	5	5	

Place Value Chart

Thousands			Ones		
hundred thousands	ten thousands	one thousands	hundreds	tens	ones
7	9	8	3	3	0

B202 B263

Thousands			Ones		
hundred thousands	ten thousands	one thousands	hundreds	tens	ones
		1	2	9	7

Copying is permitted.
Measuring Up® to the New York State Learning Standards